*Women, Work, and Worship
in Lincoln's Country*

Women, Work, and Worship in Lincoln's Country

The Dumville Family Letters

EDITED BY ANNE M. HEINZ
AND JOHN P. HEINZ

*For Rose,
with memories of wonderful times gone by, and
Best wishes!
Anne   Jack
Feb. 2016*

University of Illinois Press
URBANA, CHICAGO, AND SPRINGFIELD

© 2016 by the Board of Trustees
of the University of Illinois
All rights reserved
Manufactured in the United States of America
C 5 4 3 2 1

♾ This book is printed on acid-free paper.

Library of Congress Cataloging-in-Publication Data

Names: Heinz, Anne M., editor. | Heinz, John P., 1936– editor.
Title: Women, work, and worship in Lincoln's Country : the Dumville
 family letters / edited by Anne M. Heinz and John P. Heinz.
Description: Urbana, Chicago, and Springfield : University of Illinois
 Press, 2015. | Includes bibliographical references and index.
Identifiers: LCCN 2015028396 | ISBN 9780252039959 (hardcover : alk.
 paper) | ISBN 9780252098130 (e-book)
Subjects: LCSH: Dumville family—Correspondence. | Lincoln,
 Abraham, 1809–1865—Correspondence. | Women—Middle West—
 History—19th century. | Women—Middle West—Social life and
 customs—19th century. | Middle class—Middle West—History—
 19th century. | Middle West—History—Civil War, 1861–1865—
 Social aspects. | Middle West—Social conditions—19th century.
Classification: LCC HQ1438.M53 W65 2015 | DDC 305.409773/09034—dc23
 LC record available at http://lccn.loc.gov/2015028396

In Memory of
Professor Robert H. Salisbury (1930–2010)
who might have liked this book
and
Helen Burke Denby (1880–1955)
who preserved the letters

Contents

Preface: The Provenance and Transcription of the Letters   xi

Acknowledgments   xvii

1 The Dumvilles and Their Times   1
2 1851–1853   Family Matters   22
3 1854–1855   Cholera   32
4 1856–1857   Political Awareness   53
5 1858–1860   The Lincoln-Douglas Elections   79
6 1861–1863   The War   115
7 The Letters End   162

Notes   169

References   197

Index   207

Dumville Family Tree

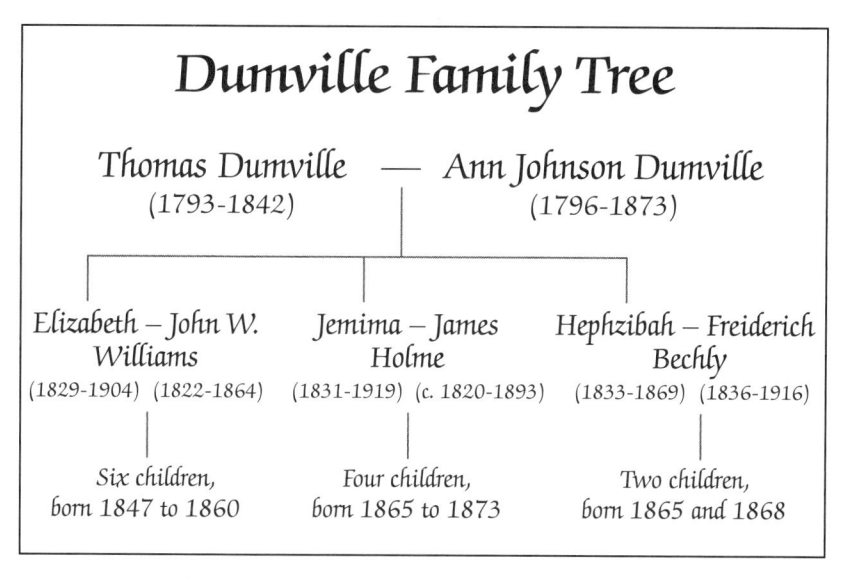

Thomas Dumville — Ann Johnson Dumville
(1793-1842) (1796-1873)

Elizabeth – John W. Williams	Jemima – James Holme	Hephzibah – Freiderich Bechly
(1829-1904) (1822-1864)	(1831-1919) (c. 1820-1893)	(1833-1869) (1836-1916)
Six children, born 1847 to 1860	Four children, born 1865 to 1873	Two children, born 1865 and 1868

Figure 1: Ann and Thomas Dumville family tree. Compiled by the authors.

Preface

The Provenance and Transcription of the Letters

The letters on which this book is based are held by the archives of the Abraham Lincoln Presidential Library in Springfield, Illinois. The collection includes ninety-four letters written by members of the Dumville family—the mother, three daughters, and the husband and children of the eldest daughter. In addition, there are twenty-three letters sent to them by neighbors, soldiers in the Civil War, and Methodist clergy. A few of the family letters appear to be copies or drafts of those that were sent, and some documents are also in the file. Of the 117 letters in the archive, one hundred are included here in whole or in part.

Because of fading of the ink, staining or deterioration of the paper, water damage, or poor handwriting, some words are illegible. We have indicated those by a question mark in brackets. In most cases, we found it possible to discern the author's intent, but we have not supplied the word unless the intent was clear. To make the letters easier to read, we added a bit of punctuation. We have, especially, indicated where sentences begin and end. Punctuation conventions were less clearly settled in the mid-nineteenth century, and the Dumvilles were sparing in their use of periods. We also created some paragraphs. Oddly, some of the earliest letters, written in 1851–53, use a capital letter on the first word of each line of text (see chapter 2 at note 17); we have retained that here. In making those decisions, we sought to preserve the character of the letters. On the theory that unconventional spelling may be an important characteristic of a letter, we retained it. Occasionally, where we thought the reader might welcome help, we inserted our interpretation in brackets. We did not alter the style or word choices. The compositions are theirs.

As noted above, some letters—those we found less informative—are not included here. We also omitted passages that were extraneous, repetitious, fragmentary, or otherwise of little use in telling the story of the Dumvilles. Deletions within letters are indicated by ellipses. Such decisions were, of course, applications of judgment, and other readers of the letters might differ with those judgments. The full collection is in the archives of the Library. Scholars who want to use the letters as primary sources should of course consult the originals.

Figure 2 will give the reader a sense of the letters as objects and of the challenges confronted in transcribing them. The cursive often cannot be put into conventional type. For example, the writers frequently include a very short line between words, at an angle, which might be either a comma or a period, or perhaps some of each.[1] One often suspects that the writer was not quite sure which it was or, perhaps, did not much care. Indeed, it is not entirely clear why *we* should care. A letter of May 6, 1862, written by a soldier, Benjamin Stead, discusses the battle of Pittsburg Landing (also known as Shiloh). He spells Pittsburg with one t and the initial letter looks very much like an F. Should we render it as "Fitsburg"? We think it looks like an F, but it might be a P, and pedantry has its limits.[2]

Some of the letters were written in standard English, or an approximation of it, and others were not. A few appear to be phonetic renditions of nineteenth-century rural dialect. The meaning is usually clear, but some passages are puzzling and may require the reader's creative interpretation. Most of the stylistic differences among the letters are attributable to the differing levels of sophistication of their authors. Some are due to maturation—the daughters' letters, for the most part, improved in spelling, grammar, and syntax as they aged. It is also clear, however, that they devoted varying degrees of care and thought to the letters. When they wrote hurriedly, the letters show it.

The Dumvilles were economical in their use of stationery. Paper was expensive. Therefore, they often wrote marginalia, and putting the several pieces together into the intended sequence involves guesswork. Indeed, there may not have been a clearly intended sequence. The paper on which the Dumvilles wrote is lightweight, without any decoration or borders, probably indicating that they chose inexpensive stock. They usually filled the pages on both sides, but rarely used a second sheet. The letter was folded into a small rectangle and the address was then either written on the outside of the sheet, if that was blank, or the page was put into a small envelope. The envelopes, unlike the stationery, were of heavier weight and sometimes had embossed decoration.

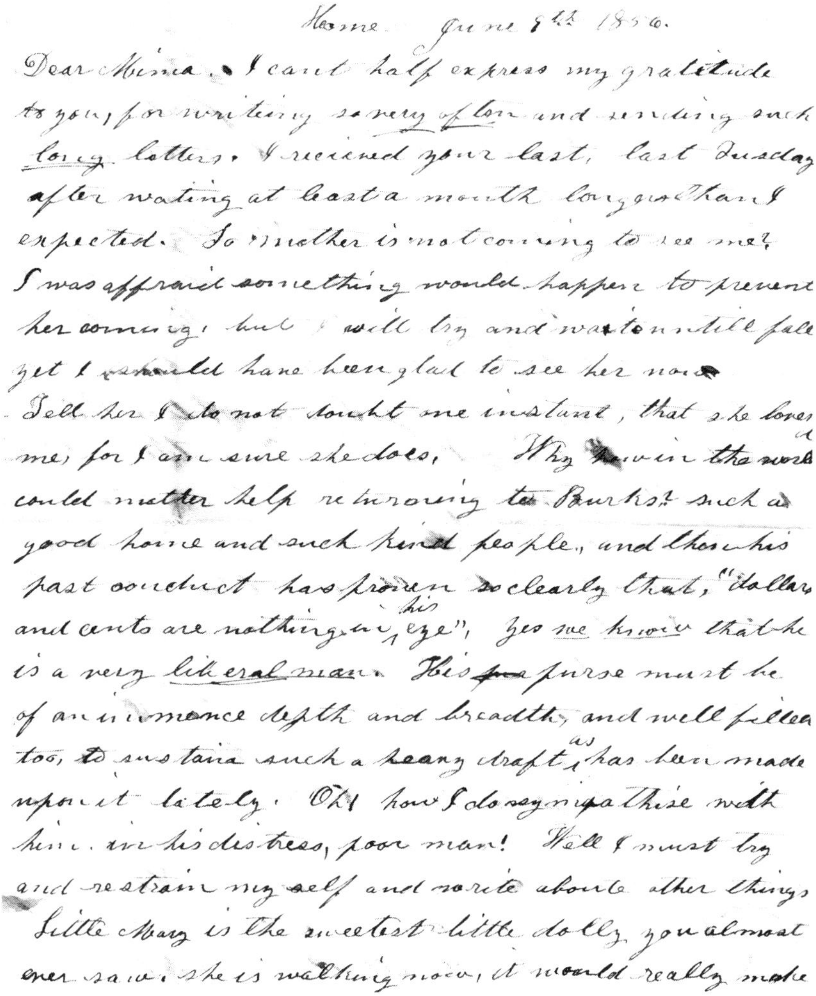

Home June 8th 1856.

Dear Mima. I cant half express my gratitude to you, for writing so very often and sending such long letters. I recieved your last, last Tuesday after waiting at least a month longer than I expected. So mother is not coming to see me? I was affraid something would happen to prevent her coming; but I will try and wait untill fall yet I should have been glad to see her now. Tell her I do not doubt one instant, that she loves me, for I am sure she does. Why in the world could mother help returning to Burks? such a good home and such kind people, and then his past conduct has proven so clearly that, "dollars and cents are nothing in his eye", yes we know that he is a very liberal man. His purse must be of an immence depth and breadth, and well filled too, to sustain such a heavy draft, as has been made upon it lately. Oh! how I do sympathise with him in his distress, poor man! Well I must try and restrain myself and write about other things. Little Mary is the sweetest little dolly you almost ever saw. she is walking now, it would really make

Figure 2: A letter written by Hephzibah, 1856. Courtesy of Abraham Lincoln Presidential Library and Museum.

With the introduction of postage stamps in 1847,[3] etiquette evolved as to how the postage was handled. This is discussed in a letter of May 7, 1854. Prior to the introduction of a national postage stamp, the recipient, rather than the sender, often paid the cost of delivery. Gradually, the process reversed and the sender paid the cost. At least two of the surviving envelopes have no stamp but a handwritten notation, "Paid 3" and "5," as do some of the folded letters that did not use envelopes. Postmarks varied during this period and, much to the disappointment of the historian, often did not include the year. Only the location of the post office, the month, and the day were consistently noted.

For the purpose of presentation and discussion, the letters have been divided into periods chosen to correspond with changes in the content of the letters. The number of letters per year increased from one in 1851 to three in 1852, four in 1853, ten in 1854, and fourteen in 1855.[4] The frequency peaked at fifteen in 1857. The reason for the increase is probably that in the earlier years two of the daughters were located near each other, so it was not necessary for them to communicate by mail. When one of the daughters later returned to her mother's home, the sisters wrote more often.

Where the letters were housed from 1863 until the mid-twentieth century is unclear. By the end of that time, certainly, they were in the possession of descendants of B. T. Burke, the employer of Ann Dumville, the mother. Burke's granddaughter loaned the letters to MacMurray College (the successor to the Methodist's Illinois Conference Female College) in the 1940s for use in the preparation of the college's centennial history,[5] and a few of them were quoted in that book. In 2001 Burke's great-granddaughter donated the main body of the letters to the predecessor of the Abraham Lincoln Presidential Library. Some additional letters that she apparently overlooked were found at her residence after her death, and those were then donated to the library by her estate.[6]

Ann Dumville lived at the Burke residence in her later years. It is possible that the letters were left behind when she died. Did Ann's daughters travel to her funeral and then deal with her personal effects? Or did Burke handle the disposition of Ann's personal property when she died? Perhaps the Dumville family left the letters with the Burkes, intending to pick them up later (but never did so), or perhaps the letters were simply overlooked and forgotten, by both the Dumvilles and the Burkes. B. T. Burke died in 1876, three years after Ann. There is a considerable collection of Burke family correspondence, and the Dumville letters were in the same boxes with that correspondence as late as the 1990s. Letters from Ann Dumville to B. T. Burke, sent while he was traveling, were among those loaned to MacMurray College by Burke's granddaughter in the 1940s. The photograph of Ann Dumville labeled "Grandma Dumville" was found with the letters (see figure 6 in chapter 1).

Some of the letters refer to correspondence that is not in the archive, and there are sometimes long intervals between letters. It is likely that in those intervals other letters were written, but all of the Dumville correspondence that has been found is now at the Abraham Lincoln Presidential Library.

Provenance and Transcription of the Letters xv

Most of the surviving letters were written in Jacksonville by Hephzibah, the youngest daughter, and mailed to Carlinville, where her mother and one of her sisters resided. The relatively few surviving letters written by the Carlinville Dumvilles may be copies or drafts made for their own records, and some letters were apparently circulated within the family and then returned to the sender. It is also possible that particular letters were removed from the file between 1863 and the late twentieth century. In any event, we clearly do not have the complete record of their correspondence.

Acknowledgments

The American Bar Foundation, Northwestern University's Institute for Policy Research, and the Adirondack Mountains provided agreeable places where much of this work was done. The ABF and IPR also supplied well-informed and helpful colleagues and essential support services. Even in the mountains, however, expert advice was readily available, and the processing of words proceeded apace. As this page is written at 2:00 A.M. on a chilly August night in the Adirondacks, a computer, a scanner, a router, and a copying machine sit beside the desk. The production of scholarly work, like much of journalism and publishing, is now a cottage industry. The separation of work from home, one of the major social changes of the nineteenth century, has reversed.

Sadly, one sees colleagues less often, but nostalgic scholars can Skype. And one sees one's mate more often. Digital devices probably mean that wives eat more lunches with their husbands, as in the day when the true woman carried a lunch pail out to the field where the man was plowing. The longer-term effect of this on the divorce rate remains to be seen. Cottage industry nurtures collaborative projects within the marriage, and there is little reason to expect work relationships to be more harmonious if one is unable to go home in the evening. The electronic revolution has dealt a blow to the traditional vow "for better or worse but never for lunch."

We received valuable advice and assistance from the United Library of Garrett-Evangelical Theological Seminary, the Methodist Library of Drew University, the Pfeiffer Library of MacMurray College, the Abraham Lincoln Presidential Library, the Carlinville Public Library, the Jacksonville Public Library, the Jacksonville Area Genealogical and Historical Society, the Powesheik County Historical Society, Chris Anderson, Sandra Bloom, Robert

Bradner, Rand Burnette, Charlotte Crane, Peter DiCola, Don Doyle, David Figlio, Katherine French, Louise French, Anne Godden-Segard, Katharine Hannaford, Elizabeth Hardy, David Hilliard, David Himrod, Tom Joyce, Marcia Lehr, Eugene Lowe, Laura Beth Nielsen, Hillary Peppers, Lauretta Scheller, Christopher Schmidt, Cheryl Schnirring, Susan Shapiro, Carl Smith, Jane Smith, Katherine Sodergren, Mary Sprague, Gary Stockton, Kathleen Straka, Erin Watt, Harvey Wilcox, and three anonymous readers employed by the University of Illinois Press. These generous people and institutions should not, of course, be held responsible for the infelicitous manner in which we carried out their advice.

Cathy Zaccarine of Zaccarine Design, with whom we have collaborated on several projects in the past, produced the maps with her customary professional skill and precision. As always, it was a joy to work with her.

Our editor at the University of Illinois Press, Dawn Durante, guided our work on this project with perceptive criticism and a firm hand. Her advice, substantive and stylistic, is reflected on every page of this book. We are both indebted and grateful to her. It would have been a very different book without her counsel. She is a careful reader, and she kept two aging scholars from growing sleepy.

Julie Gay did the copyediting with skill, precision, taste, and good humor. Her many helpful suggestions added clarity and made this a better book.

We are also grateful for the reluctance of the Burkes to dispose of anything. Having in our time cleaned out an attic, however, we cannot in good conscience recommend this as a general policy.

We could close with the traditional word of thanks to the loving wife or the supportive husband, but in this case the attempt to write that provokes peals of laughter.

*Women, Work, and Worship
in Lincoln's Country*

1. The Dumvilles and Their Times

When Ann Dumville stood to speak, the meeting paused. The clergy were debating the future of the women's college, which was insolvent. Lenders were demanding payment, and the Catholic church had offered to buy the property. The meeting was the "conference," the annual gathering of Methodist preachers in the region, and Mrs. Dumville's participation was unprecedented. Women were not members of the conference, were not ministers, did not hold leadership positions in Methodist congregations, and seldom attended the conference, even as observers.

It was a large assembly. One hundred and twenty clergy were present at the "West Charge" church in Jacksonville, Illinois, the newer and more prosperous of the two Methodist churches in town. Remarkably, the clergyman presiding at the meeting permitted Mrs. Dumville to speak. She spoke with a Yorkshire accent: "Your daughters must be educated; my daughters must have an education. *We must keep the school. It must not be sold. It must not be sold.* We must give; all must give! I have a hundred dollars in Mr. Chestnut's bank in Springfield and I will give it."[1] A preacher who was present said that her remarks were "as startling as an apparition from the other world."[2] The elders of the Methodist church were moved, other pledges followed, and the college was saved. A donation of such size from the earnings of a housekeeper was a very considerable sacrifice in 1860.

Ann Dumville was a widow who lived in a nearby town. She was a devout Methodist, and she had two daughters who attended the college when they could afford it. She had arrived in the New York Harbor in 1840 with her husband and children. According to the ship's manifest, there were six Dumvilles on board—Ann, age forty-four; Thomas, forty-six; William, nineteen; Elizabeth, twelve; Jemima, ten; and Hephzibah Beulah,[3] eight (see figure 3).

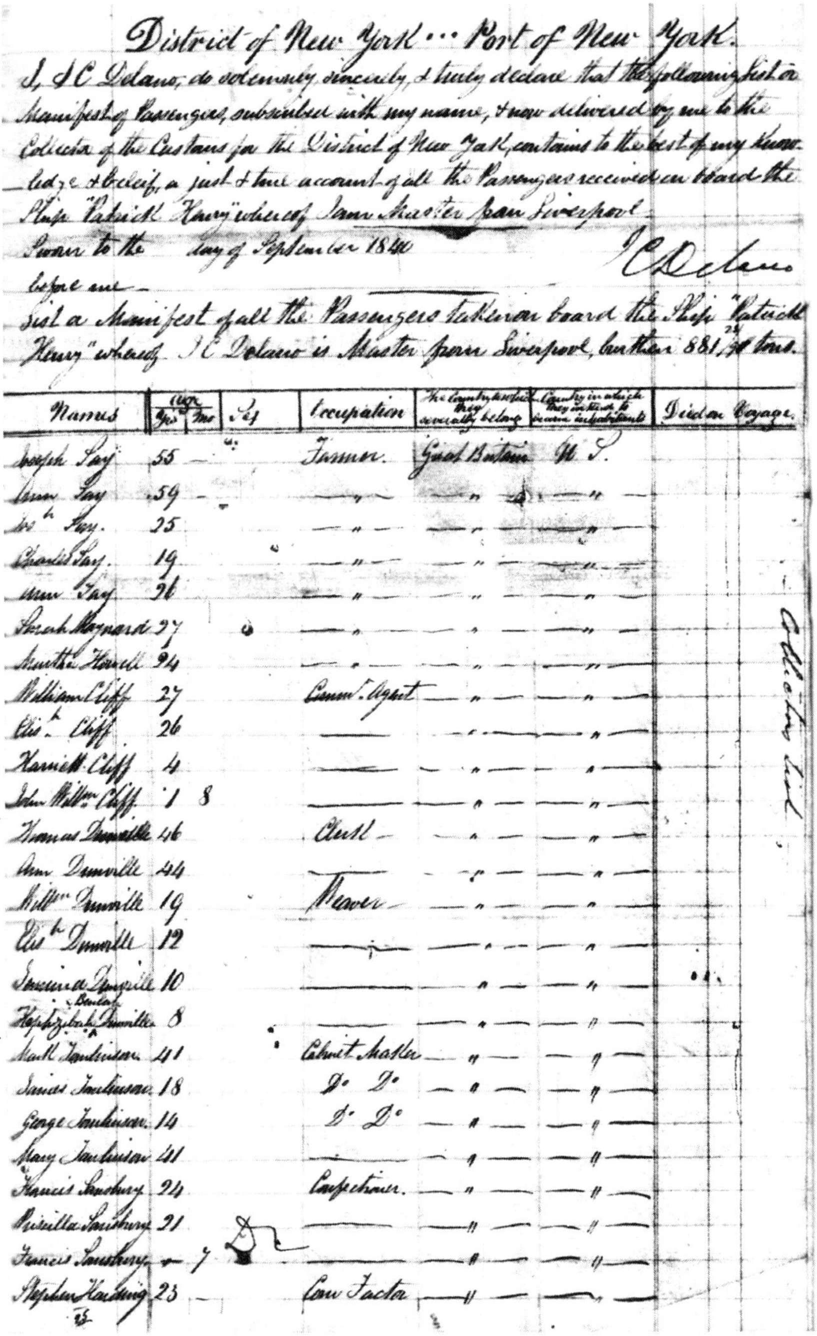

District of New York … Port of New York.

I, J C Delano, do solemnly, sincerely, & truly declare that the following List or Manifest of Passengers, subscribed with my name, & now delivered by me to the Collector of the Customs for the District of New York, contains to the best of my knowledge & belief, a just & true account of all the Passengers received on board the Ship "Patrick Henry" whereof I am Master from Liverpool.

Sworn to the day of September 1840 before me — J C Delano

List or Manifest of all the Passengers taken on board the Ship "Patrick Henry" whereof J C Delano is Master from Liverpool, burthen 881 24/95 tons.

Names	Age Yrs	Age Mo	Sex	Occupation	The Country to which they severally belong	Country in which they intend to become inhabitants	Died on Voyage
Joseph Fay	55			Farmer	Great Britain	U.S.	
Ann Fay	59			"	"	"	
Wm Fay	25			"	"	"	
Charles Fay	19			"	"	"	
Ann Fay	21			"	"	"	
Sarah Maynard	27			"	"	"	
Martha Howell	24			"	"	"	
William Cliff	27			Comm. Agent	"	"	
Elizth Cliff	26			—	"	"	
Harriett Cliff	4			—	"	"	
John Willm Cliff	1	8		—	"	"	
Thomas Dumville	46			Clerk	"	"	
Ann Dumville	44			—	"	"	
Willm Dumville	19			Weaver	"	"	
Elizth Dumville	12			—	"	"	
Jemima Dumville	10			—	"	"	
Hephzibah Bentley Dumville	8			—	"	"	
Mark Tomlinson	41			Cabinet Maker	"	"	
James Tomlinson	18			Do Do	"	"	
George Tomlinson	14			Do Do	"	"	
Mary Tomlinson	41			—	"	"	
Francis Sansbury	24			Confectioner	"	"	
Priscilla Sansbury	21			—	"	"	
Francis Sansbury	—	7		—	"	"	
Stephen Harding	23			Corn Factor	"	—	

Figure 3: Ship's manifest recording the arrival of the Dumvilles, 1840, New York, N.Y. Courtesy of the National Archives at Washington, D.C., Records of the U.S. Customs Service, record group 36, microfilm serial M237, 1820–1897, roll 044, line 17, list 696.

Thomas and Ann were husband and wife, the three girls were their daughters, and William may have been a son, a nephew, or a cousin or some such. After their arrival in the United States, we find no further record of him.[4] The father, mother, and three daughters, however, made their way to St. Louis and then, a few months later, to central Illinois, where they settled on a farm at a place called Sulphur Springs (figure 4). Thomas purchased land that was intended for the support of a colony or cooperative society, probably one that was religiously based.[5] The name of the place, with its connotations of the netherworld, might have been taken as a cautionary omen, but the settlers nonetheless bought the land.

The venture ended badly. As Hephzibah said in a letter to England seventeen years later:

September, 1859
 The death of father, which took place two years after we came to America, left us friendless indeed so far as human aid was concerned. But he consoled himself during his sickness and by thinking that the God in whom he trusted would take care of the wife and children that he would leave behind.

They had been in Sulphur Springs only a short time when Thomas died, leaving Ann with three young daughters. The colony then failed, they lost the land,[6] and the fatherless family moved to Carlinville, the county seat, where Ann found work. But, because her earnings were not sufficient to

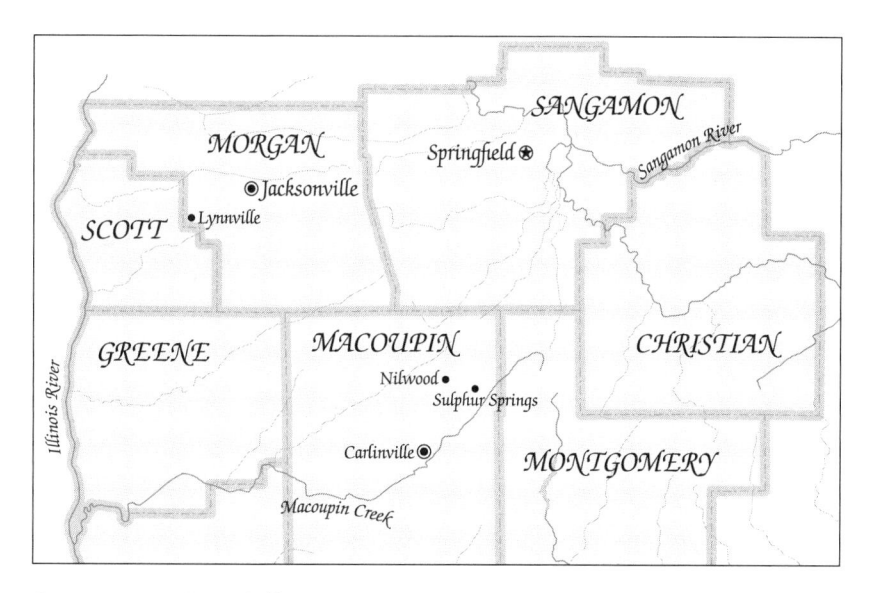

Figure 4: West Central Illinois, circa 1850. Courtesy of Zaccarine Design.

pay for the food and housing of her three daughters, it became necessary for the girls to leave her household. In 1846, when Elizabeth was eighteen years old, she married a farmer, John Williams, and went to live with him in a nearby county. Jemima and Hephzibah, then in their mid-teens, moved to Jacksonville, about fifty miles from Carlinville, and lived with the family of William Stribling, a farmer and Methodist minister.[7] The Stribling farm, Sunny Dell, was two miles east of town (figure 5).

In order to save enough money to pay for their schooling, Jemima and Hephzibah attended the women's college[8] only in alternate years—they took courses in 1851–52, 1853–54, and 1855–56.[9] Between those sessions, Jemima taught primary-school students, and Hephzibah worked at the Stribling farm. Because of their work schedules, they sometimes missed part of the school term. The two Dumville daughters resided at the farm as some indefinite combination of boarders and servants, but this was not unusual. Don Doyle's history of social stratification and economic development in Jacksonville found that, by 1860, about half of the households had at least one boarder or unrelated lodger. There was a housing shortage in the town after the arrival of the large wave of Irish and German immigrants in the late 1840s and the 1850s, and the average house then held six or seven persons, many unrelated. About one in every six Jacksonville families had servants.[10] In Carlinville, we found an average of slightly more than five persons per household in the 1860 Census. In a sample including 103 households, one-third had one or more unrelated residents. Twenty-two of those 103 households included unrelated females.[11]

Macoupin County, where Carlinville is located (see figure 4), was organized in 1829, but settlement of the county was opposed by a Methodist preacher because he contended that "God had set apart this region as a reservation for the geese and ducks."[12] Some called the place the Frog Pond Kingdom. Jacksonville was a more substantial place than Carlinville—in 1850, the population of Jacksonville was 2,745, while that of Carlinville was only 438; by 1870, Jacksonville had grown to 9,203 and Carlinville had reached 5,808. In the late 1840s and early 1850s Jemima moved back and forth between the two towns. In the Census of 1850 she is listed as living in Carlinville at the residence of the Tillers,[13] who were farmers (appropriately enough). Hephzibah, however, spent most of her youth separated from her mother and sisters—she remained with the Striblings for sixteen years.

The daughters sent letters to Ann and, later, to each other. Ann's letters were dictated, and the handwriting varies.[14] The letters from Elizabeth's household were written by her husband, John Williams.[15] Elizabeth was barely literate, if at all. She wrote little and only with great difficulty. So far as we can tell,

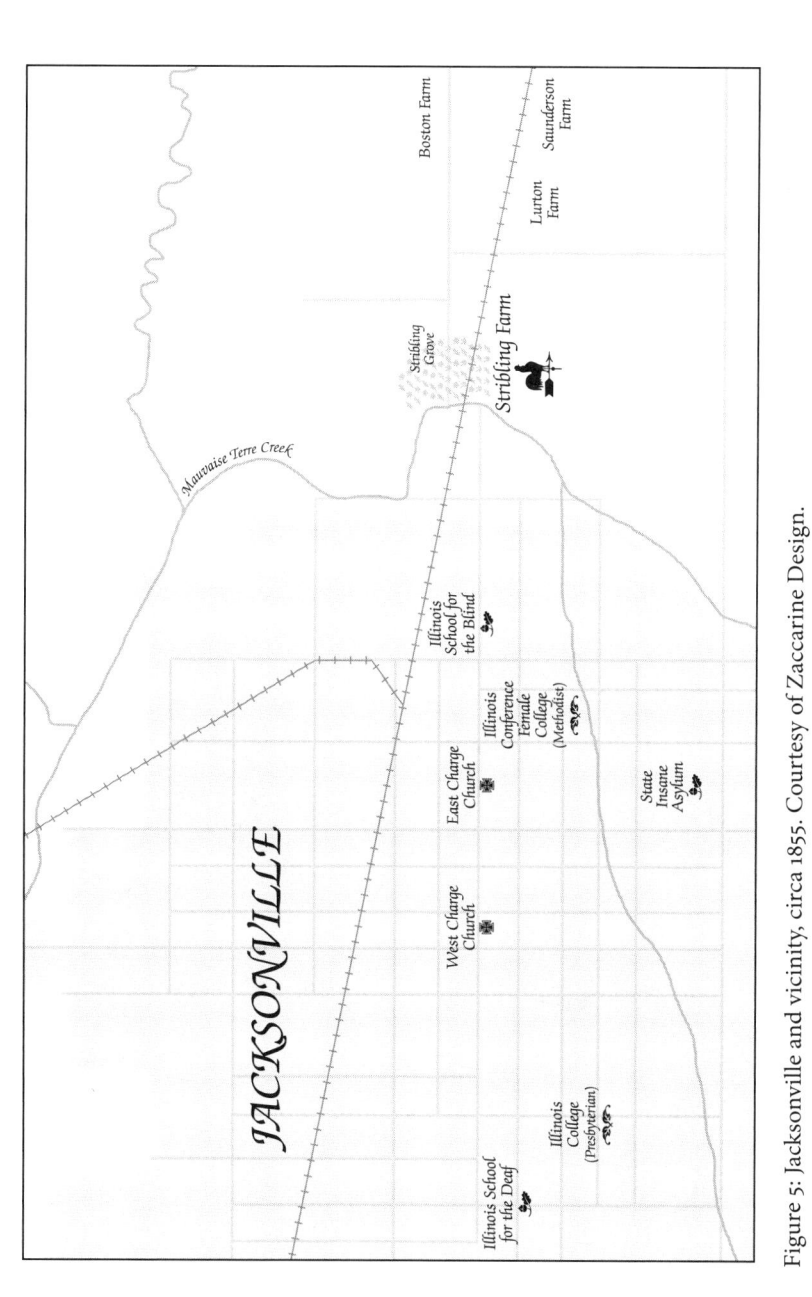

Figure 5: Jacksonville and vicinity, circa 1855. Courtesy of Zaccarine Design.

she did not read. The majority of the letters that survive were written by Hephzibah Beulah. She liked to experiment with her names—she signed her letters, variously, as Heppy, Heppe, Eppie, Hepsa, Heppa, Beulah, and (inexplicably) Belle. Her early letters, which began when she was nineteen years old, make it clear that she had not then received much schooling.

The photograph of Ann Dumville seen here (figure 6) has a revenue stamp on the back indicating that it was taken in 1865, when she was sixty-nine. She was just a bit more than five feet tall and had "an easy dignity that suggested intelligence and strength."[16] She dressed conservatively, in the attire of an elderly widow—black dress, cut full, a black silk shawl, fringed. The black was relieved by a white bonnet and neckerchief.[17] We have no pictures of Ann's husband or children. Apparently, however, Jemima and Hephzibah shared a family resemblance. A letter written by Hephzibah in November of 1856 notes a conversation in which a new acquaintance said, "I know that is Miss Dumville because she looks so much like Miss Jemima."

The Dumville women have distinct voices. The letters record their differing views on religion, schooling, politics, technological innovation, relationships

Figure 6: Ann Dumville, circa 1865. Burke family papers.

with employers, and the struggle to live. Hephzibah was a keen observer, possessed of a somewhat wicked wit, and she had a sharp eye for folly. Jemima, in contrast, was more disciplined, more conventional, more deeply religious, more serious. Their mother was devoted to her church and was a woman of unusual moral strength, courage, and will.

Hephzibah wrestled with decisions concerning her future. What type of work should she do? Even her view of the meaning of work was subject to change—did work mean carrying out domestic tasks within a family or was it labor for which she should be paid? Would she have a career as a teacher, like Jemima, or become a farmer's wife, like Elizabeth? Or would she pursue a particular skill, for example as a seamstress or cook? Was a career necessary or desirable, or was the purpose of work merely to provide food and lodging? Was education or intellectual development valued for its own sake, or was it a means to an end? If the latter, was the goal simply to find work, or was it to fulfill God's design by developing one's potential? And what were the Dumvilles' goals or expectations concerning marriage? Did they think in terms of romance? Did they hope to find husbands and, if so, of what sort? Did they want children? How far could they see ahead? How did nineteenth century serving women assess their opportunities? To what extent did they expect to be able to control their destinies? Of course, one makes choices both by direction and by indirection, and we will see some of each. Perhaps what was most important in life was not a career, or skills, or accomplishment, or even family, but living in a state of grace as a true Christian.

Religion

Religion gave Ann Dumville's life coherence and purpose. After the death of her husband, it was difficult for her to make her way on what was still the frontier of settlement. According to a Methodist preacher, a contemporary of hers, "for days together" the Dumvilles' "only food was corn cooked and beaten."[18] Ann's faith, however, was a source of comfort. An 1879 history of Macoupin County says, "[S]ister Dumville often walked five miles to church, which is but one manifestation of her zeal for the Lord of Hosts."[19] The president of the women's college described Ann as a "Methodist of primitive style, characterized by singular faith, enthusiastic without a particle of fanaticism, devout without the slightest spirit of censoriousness,"[20] and a history of the conference credits her with bringing about the founding of a church in Missouri:

> Visiting her daughter in Missouri during the war, she learned that there was a colored family living near. She visited them and finding that they could not

read, told them that her daughter would teach them and she would furnish the books. A colored Sunday School was started, soon a preacher visited them. And the result was a church was formed.[21]

Despite the fact that she had only her earnings as a housekeeper, she was a generous donor to the Carlinville church's foreign missions.[22] Ann Dumville has been called "an old-time Methodist saint."[23]

The letters reflect the centrality of religion in the Dumvilles' lives, and two experiences or transitions that held special significance for nineteenth-century Methodists are especially prominent in their comments. One of these is "conversion" and the other is "a good death," a death at which the decedent was "at peace with God." Conversion was the term used for a spiritual awakening, the experience of a definite commitment to the Word of God. In a letter written at the beginning of 1854, Jemima (then twenty-three years old) described her religious conversion at a revival meeting. Revivals, which took place over several days, were meant to strengthen and renew one's faith, and Jemima went to the meeting seeking a remedy for unhappiness. The letter tells us that she went on her own, not in a social or church group. The individual experience of salvation is a central tenet of the Methodist Church, and her decision to make the commitment was not a product of pressure from friends or peers but the result of a personal conviction that she should give herself over to God. At the meeting, she loudly declared her praise of the Lord, a conventional form of expression of faith in the evangelical tradition advocated by her mother.

Hephzibah's conversion, four years later, was rather different, and she distinguished her experience from that of her mother and sister. Her public action—standing up and going forward in front of the congregation—came after several days of struggle between her desire for commitment and her distaste for public display. Social pressure from friends who were present was important, but she felt that the crowd psychology, urging people to go forward, was not an appropriate basis for religious faith.

One needed to conduct one's life so as to be in a state of grace at the time of death and, at the end of life, to welcome the transition to Glory, "going to meet one's Maker." Preparation for a proper, peaceful death was important. It might come at any time. In Methodist publications, the faithful were given examples of good deaths, including that of John Wesley, which was depicted in a widely distributed print. Because of the influence of these models, accounts of both conversions and deaths came to follow standard forms.[24]

Deaths occurred so often that they were met with acceptance, and religious doctrine encouraged that acceptance. Of the ninety-four letters written by members of the Dumville family, 60 percent include a reference to death or serious illness; 40 percent refer to death.[25] The Dumvilles appear to have attended to the mortality of a broad segment of the community. Of the twenty-nine persons whose deaths are reported in the letters, eighteen are mentioned only when they die.

The Dumvilles heard both resident and circuit-riding ministers preach at church services, revivals, county fairs, school programs, and other community events, and they developed friendships with some of the preachers, but the circuit riders covered a large territory and were given new assignments every year or two. Gradually, congregations were established when they were large enough to support a full-time minister. The circuit riders provided a connection between the broader Methodist Church and the developing communities.[26] With constant travel and no permanent home, circuit riders could undoubtedly be quite lonely, and Hephzibah appears to have felt that some of them had an interest in selecting a mate. Since she was of marriageable age, was the daughter of a widely respected member of the church, and was living in the household of a prominent local preacher,[27] it is likely that she was regarded as a suitable candidate to become a preacher's wife. A few (but not many) of the letters reflect this.

Like any other continuing institution, the church was concerned with maintaining the organization. In addition to recruiting members, it monitored the conduct of both clergy and congregants, and it administered discipline. The Methodist "General Rules" said that it was "expected of all who continue therein, that they should continue to evidence their desire of salvation . . . by avoiding evil of every kind, especially that which is most generally practiced."[28] Members were sometimes expelled from the church, usually for misbehavior such as drunkenness or gambling. There was discussion within the congregation about each case, a sort of hearing. The Rules provided:

> If the accused person be found guilty by the decision of a majority of the members before whom he is brought to trial, and the crime be such as is expressly forbidden by the word of God, sufficient to exclude a person from the kingdom of grace and glory, let the minister or preacher who has the charge of the circuit expel him . . .[29]

An 1859 letter written by Jemima reports that a neighbor who had separated from his wife "withdrew from the Conference to keep from having a trial and being turned out."

Although women were not elders or deacons of the church or members of the conference, they could be missionaries and lay preachers, and they did much of the fundraising. Missionary work was an important part of the activities of the church, and the Dumvilles' letters discuss their interest in such service. An 1853 letter refers to plans to go to Texas, apparently as missionaries, but the continuity of the letters makes it clear that they did not actually do so. Methodists had started missionary work in Texas in the 1830s. A history of Methodist missions published in 1879 commented: "Heroic work was done in Texas in those days, and it yielded goodly harvest."[30] Friends of the Dumvilles did go to Texas, but Hephzibah reported that they did not like it. Six years later, Jemima proposed a more ambitious undertaking, missionary work in Africa. The letters refer to a lecture by John Seys, a famous and controversial Methodist missionary. He and his wife served in Liberia from 1834 until the early 1840s and then again from 1856 to 1866. Between these periods in Africa, Seys lectured widely in the United States, raising money for the missions.[31]

Both Hephzibah's and Ann's letters are attentive to the recruitment of new church members. A letter written by Hephzibah in February of 1858 reported that "about a hundred have joined the church" and that "some of the very hardest cases in town have been converted." This was discussed in terms of individual salvation, of course—as the number of souls that had been saved—but recruitment was also a matter of institution building. Ann regularly celebrated the size of the collections at church services and the success of the church's building projects. This was a period when the Methodists invested a considerable amount in buildings. According to the Census, the value of Methodist church property in Macoupin and Morgan Counties increased from $5,100 in 1850 to $65,800 in 1860. In 1855, Ann Dumville reported that the Methodist bishop had attended the dedication of a new brick church with a large sanctuary and that the cost had been fully paid. "We had a great day on the dedication of our new church, great sermon, and a fine collection, nineteen hundred and fifty dollars, were raised on that day so the Lord's house is finished and paid for, and we are thankful, and rejoicing." A month later, she wrote to her daughters: "Bishop Janes dedicated our new church he preached an excellent sermon, and collections were taken up to defray all the expense and we have now a beautiful house well furnished, and a good preacher to preach in it, and all are praying for a revival."

For all of the Dumvilles, the church provided both a sense of security in unsettled circumstances—confidence that "the Lord will provide"—and a set of daily activities, a sense of purpose. In the rural Midwest of the nineteenth century, where neighbors were relatively few, religious activity supplied a community, a network of personal relationships. But cities were growing and Methodism was then in the process of transformation from a movement based primarily on a constituency of farmers and artisans to an institution that recruited congregants who had more education and more elevated social standing.[32] This division within the denomination is reflected in an 1855 letter written by Ann Dumville in which she urged her daughters to "hold fast to old fashioned religion." The populist appeal of charismatic Christianity was strong in the rural Midwest, and self-made preachers such as Peter Cartwright[33] had a receptive constituency there. Formality in worship risked the loss of its appeal to those Cartwright called "the Lord's poor."[34] While Jemima shouted her praise to God, Hephzibah "did not feel like shouting" and preferred the sermons of more intellectual preachers. It is possible that Hephzibah was, consciously or unconsciously, moving toward a more middle-class identity.

Education

The Methodist conference reported in 1852 that "the Pupils of our Seminaries and Colleges have spread themselves over the length and breadth of the land diffusing the blessings of elementary instruction, and giving an impulse to the cause of Popular Education."[35] The Illinois Conference Women's College in Jacksonville embraced the mission of training teachers, one of the few professions open to women. For a decade, from 1853 to 1863, Jemima worked as a primary school teacher. She taught first in Lynnville, nine miles from Jacksonville, and then in 1855 she moved back to Carlinville to teach there. We do not know what qualifications she presented in order to secure her positions, but her attendance at the women's college was surely an important credential.

Publicly supported education of teachers was established at the Normal School in central Illinois (now Illinois State University) in 1857. Social reformers such as Catharine Beecher and Horace Mann campaigned vigorously on behalf of common schools—especially in support of training women as teachers.[36] The motivation for this initiative was religious and specifically Protestant. Evangelicals who embraced "perfectionism" held that the faithful could choose, through an exercise of the will and with the help of God, to achieve grace and personal improvement.[37] Indeed, self-improvement was not only possible but a moral duty. The Reverend Lyman Beecher, Catharine's father, believed that it was America's destiny to "lead the way in the moral and political emancipation of the world"[38] and that universal education would play an essential role in this. The American West was of particular importance—in his autobiography, Beecher wrote, "If we gain the West, all is safe; if we lose it all is lost . . . the competition now is for that of preoccupancy in the education of the rising generation, in which Catholics and infidels have got the start of us."[39]

Hephzibah appears to have obtained most of her education through her own reading, which was quite varied. Her letters discuss Harriet Beecher Stowe's antislavery classic, *Uncle Tom's Cabin*, published in 1852, and Milton's *Paradise Lost*. The fact that she read *Paradise Lost* is, perhaps, surprising, not only because the text is difficult but because it deviates from standard Christian doctrine. Much of her reading had a Methodist theme—the biographies of prominent Methodist clergy, a diary of a British soldier who was killed in the Crimean War (he was a devout Methodist), a retelling of New Testament stories put in the form of a novel, and a memoir written by a southern preacher who opposed secession.[40] Books were available to Hephzibah in the Stribling family library, which included Macaulay's history of England, a five-volume work, and in the library of the Phi Nu literary society at the college, but books were expensive and the selection limited.

The curriculum of the college included courses in Latin, French, mathematics up to analytic geometry, physiology, botany, chemistry, astronomy, geology, rhetoric, and one survey of world history.[41] The senior year included a heavy dose of religion—"Natural Theology," "Evidences of Christianity," and "Moral Science"—perhaps as fortification against the temptations of the outside world. Apart from something called "Parsing in Prose and Poetry," however, there was no instruction in English literature. Although *Harper's Monthly Magazine* was founded in 1850 and the *Atlantic Monthly* in 1857, and both published distinguished fiction, these magazines had little circulation in central Illinois.

The lack of attention to literature probably reflected a cultural bias against, perhaps even a distrust of, fiction. A contemporary observer reported that Midwesterners of the 1840s and 1850s regarded stories that were not "true" as "a pack of lies."[42] *Uncle Tom's Cabin* was apparently put in the category of moral instruction and thus granted an exception. Lawrence Cremin's history of American education notes that John Bunyan and Daniel Defoe, "with their explicit and implicit counsel about how to live and what to teach, could still be found beside the Bible in many a household."[43]

As new technologies reduced the cost of publication, however, the Midwest became a significant market for books, magazines, and newspapers.[44] The commonly cited estimate is that white adults in America had a literacy rate of 90 percent in the 1850s, as compared to only 60 percent in Great Britain.[45] Visitors to the United States commented on this.[46] The Associated Press was founded in 1846; larger newspapers in major cities used its services; new steam-powered printing presses sped the production of papers, and the telegraph and the railroads greatly aided the gathering and dissemination of news. A letter Hephzibah wrote in 1859 to a cousin in England notes that the telegraph and railroads had facilitated "transmitting intelligence."[47] Fiction was serialized in local broadsheets.[48] A weekly newspaper began publication in Jacksonville in 1851, and the *Jacksonville Sentinel*, a daily, began in 1857. In Carlinville there was a weekly newspaper as of 1852, and a second weekly started in 1853. Hephzibah gleaned both local and national news from the papers and passed it along to Jemima and Ann. Her retelling of the stories may well have provided some lessons in English composition.

Education was, of course, an important indicator of social class, then as now—perhaps the most obvious indicator. A new middle class, separated from farmers and manual laborers, was emerging in the mid-nineteenth century, and speech patterns, grammar, penmanship, familiarity with the classics, and skill in basic arithmetic all identified those who belonged to it and those who did not. The Dumvilles exemplify both the possibilities and the limitations in this transition. Because the family lacked the resources necessary to meet its needs, the children were put to work in order to provide support, and the necessity to work then interfered with schooling, thus limiting opportunities for future advancement. This was, of course, a common pattern. In the nineteenth century, servants and manual laborers seldom earned enough to provide more than subsistence. The labor of the children helped to feed the family.[49]

Social Mobility

By 1861 Hephzibah blamed the Striblings for the "deficiency" of her education, and she felt that she had not received much benefit from her relationship with them. She was listed in the Stribling household in both the Census of 1850 (as Hefryeba Dubville) and 1860 (as Helter Dunville) but with no indication of her status in the family. She did not receive regular wages and did not know how much she would be paid when she left the Stribling household. This lack of certainty troubled her, but she was reluctant to raise the issue. As we will see, it eventually became a matter of contention.

In the mid-nineteenth century, hired household work was mostly done by "help" rather than by servants, especially in rural areas. The help were often daughters of neighbors or were girls from farms who came to town to work and go to school. These young women were customarily paid a small amount but were treated as family members. As Faye Dudden's study of serving women has observed, "the hired girl's treatment reflected her status as a member of another family," one with "independent standing."[50]

In addition to doing household and farm chores, Hephzibah often cared for the Striblings' five grandchildren, who lived nearby in the town. The

Striblings' son-in-law, James Lurton, was the owner of a dry goods store that advertised heavily in the Jacksonville newspapers.[51] Whether an employment relationship existed between Hephzibah and the Lurtons is unclear, but it seems likely that childcare was a part of her Stribling family duties. There were times, often in the spring, when major housecleaning or home improvement projects were undertaken, and Hephzibah then shared tasks with her employer (for example, mending carpets, making soap).[52] The fall harvest was also busy. But sometimes, especially in winter, it was rather quiet, and she could then pursue her own interests—going to school, sewing for herself and her family, reading.

Godey's Lady's Book, published from 1830 until the end of the century, was a popular source of information on homemaking and on the latest fashion trends from Europe.[53] The circulation of *Godey's* grew from about 25,000 copies in the early 1840s to 150,000 in 1860.[54] Anne Rose's research on the development of commercial markets concluded that, "with unprecedented deliberation, a middle class created itself in the likeness of appearances and manners popularized in print culture."[55] *The Ladies' Repository*, a Methodist periodical, was loosely modeled on *Godey's*, and Hephzibah read it regularly. It included articles on the home and childrearing, as well as literature and religious material. Both *Godey's* and *The Ladies' Repository* included high-quality steel engravings, and at least one in each issue of *Godey's* was hand colored. Women's magazines both responded to and helped create consumer markets, and they provided role models for their readers.[56] As the number of educated women increased, these magazines prospered.

Because the pursuit of fashion required at least some leisure and disposable income, it was a visible indication of status.[57] The magazines provided sewing patterns that disseminated fashion and broadened the market for it[58] (see figure 7). The letters reflect Hephzibah's interest in fashion. She was concerned about the suitability of her clothing and was aware of current styles. At the college, Hephzibah and Jemima associated with and adopted the social values of the daughters of substantial, established, prosperous families. They went to picnics, parties, concerts, paper readings, and the meetings of the Phi Nu society and of Belles Lettres, all of which were schools for proper deportment and for the inculcation of middle-class norms.[59]

Women often demonstrated elevated social standing through the pursuit of artistic crafts. "Fancywork" was a symbolic occupation. Embroidery and quilting could be done in the home, they required discipline and dedication, and they were clearly separated from menial tasks. Early in 1857 Hephzibah wrote that she intended to spend her time "quite profitably by leasurely reviewing my last winters studies, and reading good books and finishing my

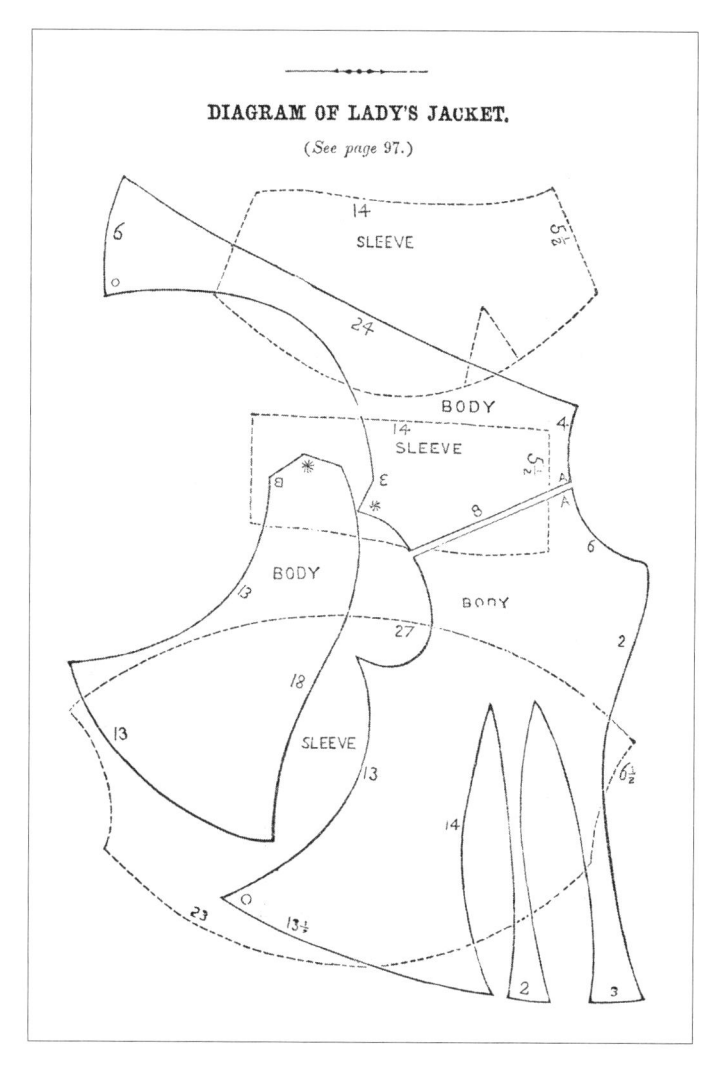

Figure 7: "Diagram of a Lady's Jacket." Pattern from *Godey's Lady's Book*, 1858.

quilt."[60] Sewing was also a social activity. In 1856 Hephzibah reported that she had been "invited to a sewing," saying, "I enjoyed myself very much."[61] Needlework, watercolors, and the crafting of objects made from human hair were all seen as expressions of esthetic tastes, as well as evidence of leisure. Hairwork was regarded as especially empathetic because it incorporated the substance of the person (see figure 8). A gift of an object made of one's own

Figure 8: "Hair Bracelet" as illustrated in *Godey's Lady's Book*, 1858.

hair was a personal expression of attachment, suitable as a betrothal present.[62] By the 1850s and 1860s, commercially produced hairwork was available, but homemade work was obviously a better demonstration of commitment and domesticity, and Hephzibah wrote to Jemima requesting her to send some of their mother's hair and some of her own.[63]

The Dumvilles were immigrants, a label that now implies "the other,"[64] but in the mid-nineteenth century a very large share of all American families had recently arrived. In 1846, the potato crop failed in Ireland, and crop failures on the European continent in the following two years and the political warfare there in 1848 further exacerbated living conditions. The resulting unprecedented wave of Irish and German emigration to the United States brought both social change and political controversy.[65] Until the mid-1840s the annual number of immigrants remained below 100,000,[66] but the population of Illinois doubled in the 1850s, a rate of growth three times that of the nation as a whole. In 1850 the population of Chicago was 29,963. Only five years later, it had grown to 80,028, and in 1860 it reached 109,260.[67]

The Dumvilles had arrived before the great influx, and that was no doubt to their advantage, as was the fact that they were English. An analysis by economic historian Joseph Ferrie of U.S. Census and immigration data indicates that English and German immigrants fared better during the 1850s than did those from Ireland.[68] The Midwest was probably more open to immigrants than Boston or Philadelphia;[69] in the Midwest, social rules permitted more latitude for variety. The Dumvilles, in any event, looked like, spoke like (except, perhaps, for their accents), dressed like, and worshiped like the established families. They shared the common understanding of the criteria for membership in the community. They knew what was expected of them and, in the small ways in which they were different, they sought to adjust their behavior and acquire proper credentials.

Politics

Fourth of July celebrations in Jacksonville receive repeated mention in Hephzibah's letters, and she describes them in detail. Her account of the 1859 parade is especially vivid, but she also gives close attention to the picnics and speeches in 1860. She mentions the reading of the Declaration of Independence, the "Patriots of seventy-six," and veterans of the War of 1812. Despite her birth in England, Hephzibah's choice of allegiance in these old wars appears clear. She wrote that an Independence Day included "music and dancing, swearing and drinking, and fighting and such things as are common on the Celebration of a day of which the American people are so proud." The letter is wry in tone, but she enjoyed the day.

As she matured, Hephzibah followed the politics of the time closely, and she was clearly a partisan in the elections. She was upset when Buchanan won the presidency in 1856 and celebratory when Lincoln was elected in 1860. Of course, the issues of the day were extraordinarily compelling and consequential. Moreover, the citizens of central Illinois were close to the principals; Lincoln was in the neighborhood; Stephen Douglas had been the local prosecutor in Jacksonville. Campaign rallies, public speeches, and sermons on the evils of slavery were frequent occurrences, and the local newspapers were full of commentary. It would have been difficult to remain oblivious, and the Dumvilles clearly were not. They were engaged. They cared about the future of their adopted country and the preservation of the Union.

The increasing political conflict over slavery, however, threatened the stability of both the nation and the local community. Jacksonville had been settled by Southerners, primarily from Kentucky and Tennessee,[70] but there were strong differences of opinion concerning abolition.[71] The Illinois legislature, dominated by representatives from southern and central Illinois in the antebellum period, passed highly restrictive fugitive slave laws in the 1830s and 1840s.[72] Even within the Methodist Church, abolition was a contentious issue. At the national level, Methodists split between North and South in 1844 after disagreements about slaveholding by clergy and the authority of bishops. Remarkably, despite Ann Dumville's strong and constant devotion to the church, her abolitionist sympathies led to her expulsion from it, briefly. The *Minutes of the Illinois Conference* reported: "Her deep devotion and zeal were not appreciated by members of the church. She was an abolitionist, and that was enough in their estimation to neutralize all her other excellences. For this she was turned out of the church."[73] There is no discussion of this in the letters. By the time the letters were written, she was again in good standing in the Methodist congregation in Carlinville and still an abolitionist.

The Dumvilles gave increasing attention during the 1850s to the Midwest's conflict concerning slavery.[74] The Missouri Compromise of 1820 had admitted Missouri to the Union as a slave state and Maine as a free state, while prohibiting slavery in other Louisiana Purchase lands at a latitude north of 36 degrees, 30 minutes. The Kansas-Nebraska Act of 1854, however, repealed the Compromise. Despite the fact that both Nebraska and Kansas were north of 36 degrees 30 minutes, the repeal permitted voters of those territories to decide whether slavery would be legal within their borders. Senator Douglas, Democrat of Illinois, was a principal author of the Kansas-Nebraska Act and argued that "popular sovereignty"—decision by popular vote—would help preserve the Union. But opponents, notably the newly formed Republican Party, made the extension of slavery into the territories a central campaign issue.

In the 1856 presidential election, Millard Fillmore, the former president, was the candidate of a third party, the American or "Know-Nothing" Party, and Hephzibah declared herself to be a supporter of Fillmore and the Know-Nothings. The party was anti-Catholic, anti-Mormon, and anti-immigration, and those positions were congruent with Hephzibah's views. Irish and German immigrants were concentrated in large cities[75] and by the 1850s were a majority in St. Louis, Chicago, and Milwaukee.[76] Almost all of the Irish immigrants and about half of the Germans were Catholics. The anti-immigrant and anti-Catholic policies of the Know-Nothings were, thus, specifically anti-Irish and anti-urban, and nativist sentiment was strong in rural areas such as central Illinois. Many Jacksonian Democrats, wedded to agrarian values and uncomfortable with industrialization and urbanization, became identified with the Copperheads or "Peace Democrats," Northerners who opposed the Civil War. Some Copperheads clearly supported the Southern states and the institution of slavery, but others simply wanted peace and advocated negotiation. Often, indeed, they resisted not only the war but social and economic modernization.

Although Hephzibah declared herself to be a Know-Nothing in 1856, her sentiments changed as the struggle between North and South became more intense. By 1858, all of the Dumvilles were abolitionists, and Hephzibah transferred her allegiance from the Know-Nothings to the Republicans. This was a typical pattern. Those parties shared antipathy toward Irish and German immigrants, especially Catholics, and Lincoln actively courted Know-Nothings.[77]

The Civil War

After Lincoln's election to the presidency in 1860 and the subsequent secession of Southern states, the Union tried to blockade the South's ports and to maintain federal control of Fort Sumter in Charleston bay. The Confederate attack on Fort Sumter on April 12, 1861, was the beginning of open warfare between the Union and the Confederacy. As one might expect, from 1861 to 1863 the letters give considerable attention to the war. The Dumvilles knew soldiers from both Jacksonville and Carlinville, and they corresponded with some of them. The archive includes a few of the soldiers' letters. Given the very large number of deaths of Union troops, it is rather surprising that none of the letters written by the women report war deaths.[78] The men's letters do, however. The men were, of course, closer to the battles, they saw the consequences, and they were keenly focused on the risk. A soldier's letter of May 1862 closes with a prayer that, if he was "not permitted to meet on earth, I hope and trust to meet you all in heaven." The only injury of an acquaintance discussed by the women is a report by Hephzibah in April 1862 that a friend "was struck by a ball in the cheek." (Apparently, the musket ball did not do great damage. It may have been spent.) Hephzibah and Jemima were active in trying to maintain morale. The women encouraged the soldiers, sent letters and packages, sewed bandages, and commiserated with worried and grieving families.

Gender Roles

In a sense, the domestic service positions held by the Dumvilles were like the work of most women in the nineteenth century. Their duties included many of the tasks of motherhood, such as childcare and maintenance of the home—Hephzibah and Ann were homemakers, although working for another family. In early frontier economies, the principal economic unit was the family, but as industrialization and urbanization proceeded and the market economy developed, work formerly performed within the home increasingly moved into the public sphere. When it did, the roles of men and women became more distinct both in their work and within their families. Home remedies for illness were replaced by doctors and hospitals, and reading at the kitchen table was replaced by teachers and schools. When these services moved outside the home and were "professionalized," the professionals were usually men. This was less true of teachers and dressmakers than it was of doctors, cabinetmakers, and tailors, but the work that was left within the home, the woman's domain, became less honored and was perceived as less consequential. For the most part, it consisted of cooking, cleaning, and childcare, and these tasks were then defined as "women's work," not a prestigious category. The homemaking movement attempted to ameliorate these effects by claiming professional status for the wife and mother, the "home manager."[79] It was not entirely persuasive.

Domesticity was an ideology that elevated the woman's role, but it sharpened social class lines because women could afford to specialize in domestic arts only if their time and labor were not needed for work in the fields, a shop, or a mill. As we will see, Ann had some management responsibilities at the Burke household, perhaps because her employer was a widower, but there was an important social distinction between wives managing their own homes and housekeepers employed as servants. Hephzibah's role at the Striblings was clearly subordinate. Jemima's work as a teacher, defined as a "nurturing" role, was one of the few "professions" open to women. The education of women was heavily oriented toward the training of teachers, who were very poorly paid.

In the 1850 Census, occupation was recorded only for adult males. By 1860, the Census sought to record the occupations of both men and women, but those of women were not consistently reported. Many were listed as "at home." Although hired men in the Stribling household were recorded as "laborer" in both 1850 and 1860, Hephzibah's occupation was not entered at either time.[80] The Census practice reflects the "silence" of women in a patriarchal society.[81]

The Dumville letters tell a story of striving—for social acceptance and economic security, and for salvation. There was tension in antebellum America between religious values and the attractions of the market for consumer goods. In the broader society, the culture was increasingly dividing along lines defined by social class. Cultural historian Anne Rose observes that "middle-class social arrangements were seductive" and that the desire for social advancement usually won.[82] What scholars have called the cult of domesticity was a way of resolving this tension.[83] It permitted the home to be defined as an island of peace, tranquility, and moral virtue, apart from the corrupting influence of the market and the quest for status. With the movement of workers from farms and cottage industries to factories and offices, so that there was less need for a large labor force in the home, family size decreased and parents made a greater investment in the education of the next generation. The relationship between education and social standing was well understood.

Most published letters—indeed, most that are saved long enough to be published—were written by public figures, noteworthy scholars, or famous authors. The Dumville letters are a small counterweight to the dominant elite, masculine perspective. While men wrote letters that dealt with politics and business, women were the primary authors of family correspondence that recorded joys, challenges, and sorrows. Most women's letters have disappeared, of course, as have most letters written by men. In many cases, no doubt, this is not a great loss, but some family correspondence is very informative about the nature of daily life.[84] The Dumvilles saw and felt the ravages of cholera and typhoid, which were constant threats; they confronted the conflict concerning slavery and the resulting dissension within their communities; the vicissitudes of weather governed their finances as crops flourished or failed; rapid population growth, driven by a wave of new immigrants, transformed the norms and social structure of their towns. It was a life of privation and risk, but the letters are remarkably hopeful.

The literature on the lives and work of serving women such as Hephzibah and Ann is sparse,[85] and the Dumville letters provide telling detail. We can read the letters as lessons in American social, political, and cultural history, as essays on the comfort provided by religion during personal loss and national conflict, as a comment on the roles of women, as a picture of the antebellum Midwest, or as all of those things.[86]

2. 1851–1853

Family Matters

The early letters focus on local news and day-to-day activities—they give accounts of shopping, sewing, reading, and travel, and they report marriages, the quality of Sunday sermons, and even the occasional family quarrel. At this relatively early stage of the daughters' lives, the letters also give considerable attention to schooling. Ann's letters encourage education, Jemima's report her pursuit of it, and Hephzibah's lament her lack of it. It is not clear how far either daughter progressed at the college, but Jemima refers to taking exams. Hephzibah does not appear to have reached that point.[1] In 1852, Jemima received a brief letter offering a teaching position. The man who wrote was a Methodist, and it seems likely that the church's network helped her get the job. The nature of the school is not mentioned, nor is it clear what grades she was to teach. Her students probably ranged in age from perhaps six or seven to twelve or so.

A few accounts of schooling in Illinois in the mid-nineteenth century provide a picture of teaching methods in the elementary grades. The autobiography of lawyer and businessman Daniel Harmon Brush, which describes his education in Illinois in the 1830s,[2] notes the use of competitive spelling bees and of reading aloud before an audience of fellow students. The students were required to memorize facts, dates, poems, and multiplication tables, and then to recite. Recitation is also mentioned in some of the Dumville letters written by younger children.[3] Teaching methods were adapted to accommodate students varying in age and ability, all in the same classroom. Older students were often assigned the supervision of younger ones.[4]

As it happens, Lawrence Cremin's classic history of American education uses a Carlinville man, John McAuley Palmer, as a case study. Palmer, who is mentioned in later Dumville letters, became a major general in the Civil War, then governor, and then a U.S. senator.[5] Cremin also discusses the education of another resident of Macoupin County, James Henry Magee, an African American scholar, newspaper editor, and minister in the Baptist Church. Cremin concludes that "the educational biographies of Palmer and Magee . . . patently illustrate that individuals made their own way, irregularly, intermittently, and indeterminately, through the educational configurations of the nineteenth-century frontier, going back and forth across the permeable boundaries of household, church, school, and apprenticeship, largely self-motivated and largely self-directed."[6] The Dumvilles' experience fits this pattern.

Little education above the elementary level was available in Illinois until after the Civil War. A few private colleges, seminaries, or academies were established before 1850, but the number of students was very small. According to the 1850 Census, Macoupin County then had one academy or seminary with two teachers and forty-five pupils, and Morgan County had one college (Illinois College) with six teachers and ninety pupils and two academies with fourteen teachers and 291 pupils. Some of what took place in these schools was, however, secondary or even primary education. While higher education was unusual, Cremin reports that in 1850 about 90 percent of the Macoupin County children between ages five and fourteen attended some kind of school, at least part time.[7] Prior to the establishment of free public education in 1855, private religious and secular schools were the available educational options.[8] Nonetheless, Hephzibah and Jemima, daughters of a housekeeper, both completed sufficient schooling to take courses at the Illinois Conference Female College in the 1850s.

Given the Dumvilles' concern with education, the letters include remarkably little about either the content of their courses at the college or the quality of the teaching. Perhaps the courses were so basic and standard that they did not require comment—perhaps, that is, it was well understood that students would learn to express themselves properly and do simple algebra. The college offered more than that,[9] but the Dumvilles did not, so far as we can determine, pursue instruction in the arts. They did, however, go to concerts and to meetings of literary societies at which poems and essays were read. As the letters make clear, these meetings had social as well as educational purposes—indeed, they may have been primarily social occasions.

In a later letter, Hephzibah described herself as "a dear lover of music."[10] Jemima played the piano.[11] In the middle of the nineteenth century, however, Methodists had a cautious attitude toward the arts.[12] Pictures with religious subjects were approved, unless people were depicted in a state of undress, and Methodists were enthusiastic about hymns—the right hymns.[13] But other music was viewed with suspicion; entertainment was a frivolous pursuit, or worse.[14] W. W. Sweet, a Methodist historian, said that "more devils lurked in catgut and horsehair [a reference to musical instruments and the bows used to play those instruments] than Luther ever dreamed of."[15] The proper purpose of music was to express religious faith. Hephzibah's enthusiasm for concerts appears to reflect her independent judgment and her willingness to challenge authority.

Thomas Augst's examination of the letters of young men suggests that some mid-nineteenth-century letters "intensified familial relationships primarily by serving as a medium for moral admonition and guidance."[16] In much the same way, Ann Dumville's letters to her daughters emphasize religious and moral values. A letter written by Ann to Jemima in 1853 expresses commendation for Jemima's employment as a teacher and endorses the practice of opening the school day with prayer. Hephzibah's letters show that she was troubled by her separation from her mother and sisters and that she sought moral instruction from her mother for as long as the letters continued. Her first letter, written in 1851, sought to reinforce the family ties—her mother had probably scolded Hephzibah for failing to write. Unlike later letters, this first one does not discuss a wide range of topics or provide factual detail—Hephzibah refers to family but mentions neither friends nor neighbors, nor her reading, nor concerts at the college, nor Christian values. We learn little about what was going on in her life or what she thought about events. Despite expressions of love, this letter is relatively formulaic and impersonal.

Family correspondence was a duty given primarily to women. Young ladies were expected to learn how to compose letters in proper, polite form, and manuals were published to provide instruction concerning both the form and the content regarded as appropriate. The first letter makes clear that Hephzibah was not then an experienced or confident writer—indeed, she expressed doubt that she could produce a letter "fit to be read." She was, apparently, conscious that she was both practicing the art and conforming to social conventions of the time. Writing a good letter was a mark of social attainment.

From: Hephzibah
Envelope address: Miss Mima Dumville, Carlinville Illinois

Jacksonville   June 1th, 1851

Dear Mother I have often thought of writing to you
And[17] indeed I have twice attempted it but not

Being pleasd with my letters I laid them
Aside and though[t] that I could not write one fit
To be read and it was not worth wile trying
I forgot then that a mother recives with pleasure
Every token of affection from her child be it ever so
Small or ever so poorly offerd she can as no one
els[e] can look over the imperfecttion of her
Childeron and now dear mother you must not
Say again that you are afraid i doo not love you
for I love you better than any other person in
This world—I went to se[e] the girls[18] last
Saturday week and staid till Sunday evening.
I should have staid longer but matters at home
Were so pressing that i could not. They ware
All well and apparantly in good spirits. It is
Needless to tell you how many cows they milch
For Jamima towld me that she intended to write
To you soon and she will be sure to tell you
All aboute them things. Write to me as soon as
You get this and tell me when you are coming
To se[e] us. Jemima with myself[19] sends our love to
you and best respect to all our friends adiu[20] your
affecttionate daughter Hepsa.

From: Hephzibah
Envelope address: Miss Mima Dumville, Lynnville, Illinois

Jacksonville   Jan. 1th 1852

Dear Sister Mima
I am very sorry
Indeed to hear that John[21] has a sore
Thumb and Grandma [Stribling] says it is not worth
While to lance it unless you lance to the
Bone, that it will be the best thing you
Could do. I have been comeing ever since
Grandma came home but the roads
where impassable for 6 weeks after her
Return. I made preparations to come
And spend the Christmass but the weather
Was so unfavorable that I could not.
Intended to come yesterday but was
Prevented by the roads being so muddy.
You need not look for me untill you see

Me but I shall come as soon as I can.
I am well at present but Mr. and Mrs.
Stribling are as usual unwell. I do not
Think their visit did them any good.
Miss Parker wrote a letter t[w]o you two or
three week since and [h]as asked me
If I thought you had recieved it.
If you have pleas favor her with an answer
Is my request. I recieved a letter from
Mother while Grandma was gon[e] to
Kentuckey[22] but have not heard from her
since. I in turn must beg you to
excuse my bad writeing.

So Wishing you
A happy New Year.
I remain your affectionate Sister Hep.

From: Hephzibah
Envelope address: Miss Jemima Dumville, Lynnville, Ills

Postmark: Jacksonville, July 24

At Home July the 18th 1852
Dear Mima
I did not recieve your letter untill last Wednesday
And I was so buisy that I could not write or go to town
Untill yesterday. I went to Mr. Brown's to get a
Letter for you and he looked in his books but said
That your name was not there to be found. He said
Furthermore that Mr. Jaquess[23] could not give you a
Letter as he was not the Pastor and that the only way
Was to join the church again on [?] probation.
I selected a dress for Lizzy it is all brown except
A small white leaf and will I think make a very neat dark
Dress. Mr. Lurton said if she did not like it he would
Take it back or if it should faid, but he was shure
It would not she should have another. I obtain'd
Some net for Mother's cap and of cource charged it to
you they that have the cape aught to pay for the cap.
Bye the bye I intend to make it up and wear it un
till I have an opportunity of sending it to you
As I could not get anything to pleas me at

Lurtons Store. He had a peice of beautiful Corn
Collard [colored?] Tissue but there was just one dress pattern.
And he could not cut that. He had another peice
of the same kind of goods. It was green but there
Was just two dresses of that so I could not
get it eather and I would not have the pink
Tissue it was so pale. So to make up for
the loss of cape Grandma bought a pair of
very nice gloves and a nice hankerchif that
Cost more than the cape would have cost.
I have not heard a word from Mother and I dont
belive she intends to come at all at least it would
Seam so. We are all about though in complaining
Moode. William Lurton has just got well of the
Meazeles and has now got the hooping Cof. Joanna
And the baby has just taken them. Sis is very sick
her face is perfectly coverd with them. Willie
Jaquess has got them also. . . .

I went to the deaf and dum[24] examination and would
have gone to the Commencement but I had no
Company I saw the Odd Fellows[25] march on the
Seventh and also on the 17 and what is more
I saw [Damaris?]. She was well. You will have
Heard of the Marriage of Mr. E. Rutledge
And Miss J. Furgus before this. They were
Married on the 8 in Colledge Chappal
At 6 o clock in the morning by the Rev.
J.F. Jaquess
You have also heard of death
of Mr. Louis his last words were
Glory he has left a Widow and
Six Childeron to mourn his loss.

I have not told you half I wanted
to tell but I have not time to write
Any more at present

I did not write this with A
puddin stick, though I might
Almost as well have done so.
I could not have written much
Werce. The Candle flyes and my

Cap plague me so that I cant
Write any more at present.

Adios
Beulah

From: Thomas Huckstep [Lynnville]
To: Jemima

Oct 24th [probably 1852]

Esteemed Friend,
    I write these few lines hoping that they will find you in good health. John Adkinson is desirous to know if you would go down there to teach a School to commence on the first day of April. If you condescend to go, please do inform me by return of post so I then can give an answer.

Yours respt
Thos Huckstep[26]

From: Hephzibah
Envelope address: Miss Jemima Dumville, Geneva, Ills

At Home   February 26th 1853

Dear Mima, Your requiste me To be shure and pluck the beam out of my own eye before I try to see the mote's in the eye's of others.[27] very good advice, I thank you, And the only fault I have to find is that You do not second your prescept by your Example. For I think you had a very large beam in your eye when you refer'd me to the conduct of Mr. Stribling. I have been A witness of his conduct for the last 6 year And have always seen him a consistent Christian "concistence thou arte a jewel!"[28] And I think you have been acquainted with him longe enuf to know it for yourself. I would like to know what Mr. Stribling has said Or done to you or any boddy els[e] that has Caused you to think so very very unfavorable of him. I think that you ought to be amonge the last to say anythinge against Either him or his Lady. I supose you have for gotten their kindeness last winter, tis true you may have had some little inconveniencess but where will you go and find them not, I am shure they did everything in their power to meak you Happy and gave you all the opportunity possable to learn, knowing that you had had a very poor chance, and this is the thanks they get for it. They ask no reward or even thanks but they did not expect you to join there Persecutetery [persecution?], I am sorrey that my Sister has proven her-self so ungraitfull "You say he did not so much as come in the house let along Preach for us" I will tell you his reasons first, he did not recieve Mr Hindall's[29]

Invitation untill the day before he came for Me, 2nd he was so unwell having taken a severe cold the day he took me to see you the day being so unfavaorable and the day after going to fill Father Hindall's appointment At Mount Zion, 3rd there was no one to s[t]ay with Grandma. . . .

. . .

Remember Sister I am not writing these thing to hurt your feeling. I only want you to know that you have hurt mine for it dose hurt my feeling for anyone to speak ill of those I look upon as among my best friends. I attended a meeting at Salem on Sunday only not haveing a chance to go at night I went to [?] Mrs Carr's Funorel [funeral?] on Thursday, and to the Colledge on Wednesday night to hear the paper read and on Thursday morning to Mr Saundersons[30] and Miss Hanna's Wedding and a jolly one it was but more of this bye and bye, no more at present, your affectionate Sister Heppy

[on back of envelope] I saw Mr. Jaquess not long since he sent his Compliments to you Mima
Heppy

From: Ann, Carlinville
Envelope address: Jemima Dumville, Lynnville, ILL

Carlinville Macoupin Co. Ill. May 2nd, 1853

Dear Jemima

    I was much rejoiced to receive a letter from you some two weeks ago. Especially was I pleased with the cheering intelligence it contained of your success in both temporal & spiritual matters. I rejoiced to find that the Lord had given you to see your duty and give you at the same time grace to discharge. This will not only secure your own religious enjoyment but wil prepare you to exert a sanctified influence upon all with whom you are called to associate. I am glad that you have received by your own exertions an education sufficent to prepare you for usefulness in an enlarged circle. There is scarcely any position in life so desirable to one who wishes to be useful as that of a teacher—to you in this capacity is committed the destiny of young minds. To you it is given not only to impart to them a knowledge of the sciences but impart those precepts that will bring them in possession of knowledge far more precious: a knowledge that maketh wise unto salvation. In the position you occupy you may if faithful and prayerful become an instrument in the hands of God not only of prepareing many for usefulness here but instrumental in leading many souls to Christ that shall be stars in your crown of rejoicing in the better world.

    I was glad to hear that you opened your school with prayer because precept will do but little good unless it is enforced by good example. I doubt not but that in victory you have gained. Your happiness has been greatly increased. You must remember that you are still in an enemys hand. Your conflicts are not yet past for there is no point of rest between conversion and death the Cross must always be borne: remember that you have the promise of your heavenly Father to rely upon and if you bear the cross now after a while the cross will bear you. I expect to be at your brother Johns in about two weeks I would be much pleased if you could come there while I remain I will not remain long you must be sure and come if possible.

Your Affectionate Mother
Ann Dumville[31]

From: Ann, Carlinville
Envelope address: Miss Jemima Dumville, Lynnville, Morgan County, Ill

Carlinville   September 26, 1853

My dear daughters,

I have just written[32] a letter to my daughter Heppsy, and now write you a few line. I am well and have been through the season, and was truly glad to hear by Heppsy letter that you were all well, for which I do most heartily thank the giver of all good. Heppsy letter informed me you intend going to Texas next fall.[33] Now my dear children I must insist as a mother has a right to that you all give up this Texas trip, for you are all doing well where you are and I think you ought to be satisfied. When I came home James McClure[34] insisted upon my letting him have my money. Tell Jemima she must let you have her money & I will provide her with money to go to school. I want her to come down as soon as she can and when she wants to go home James McClure will go with her to Harris' Point[35] and bring her things here to put them on the railroad[36] or take them safe to his house as she may desire, and I want her to come and stay with me and fix up my winter clothes, and spend what time with me she can. We have had a good deal of sickness here this season, though all the sick are getting better. Old Mrs. Boston and old Mr. Sherrill died about two weeks ago. Now my dear children I am daily living to God and find great solace and consolation in his service and delight in his service daily and will pray for you all daily and ask God to direct you aright in all things and have faith that he will answer my prayers in your behalf, and may you still be put out of the notion of going to Texas, for my wish and desire is to remain here and to have you all remain here likewise.

Give my love to all inquiring friends, and Jemima must be sure and come if she can. rite soon. Accept my dear children, my best love, and best wishes for your temporal as well as your spiritual welfare.

Affectionately, your mother,
Ann Dumville

From: Hephzibah
Envelope address: Miss Jemima Dumville, Lynnville, Morgan County, Illinois

Home, Sunday evening, Sept 26th 1853

Dear Sister,

. . . Grandma wants me to go to school but on account of sickness in our family we are in the back ground with our work we only began drying fru[i]t last week and I think we shall finish this if we keep well. Grandma is just able to help me a little.[37] I only had two chills but they tell me I look as if I had been sick a month. When we get dun [done] our fruite I have to make two dresses and make some other sewing and knitting before I can starte to school.[38] I can't go before three week or a month. I don't want to have much to do in that line when I begin going to school. Be sure you get all your sewing dun before you come and if you have time to come and assist me I shall be glad but not unless you have time to spare. We must get to school sooner this winter than we did before and have our lessons better. . . .

Respectfully, Your Sister,
Heppy

3. 1854–1855
Cholera

The darker aspect of the letters is their focus on illness and death. In one year, 1854, Hephzibah's letters discuss the deaths of seven people who are named and several who are unnamed. In 1854 and 1855, there was a cholera outbreak in central Illinois—the number of cases in the area increased from one in 1850 and twelve in 1852 to twenty-four in 1854 and seventy-one in 1855.[1] The transmission of cholera through contaminated food and water had been established in England shortly before,[2] but public health measures to limit its spread had not yet been implemented in Illinois.[3] Professional medical care was available, sometimes, but the causes of disease were not well understood, and, apart from quarantine, measures to limit the spread of contagion were largely unknown. Serious illness and accidents, affecting young and old alike, were frequent occurrences. Medicine was primitive, cures were few, and there was little or no regulation of occupational safety.

A letter written by Hephzibah in 1854 discusses the death of Elizabeth's five-year-old son, Logan. The letter is moving and heartfelt, but it begins oddly. Although the main subject is Logan's death, there is first a rather long discussion of the shipment of a trunk, of the separate mailing of the key to the trunk, of when the mail would go out, and of whether the trunk and the key would arrive simultaneously—all of this before the letter tells us that Elizabeth was so upset that she "could scarsely speak." We are not told why Hephzibah was called to the Williams farm, nor why Elizabeth could scarcely speak, nor why Hephzibah "sat up till morning." The child is unnamed until the account reaches his burial. The narrative of the letter is therefore frustrating to the unacquainted reader, but the family, the recipients of her letter, surely knew what it was about. The difference between the detail and sequential description in the discussion of the shipment of the trunk and the emotionally laden but inarticulate story of the death is striking. In the latter, Hephzibah gives a participant's somewhat garbled account of the family's anguish. Then the tone of the letter shifts again. She moves from the first person to the role of reporter—Mr. March died after failing to take his medicine, the sister of Congressman Richard Yates was to be married, and a new farmhand had been hired at the Striblings. The family would want to know.

Family correspondence has many purposes, and, despite personal tragedy, the letters of 1854 and 1855 continued to comment on everyday problems and frustrations. One of the most serious of those was that travel was difficult and sometimes impossible. A trip of more than a few miles was a major undertaking. The roads were unpaved, muddy, often impassable, but railroads were being built, and in the early 1850s there was one line from Springfield to Jacksonville and another from Springfield to Carlinville[4] (see figure 9). The Dumvilles could then travel between Jacksonville and Carlinville by changing trains in Springfield and riding two legs of a triangle, a total journey of about eighty miles.[5] Railroad accidents were frequent, however. As a result, Hephzibah seldom saw her mother or her sisters. Letters were, therefore, all the more important.

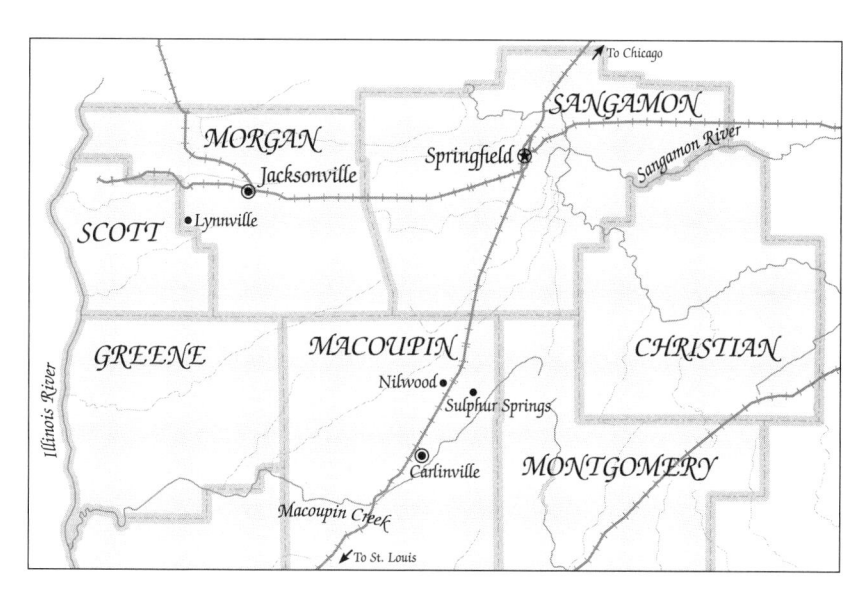

Figure 9: Illinois Railroads, circa 1855, based in part on Arthur C. Cole, *The Centennial History of Illinois: The Era of the Civil War, 1848–1870*. Vol. 3. Springfield: Illinois Centennial Commission, 1919. Courtesy of Zaccarine Design.

Photography was a partial, although inadequate, remedy for the separation of the family. In January 1855, a few months after Elizabeth and John Williams and their children had moved to Iowa, John wrote to Jemima saying that Elizabeth wanted a photograph so that she could "see" her family "here in this wild country." Although most discussions of technological innovation in the mid-nineteenth century give principal emphasis, understandably, to the coming of the railroads and the telegraph, the Dumville letters illustrate the considerable social impact of photography. Only two of the letters mention the telegraph, while eleven discuss photographs. The benefits of photography were apparent and immediate. As John's letter illustrates, "likenesses" served to remind the Dumvilles of the appearance of absent relatives and friends. Family members could, by exchanging photographs, see how the children had grown. Family portraits, formerly the province of the wealthy, now were within reach of most people,[6] and putting a photograph on the parlor table, as Hephzibah reports she had done, constituted a public statement of social status and moral character. The content of the image reflected norms of neatness and fashion.[7] The letters discuss the appropriateness of particular styles of dress to be worn when having a photo taken, and the Dumvilles were aware of which colors would "take well"—that is, produce a pleasing black-and-white image. Like the introduction of railroads and the telegraph, photography was an innovation in communication that changed social interaction and personal relationships.

In addition to changes brought by technological innovation, the Dumvilles confronted the challenges presented by pressing social issues, including the abolition of slavery. As noted in chapter 1, the conflict within the Methodist Church concerning abolition had direct impact on the Dumville family—Ann had been excluded from the Methodist church, temporarily, because of her abolitionist views. In 1836 the Methodist General Conference rejected "any right, wish, or intention to interfere in the civil and political relation between master and slave," and the hierarchy of the church then actively discouraged abolitionism.[8] At the General Conference in 1844, however, a preacher was suspended from the ministry "for refusing to manumit certain slaves which came into his possession by marriage," and Bishop Andrew was "requested to desist from the exercise of his office, on account of his connection with slavery."[9] As a result, the church divided, North and South.[10] The first conference of the Southern Methodists was held in 1846, Bishop Andrew presiding. The Methodist Church South had jurisdiction over its own congregations, but some Northern conferences maintained contact with missions in the South after the split because Southern Methodists were often unwilling to provide ministry to slaves. In his autobiography, Peter Cartwright commented,[11] "If the Southern preachers failed to carry the point they had fixed, namely, the tolerance of slaveholding in the episcopacy, that they would fly the track, and set up for themselves. And in that event, many souls would be injured, and perhaps turn back to perdition."

In the two decades before the Civil War, conflicts within the Methodist Church concerned not only slavery but the liturgy. Camp meetings were an attempt to harness the disorder of the frontier,[12] but the revivals were social occasions, and they sometimes became raucous.[13] Second-generation church leaders sought to make Methodism more appealing to the urban middle class.[14] The newer leaders wanted to regularize and routinize worship services, making the liturgy more formal and dignified. As Nathan Hatch's history of American Christianity has observed, "Methodists domesticated the camp meeting, deemphasized its emotional exercises, and restricted its spontaneous exuberance."[15] Traditional Methodists, however—especially frontier circuit preachers such as Cartwright—resisted the change because they relied on fervor and charisma in their recruitment of converts,[16] a technique that was less effective in the cities, where the congregations were increasingly made up of merchants, clerks, and professionals rather than farmers and laborers. As urbanization progressed, therefore, conflict arose between circuit riders and the resident clergy, who usually had more education.[17]

Indeed, many of the circuit preachers actively opposed theological education. Cartwright said, "I would rather have the gift of a devil-dislodging power than all the college lore or Biblical Institute knowledge that can be obtained from mortal man."[18] In 1856 Dr. John Dempster, who founded Garrett Biblical Institute in Evanston, Illinois, reported that "at least two-thirds of our entire ministry" had opposed efforts to establish a Methodist seminary.[19] The Methodists, however, created many colleges and universities. They opposed education only for the clergy—they believed that God chose preachers and that "God never called an unprepared man."[20]

Circuit-riding preachers largely depended upon charismatic appeal in order to secure their livelihood. Their regular compensation was minimal, but they often received free hospitality. While circuit preachers had nominal pay of $100 per year, they often received much less than that, sometimes as little as $20 per year,[21] supplemented with a commission on their sales of Methodist publications.[22] Social historian Katharine Dvorak's analysis of the role of charisma in the Methodist church argues that the support of clergy through voluntary gifts was more consistent with the charismatic character of their message than a regular salary would have been.[23]

Much of the work that was essential to the organization and maintenance of the church was done by uncompensated women. In the church, as in the broader society, men were assigned the public roles and women the domestic. Historian of religion David Hempton observes that "the Victorian cult of domesticity was at least in part a Methodist creation."[24] As noted in chapter 1, publications such as *Godey's Lady's Book* and *The Ladies' Repository* actively encouraged domesticity. The ideology of domesticity provided a rationale for the subordinate, dependent status of women, and Hempton's history observes that Methodist publications increased their emphasis on female domesticity during the first half of the nineteenth century.[25] The attention that the letters devote to domestic tasks is consistent with this ideology. For the Dumville women, however, work outside their own homes was a financial necessity.

When Hephzibah was doing housework at the Stribling farm and Jemima secured a teaching job in another town, letters helped to hold the family together. Marilyn Motz's research on women's letters suggests that women looked to their "female kin" to provide "lifelong emotional and financial support."[26] Since work inside the home, domestic work, was very poorly compensated or, more often, not compensated at all, women were in a dependent status. The separation of public work from private work changed the social meaning of both class and gender, and family correspondence then reflected and reinforced the distinct roles of men and women, mothers and daughters, landowners and servants. Because women wrote most family letters, not only in the Dumville family but more generally, the relationships that those letters reinforced were primarily those with other women.

From: Jemima
Envelope address: John W. Williams

At Home   Jan 30th 1854

Esteemed and Beloved Sister

After (I suppose) about 2 houres hard riding I safely arive at Presbeterian College [Illinois College, Jacksonville].[27] And walked from there to school. And you may know how I felt for I presume that you was aware of my troubled mind and remained so untill nigh[t]. As the protracted meeting was still in progress I staid in town to attend me[e]ting. After preaching was over we went to the College and had a happy time. I never saw Brother [?], so happy. And many others. And all my trouble was known by the Lord. I made a full surrender to God desire him to take me entirely into his hands, and do with me whatever seemed good in his sight. And I was then enabled to shout his prais with a loud voice. Since that I cannot grieve about my helpfless condition as before. I feel confident that the Lord will provide my way before.

I received a letter from Mother a short time since. She was well and was anxious for sister and I to go and see [?] And I expect us to start 2 weekes from to day if not prevented by providence. And perhaps may stay all summer. I should have written to you sooner but I have been so anxious to be prepared for examination that I have not had time. It commences next Tuesday. I should be very happy to see you all before I have but if you come you need not bring my clothes untill I know where I am going except my shoes.

I have prepared you some turkey wings. And should be very glad to see you to come. Dear Brother If I may so call you I was very much hurt at your treatment to me, when I was at your house. And I hope it never will be so again. And if I have merited such treatment I don't know when it was and if you will explain it to me as a Sister and a Christian I am ready to [four words illegible]. I want peace to exist amongst us as long as we live and when friendship can no longer exist among us if prepared I should hope to die. And be out of my trouble. I hope you will come and see me before I go. And come . . . with more agreeableness than we parted. I must close. I stayed away from prayers to finish my letter and they sing so delightful or some other way that I scarcely know what I am wrighting. Brother Heard & Father Stribling are the singers, and I presume you have heard them. One of our School girls died last Saturday but went home to heaven. There is another one sick with typhoid fever. Nothing more. I remain yours, if you please I should like to receive a letter from you if you do not come.

Jemima Dumville[28]

From: Hephzibah
Envelope address: Miss Jemima Dumville, Carlinville, Macoupin County, Ills

Home   Thursday March 30, 1854

Dear Mima,

I very much hoped when I received your letter that I should have sent your clothes to you before this time.[29] But as I did not get those from brother Johns until Sunday (and then I brought them myself) and had to get a Trunk Monday bring it home and pack up your things. . . . Lizze wants you to knit Mother a pare of hoes of the ligh[t] blue and deep blue mixd and keep the other for your self. She wants you to get a dress for Martha and make it before you come home.[30] I have a grait deel of news to tell you but I am sure you will not feel like hearing it now so I only will say that Mr. Walter and family have returned from Texas and give a dreadfull account of the country.[31] We are as well as usuall. Grandma has a cold but is so as to keep about. I am afraid to send your eye water and your inkstand is at Mrs. Lurtons. I send you Mrs. Tillers gift because I thought you would like to take it with you when you went to see her. Be sure you send us word how you fared and how they all looked at you. You will find a letter in your Trunk. Which will tell you why I went to Sister's. Let me hear from you by next Thursday. I remain your Affectionate sister, Heppe

CHAPTER 3

From: Hephzibah
Envelope address: Miss Jemima Dumville, Carlynville, Macoupin County Ills

Home   Thursday Morning May 4, 1854

Dear Mima,

I received your welcome letter last Thursday And I assure you it made my heart glad, for, I had to tell the truth, I been thinking rather hard of you. For neglecting me as I thought I had been so carefull in sending your Trunks and key so as for you to get them boath at once. I could have sent your Trunk, some days before, but thought it would get there before the letter. And you would be uneasy if it did. Your trunk went as fare as Springfield the same evening it was taken into Town. so B. said. While the Mail did not go out till the next morning. But you have gotten them and that is enuf and I am glad you have.

I have not heard from sister since I left them. I wrote to her two days before I received yours, and requested her to write soon and let me know whether she had heard from you. I have been expecting her to visit me. She has not done so as yet. You must write to her. I think you can comfort her better than I.[32] You are better acquainted with her and have been more with the children. I feard very much that I should be sick after getting to Brothers the day they came for me. As it was between three or four oclock when Jesse H reached here, And I was washing and Grandma was not at home. J. went for her, and by the time she got here and I got redey [ready] it was near five oclock. The weather was cold and I had to ride on horse-back. I reached Brother's about seven I think. Sister met me at the door she could scars[e]ly speak, Dear Lizze! I thought I would sit up all night (though there was Mrs Tuggle, Miss L. Grey, Miss. S.A Williams, and Mr. Coates and another gentleman.[33] I sate up untill near ten when I became so sick I had to lie down. Sarah[34] gave me some water. I soon went to sleep, and slept until half past one. I felt quite well so sate up till morning. Margret[35] was a sleep when I got there. In the morning I went to her as soon as she waked, and looked in her dark ernest eyes. She seemed as though she did not know wheather to laugh or not. I asked her if she knew me & she said yes; I then asked her who I was? Aunt Jemima she replied.

When at the burrien [burying] and the cold clods was rattling on our Dear Logan's coffin. Charly Horiel [Horrell] exclaimed. "I don't want Logie put down there" two or three times, so that his Father had to teak [take] him away. Oh how my heart echo'd to his words!

Little Charly has a brother and so [h]as his cousin Charly. Sarah W was to teach school aboute 2 miles from Johns in a school-house on the left-hand side of the roade to the grave-yard and close to a large white house, Where she is to board. She was on her way home from Winchester where she had been to attend school. I don't know what she gets a month.[36]

Mr. March[37] came home from St. Louis on Saturday the 22 of April. On Sunday he was taken sick but not so bad but that he could tend to his business. On

Wednesday evening he called at Dr. Shirley's office and asked for some medsin [medicine]. Told the Dr he wanted something to cure him rite—that he had not time to be sick. The Dr. gave him some and told him to go home and go to bed that he was worse than he thought. I don't feel any pain said Mr. M. You are worse than if you did feel pain.

In stead of going to bed, as the Dr. said he eate for his supper, three hard fried eggs and some ham and pie and did not take the medsin at all. So he very soon grew worse and sent for Dr. Long when he got there he sent for Dr. Prince for assistance. They found they could do nothing for him and, told him if he had any matters to araing [arrange] he had better do it, for, he had not longe to live.[38]

He replied that he did not expect to be called so soon but as it was so, he was resi[g]ned. And then gave some general directtions to his family he made some acnoligement [acknowledgement] to Mr. Pittner. He died Thursday evening aboute six and was buried the next evening. He left a wife and eight children. His disease was cholera.[39] The Sunday after his death the youngest child Harriet was taken sick and died on Monday and Ella has been sick ever since her father was burried and has not been expected to live but is now getting well. I have not heard of any of the others being sick. The Misses J and E March are bo[a]rding there now. Uncle Wesly is going to get married. Miss Yates is the Lady, I believe, sister of the Hon. Richard Yates.[40]

We are all aboute, though somewhat complaining. Mrs. Walter spent the day with us last Wednesday. She has been sick almost ever since she returned[41] with something like Rumatisem in her ear and face in fact they have all been sick especially the two youngest children. They are getting well now. Mrs Walter and Margret send there love to you.

Mr. Patterson has not returned, he would have come back with Mr. W. but he had ingaged to crop on the shears [share crop] with a man there. Mr. Stribling recieved a letter from him not long since, in which he said the longer he staid there the more he disliked the Country and the people and did not think he would stay there much longer. Peter[42] is not here now he left soon after I came home and went to Mr. Richardsons. A young man by the name of Josiah Belt is with us in his place. He is from Maryland. My sheet is full and I have not written half I want to write. I must stop for the present. Yours sincearly Hephzibah.

From: Hephzibah
Envelope address: Miss Jemima Dumville, Carlynville, Macoupin County

Home   Sunday morning May 7, 1854

Dear Mima,

I could not write all I wanted on one sheet so I will send two.

The first time Miss Brown came to see us after I came home was four weeks ago. She came out on Friday and staid untill Monday. She came out last Saturday week and staid until Monday again I delivered your message the first time she came and the seccon[d] . . . time In return, she requested me [?] I wrote to you to give her love to you. She came oute again Tuesday evening with Miss E Trotterm Miss J Wall and the Misses A and S Becraft and took tea with us. Amanda is to graduate in July. Examination begins in eight weeks. Miss Wall is to start for Warsaw [Illinois] tomorrow, as the Lady with whom she lives is sick, and wants her to go home. She dose not want the Catholics to know that she is going. She is much more lively than I thought. If Miss Brown writes to you, which I think she will, you must be sure to write soon, . . . for, she will not have a sister's patience. Be sure you pay the postage on your own letter, as it is looked upon as a matter of politeness between ladies when corresponding for each one to pay the postage on there own letters.

Besides it is a saving plan, for what [you] would pay the postage on three letters . . . when taken out of the office, will pay for five when put in the office. I mention this because I think you will take such a hint from me, better than you would anyone else, in fact I would not like anyone else to say anything about it to you.

Grandpa is gone to preach the Funeral sermon of Mr. Deaton who died aboute two weeks since, a very pious old gentleman. He fell oute of an apple tree which caused his death. There was a young man died at Mrs. Poesy's [Posey][43] not long since, of the Lung fever by the name of John Poe. He and a granddaughter of Mrs. P. was married the 29 of March I think it was. Jane was the Bridesmaid. Four days after his marriage he and his Bride came to Mrs. P. He was taken sick the next day and after a sickness of ten days he died. Leaving a bride of 18 summers he had only been married two weeks when he departed this life.

He suffered very much, but was quite regined [resigned].

I want to tell you about Sarah Hurst now. There was a Ball in Town not long since and Mary Dixon and Hannah Caughenaugh [Cavanaugh?] went and Danced, someone as[k]ed Sarah if she was going? No she replied; my class meets tonight and I am not going to leave it to go to a Ball. Was not that a noble reply?

Mr. Pitner[44] was turned out of the church in March, for selling men and women into perpetual bondeage, as the people said.[45] He takes it very Hard, he sayes he has had a great deal of trouble, and we know he has for his sister was burned to death, and his two sones was drowned just at the time they began to be of some service to him[46] but he says that this afaire hurts him worse than all the others, as he knows he is innocent of the charge brought against him. He left his family in the depth of winter and went to Tennessee with the full intention of liberating the negros and had written to his Brother in law for him to be there so that they could be divided but he did not come and law according to the Laws of that State, such property could not be divided unless all the heirs were there. They were not there and could not be. According to Law they were sold, and the mony that fell to his wife was given to him. But they were not sold with his consent. In fact, he did all he could to prevent it. But what could he do? They (the negros) were not willing to go to Liber[i]a. He could not set them free there, for that was contrary to the Law of the place. He could not bring them here and set them free here. It is contrary to law here. So what could he have done with them even if he had them in his poses ition[possession]. The Brethren here was not pleased with him so they thought this would be a good time to show there dislik[e] and they did so. I cannot tell you all the particulars about it but I believe Mr. Pitner is as good a man as any of his accusers. He says one consolation is they cannot keep him oute of heaven, if they do put him out of the church. He has made an appeal and his case will be reconsidered nesxt month. I hope he will be admitted into full membership again.

I want you to tell Mr. Plain[47] aboute him. You know we spoke of him as having sold slaves to Mr. P, so we heard, but it was a fals reporte and I don't want to spread any such reports about anyone.

Sister Lizze wants Mother's miniature taken and if you can have it taken in Carlynville I wish you would attend to it and have yours taken also. Tell Mother to send me Sister Mary's address[48] in your next letter. . . . My sheet is full so I will sease. Your affectionate sister Beulah.

From: Hephzibah
To: Jemima

Home   June the 8th 1854

Dear Mima,

You perhaps remember, one evening while I was at Mr. Burks [Burke's], something was said aboute, Abolitionists, and the way they treated the negroes when they had them in there power. Mr. B seemed to think that they were the graetest enemys the slaves had. I said I thought so, and gave Mr. Pittner's case as an instance. I said, "he had gone to Tennessee and sold slaves and brought the money home with him," this was what we heard but it was a fals reporte. You both may have forgotten the matter, and think it a trifling afare, but I feel as though I did him injustice to speak thus of him, and want you, if you please, to correct the error.

I recieved your letter last Friday and wrote an answer Monday but didn't send it. Sister was here not long ago. They were all well. She told me to tell you that Mr. L. Huckstep was married. Mr. W. Mathers and Miss Yates were united last week and Mr. McDonald and Julia March. I think the Cholera has subsided, at least I have not heard of any more cases since Mr. Pittner got well, he and two of his childeron had something like it, but are all well now. Mathiu Bosson is no more, he died of the breain Fever. His father is almost blind with the sore eyes so I heard last week.

I wish you had written how you was coming home and if ma was coming with you. If she dose, get her to bring her brown Marino dress that she brought from England with her. She has one hasn't she? If she dose not come with you persuade her to dress up respectable, and have her likeness taken and send to us. Pray don't let her ware her Liney[49] dress. True we love her as well in liney as anything else, but I think there are times when she ought to wear something better.

I can't tell you much aboute the Fassion. Capes are worn very much but sacks are worn also if anything more than capes are. I had a mind to send you some patterns but I thought it would not be worth while, you would be home so soon. Don't cut up your scarf to make a cape of it. [It] will not look as well as a white brage one,[50] and then it will be to warm for summer. I have made me a white brage cape, circular and put a fold of the same on it for triming. Most persons trim with blue ribbon and I have made another oute of my scarf and trimed it with white ribbon.

Dresses are worn low in the neck, open sleeves are still used some but Mrs. Lurton and Grandma have made there's Bishops[51] with a plain peace at the top with a cap large enuf to cover it. I don't know that you can understan what I have said for I am not good at description, but you will be here soon and then I will show you. I am very glad you are coming home. . . . Almost every day I say, Ah I wish I could see Mother and Mima. Excuse my blunders if you pleas, give my love to all my friends and come home as soon as you can. Ask Sophia to excuse me for not paying the postage on the letter I sent to her, the reason was Mr. Stribling put it in the office, and there was no person in so that he could not pay though I gave him the requisit amount to pay it. I was very sorrey, but I could not help it. Heppe

Ask Mother to look over father's papers and send me his Odd Fellows card if she can find it. I'll take good care of it. Don't forget Sister Mary's address. yours Hephzibah. My pen is so poor I can't write.

From: Hephzibah
To: Jemima

Home   Monday morning August 14th 1854

Dear Mima,
I did not expect when i wrote to you last, Wednesday to write to you so soon again. But I received a note from brother John requesting me to write immediately and request you to come home, as he is going to start to Iowa the 22nd of this month and Sister wants you to come and stay with her. He is going to see the country, I suppose, as he has taken a notion to *move*, he will have to do it if he only goes across the road. I hope it will be for the best anyway. They were all

well. I have not heard from the cholera lately but I expect it is allmost gon. Mr. H. Saunderson is very sick with fever Billious I think it is. Brother said in his note that he had heard that now it was in Carlinville. If you will take charcole pulverised a tea spoon ful every other morning it is said to be a sure preventitive of cholera it won't hurt you if it dose no good and for a cure take an ounce of pulverised charcole an ounce of laudenum and an ounce of brandy mixed well shaken a tea spoon full every five minuts.[52] I write this because you might not have noticed it though it has been published in several News Papers. I did not tell you in my last that Aunt Molly fell of[f] the Porch[53] some time since and was hurt very much, she can not sit up much and has to be wa[i]ted on all most like a child. Did Mother think my last letter too silly? I did not think it wrong to write a little nonsense. You know I don't do so very often. I told Grandma a few things that I wrote and she said she was afraid you would think I was no better than I ought to be. I say the last part of the sentence And I expect you know it. Well as Goldsmith [1730–1774][54] says,

> "I strive the neighborhoo to please / with maners wondrous winning; / and never follow wicked ways— / Unless when I am sinning.

I have only made a little variation in this verse. I thought when I began this I would only write a few lines but I am writing yet you see. Give my love to Mother and tell her to write to me when you come home I wish she would come with you. Come home soon, Mima. Good Bye from your would like to be good, but very bad sister, Belle D. [Hephzibah][55]

From: Hephzibah [Belle]
Envelope address: Miss Jemima Dumville, Lynnville, Illinois

At Home   Oct 31st 1854

Dear Mima

Are you very ill with the blues,[56] I tried them a while but found they did not pay so I conclude It best to get rid of them. And advise you to do the same. I have not seen or heard from Mother, neither have I heard wheather Brother has started. I should like to know very much. If you are able to be oute of bed I should like for you to write and tell me, and can take time from your correspondencts elswhere. . . .

I know Maggie will be disappointed. I told her I would send her something. . . . Grandpa and I went to Salem on Sabbath to hear the Rev Cloud preach. He is the senior on the Cirqute [circuit]. We have two others. I think they intend to rouse us or try very hard on.

Bye the way, Mima, Mr. Littler was there at church. I mean he dose <u>love</u> to <u>be</u> at Mr. Pittner's but whether Mr. Pittner <u>Loves</u> for him to be <u>there</u> is another part of speech. Perhaps if he cannot succeed there he will come this way, as I am a "faultless young lady," but I think he will hardly find rest for the sole with his post in this neighborhood. I think he had better go onto his circuite, and spend his time in preparing sermons than in paying address to young ladies. There was preaching at Salem last Friday Saturday Sunday and Monday nights. I need scarcely tell you I was not there. Mr. Cloud's text for Sabbath Nehemiah 6 chapter 3 verse "And I sent messingers unto them, saying I am doing a great work, so that I cannot come down: when should the work cease, whilst I leave it and come down to you?" I suppose they think there is need of a great work being dun at Salem.[57] I have read some in the Invisable World,[58] the evening I left you. I read two of most frightful storys in it, and went to bed without a candle. Though I was thinking aboute it all the time I was not the least alarmed. I more believe then disbelieve the statements like Mr. Wesly I think there has been murders, and because I have not seen anyone murdered, is no reason why I should disbelieve the fact. So I think very likely there has been gostes [ghosts] but I never expect to see one.

I have been reading a book which I think is far more interesting than the book above named. It is intitled the Autobiography of the Rev J. B. Finley or Pioneer Life in the West.[59] It contains some thrilling accounts of the adventures the early settlers of Kentucky, Ohio and Illinois had with the Indians and wild beasts that there roamed the forest, and tells some very amusing anacdotes of there hunting expeditions. I wold tell you one or two but my paper will not admit of it. I wrote a letter to Grace last night, is it not astonishing? Perhaps I may write one to Sophia this afternoon, I have not recieved hers yet. I may write one to Mother also. The Miss Carrs gave a party not long since but they had not manners enuf, to invite me. But who car[e]s? I don't. His Lordship Maybery and Her Majesty Mary M. Walter Maybery had the honor of conducting the Misses Margret Jane and Frances Posey to and from the party. . . .

Yours Belle

[in margin] . .You need not look at the fly specks unless you want to

From: Hephzibah [Belle]
Miss Jemima Dumville, Lynnville, Illinois

Home   Dec 22th 1854

Dear Mima,

This is the last day of your school and I suppose you are glad of it? I know I am, for now you will come and stay with us won't you? don't make your visits too long with your friends. "Short calls are best you know" the fly said when it lit on the hot stove."

There was a Miss Adams died at the Colledge last Saturday. They thought she caught cold the night of the Concert and she had had the milch sick before she came to school. She was one of the girls that sung and plaid at the Concert and did not eat any supper so after it was over they ate Oysters in there own roomes and it is suposed she ate to[o] many wich caused inflaimation of the bowels. She was taken home on Monday on the cars to be buried. . . .

Write to me if you don't come soon, even if you have to bring it in your pocket.

Grandma sends her love to you.

. . . Come home soon, Mima. Your devoted Belle

From: Jemima Dumville

January 17, 1855

L. Lawson	122.	$5.08
Mr. Donald	148	6.12
Mr. Todd	89.	5.00
Mrs. Lawson	26.	1.25
Mr. [Marlin?]	25.	1.9
Mr. Dean	60	2.50
Mr. Flynn	142.	6.11
Mr. Johnson	120.	5 00
Mr. [Canatsy?]	88.	2.42
Mr. Summers	99.	3.10
Mr. T Lawson	92	3.83
Mr. [Worwell?]	28	1.25
Mr. Patterson	194	6.87
Mr. Murphy	17.	1.25
Jemima Dumville		

I hereby certify that the above number of days are correct to the best of my knowlege and also the amount of dollars and cents which the aforesaid days come to.[60]

this 17th of Jan A. D. 1855

From: John Williams
To: Jemima

Pow[eshiek County], Io   Jan 28, 1855

Deare Sister

We received youre favor in due season and was glad to hear of your good health and the health of oure old neighbors, in general. We are all well at this time and have no reason to complaine. We live in a rough style and we are all geting quite fat for we have lots of corne [?]. through the week and Sunday wheat bread & quails for we have caught 9 today and we have some church privaliges here by going 3 or 4 miles. We have a school this winter in a quarter of mi. Sarah + esra[61] is going. They like to go and is learning quite fast. I have been engaged this winter making rails and have some logs ready to haul to the mill for building purposes. We desire to run a prairie teame the coming season. We have foure yoke of oxen and would like to have one more but we are to[o] poore to b[u]y. When you get more [?] horse than you can maintain just ship a cargo out here and we won't more than condsend to thank you fore youre favor. . . .

Eliza is dissatisfied here and wants to come back. She don't like the people nor the appearance of the country. Tell H.B. [Hephzibah Beulah] we have been looking for a letter from hur in vaine but hope she will rite soon if not sooner. Eliz wants you to send youre mineature so she can see you but here in this wild country you will go & see Eliz & Annis Horell for hur—tell them & all the wourld & the rest of man kind to rite. I may not stay in this state very long as I find theire is some objections to the country more than a meare passenger can possibly find out. The last week has been close winter. The snow is 2 or 3 inches. Yesterday and part of tody was quite snowey the temperature has been from 30 to 6 below zero. Taking the winter together it has been pleasant. The children often talks about you and wants to see you. If we never see each other in this world let us live so as to meet in heaven. Now I must close as I have walked 6 or 8 miles to meeting and did not comence to rite till 7 oclock. It is near 10. We have received one letter from Mother D one from father & one from you is all we have received yet from oure friends yet rite soon and give all the news.[62]

J W and E Williams

From: Ann
To: Jemima and Hephzibah

Carlinville   Feb 22nd 1855

My dear Children,

I am happy to inform you that I am enjoying good health, and have been greatly blessed lately and feel like shouting glory. We have had protracted meeting going on here for over six weeks. 246 have professed religion and 191 have joined our church, and tell Father and Mother Stribling I wish they were here to help me shout Glory, and I want to know how they are getting along. Mr. Maddox has professed religion and joined our church. Mrs. Wayne and her two daughters have joined the church and professed. Wm Hughes is a penitent, Shrade Cotter is very sincerely to all appearance seeking religion.

The only grocery we had in the town excepting at the depot is broken up. Part of the liquor is thrown in the streets and the good liquor was taken to the drug store. The grocery keeper's wife has professed religion and he has joined the church as a seeker. . . .

> . . . In regard to the school I feel almost confident you can get one when you come down here either in the town or country. Major [Burke] told me to write for you to come down, and I am anxious to see you to have some conversation with you. . . . I want you to come as soon as your school is out.
>
> . . .
>
> From your affectionate Mother
> Ann Dumville
>
> Give my love to poor Ep tell her I want her to seek religion with all her heart and not rest till she has found it. . . .

From: Hephzibah
To: Jemima

> April 13 [date unknown]
>
> Dear Mima
>
> Mr. Lane came in the evening and told me you wanted the watch . . ., so I will send these things in this morning to the store. I took the watch to the silversmith and he said it would cost aboute two dollars to repair it, so I did not leave it because I thought you would not like to give so much, and perhaps as it would run as it is. Yours Heppe

From: Hephzibah
To: Jemima

> Home   July 13th 1855
>
> Dear Mima
>
> . . . I have just sent a letter to town for Mother. I recieved one from her two weeks since she sent it by Mr. Chalicomb [Challacombe], when he came for his daughter. She sent also a scirt [skirt] like yours, and what do you think beside? I know you can't guess. A pair of <u>ear rings</u>. I have not the least notion of wearing them, and wrote to that affect, though she requested me to wear them for <u>her sake</u>, I don't know what to think of her. . . .
>
> I have not spoken to Grandma yet aboute the books or bedstead[63] but I expect she will not say much against it. I barely like to speak of it to her. . . .
>
> . . . The measles have been in the neighborhood. Margret and Julia Walter have had them but are well now. The others did not take them. They did not want Mayberry to take them so he staid at our house about six weeks. He left last evening for good. . . .
>
> There is no chance for me to go to school this year that I can see, but I want you to go if I don't.
>
> Yours sincearly
> Heppa

CHAPTER 3

From: Ann

Carlinville, Sept. 15th, 1855

Dear Sir [B. T. Burke, Ann's employer],
 ... Jamie is well, but has had a boil on his arm, so bad that he could not do much for two or three days. When Clark came last Monday morning, Jamie said he could not work and he wanted me to hire a boy at 1 [?] 50 per day to assist him; I would not do it, and told Jim he must do what he could and I would help him so I have had to help make mortar, carry brick and rock into the cellar. All the rock is laid, the cement is ready and it would have been finished if it has not been for the wet weather. It will be finished tomorrow evening if the rain does not prevent.

The Dutchman has brought another load of hay, 23 cwt. and he wanted to know if you had left any money for him. Send me word if must get some of Jacque [Jake] for him. I paid Mr. Easom the $20 you left for him, he has been at the house two or three times since you left. I asked him if he was at work on the fence and he said no but it would be all done before you came back.

I would like to know whether I must send the children to school or no before you come back. Miss Birks may open a school in a week or two.

Our new church will be dedicated on the 23rd of the month by Bishop Janes and Rev. Mr. Stamper.
 ...
I am hoping and praying that you will return in safety, and I have taught little Ellen to say "God bless father, preserve him from every danger, bring him back in safety, and we will praise thee"

I remain
Yours respectfully
Ann Dumville.
Ellen sends you a round kiss.

From: Ann

Carlinville, Octr 9th 1855

Sir [B. T. Burke],
 ... Jamy has been sick, with the billious fever and now the fever is broke he has the chills. It is nearly three weeks since he quit work. The first week after he left I attended to the horses, the hogs, the cows, picking up the wood by myself. Ellen and I slept in the house nine nights by ourselves.

Whilst I was walking back ward and forward with the slop to the hogs and water to the horses, with Ellen clinging to my side, prattling with childhoods innocence, it brought to my recollection the time when my own little ones were around me, and caused the silent tear to flow from my eye.

I hired Mike Cooney the first of this month in Jamy's place at the same wages until you come home, and indeed I do not want Jim again unless it is your wish for I found two pipes, some tobacco, a bunch of matches, and a jug of whiskey in the saddle house and Ellen saw him smoking in the stable.

Mike is more watchful and attentive than Jamy and can haul full as much dirt. He cannot milk, but I am learning him. Mr. Henry Hinds paid me 21$. Eleven dollars on the lot, and ten dollars interest money. Mr. Easom desires to have some money, he is working on the fence you must send word how much he can have and where he must get it from; must I give him some or Jacque. I think you will be pleased with the cellar, when you come home, every thing looks well, and we are getting along just the same as if you were at home now.

We had a great day on the dedication of our new church, great sermon, and a fine collection, nineteen hundred and fifty dollars, were raised on that day so the Lord's house is finished and paid for, and we are thankful, and rejoicing.

. . .

Yours faithful to her trust
Ann Dumville.

From: Ann

Carlinville, Octr 25th, 1855

Dear Sir [B. T. Burke],

. . .

I was very glad to find that you had arrived in safety at your sister's and I have no doubt you had a happy meeting with them all, for although your sister had "grown old and ugly" she was still your sister; I should like to see her much and I think you ought to gratify her wish to see her son's grave, and bring her with you to Carlinville as they are all broke up and are moving to Missouri it would not be much of journey from here there.

I am sorry you were so unfortunate whilst at Baltimore as to get into such a "horrible" place as a theatre, I fear you were not so much horrified at it as you intimate. You must ask forgiveness of a higher power than myself. . . .

. . . I have been glad you were away visiting whilst the cellar was being fixed and I had bricks and lime, mud and mortar to contend with, it tried my patience, let alone yours but I am amply repaid now, it looks so nice.

Jacque Plain gave Mr. Easom ten dollars, he said he had no boots to work in, and some other things he wanted very bad, he is splitting posts for fencing. . . . Old Mrs. Adams sent for me to talk to her daughter, but she is so far gone she could neither hear nor speak to me, health is the time to prepare for death.

I remain your's faithful to my trust
Ann Dumville

PS Ellen sends two kisses this time because she forgot to send any last, and she says she has a bushel for you when you come home.

We are beginning to look for you at home

From: Ann

Nov 1st, 1855

Dear Sir [B. T. Burke]

I received two letters from you today and I was very much pleased to receive them as I had not heard from [you] for some time. We were very [?] that you [?] had all shed a good many tears fearing you were either sick or dead, and Don in particular when saying his prayers, and praying for his pa could hardly call the name for sobbing.

We are all well. Don has had a boil on his finger but it is some better.

...

The first letter I got from you, I went over to Mrs. Whitaker's with; she was just getting into the buggy to go to her mothers, and Mrs. W. would hardly stay for me to bid her good bye; she was away two weeks and I had to come up town to get it answered; since she came back she has paid no attention to me, nor me to her, and I know nothing about her; Ellen went over there three or four times and always came back home in trouble generally crying.

I am tired of hearing about the pretty girls, and have no news to send you about them, except one Agnes Adams who still lives on the borders of eternity. I had much rather that you had begun to pray and seek religion in ernest, rather than to learn you were spending all your time flattering and dissembling pretty girls. I have more solid peace praying and singing with the children; than you have with all your pretty girls put together.

...

Yours faithfully
Ellen's kiss   Ann Dumville

From: Ann

Carlinville, Novbr 9, 1855

Dear Sir [B. T. Burke]:

I am in receipt of yours dated the Oct 29th and feel very sorry to find you have not received the two last letters I sent you, this is the fifth letter I have sent to you at Harpers ferry.

I have sent you every particular in those letters about ourselves and your business. We are all in good health. Ellen has not been sick one hour since you left home; we all enjoy ourselves very well thinking soon to see you at home.

I am glad to hear your sister and family are coming to Illinois. I will do my best to make them welcome as long as they choose to stay.[64]

I have made the crout as you desired, and I have plenty of potatoes Mike is digging them, they yield very well.

I have put down considerable of butter and a good many eggs. So I shall get along, with every thing until you come home, not having to buy any eatables, but a little fresh meat. Don and Ellen are going to school.

The weather is very pleasant now, we have not got up the horses yet, as there is plenty of food for them. I shall send Mike for them if the weather changes.

Our new preacher has come and preached twice on Sunday his subject in the morning was Paul's determination to count all things but loss for the excellency of the knowledge of Christ Jesus, our Lord," I wish that was your determination.

Miss Golden is dead, she died of the typhoid fever last Saturday. Agnes Adams is better. Mr. Whittaker took sick last Saturday, Dr. Hankins says it is typhoid fever, his fever is higher today than it has been yet, but the doctor says he is better. I am not alarmed nor afraid. We are sheltered by the protecting power of the orphan's father and the widow's God.[65] The most of the anxious care we have is that you may arrive home in safety. so many accidents taking place on the railway. I have nothing more to write at present.

Your's faithful to my trust
Ann Dumville.

PS There has been three men to buy land of you, they will be to see when you return.

From: Ann
To: Jemima and Hephzibah

Carlinville, Novbr 31st [sic] 55

My dear Children

I was much pleased to receive a letter from you, and glad to know you are going to school, and hope you will make the best use of your time.

My health is moderately good, but I have a very bad cold, but I trust it will pass away without any serious difficulty. I have had a letter from Iowa. Eliza had been sick with the billious fever but was better, but they are very much disatisfied and intend to sell out as soon they can, but I intend to let them do as they like. I gave them good advice before they went away and they did not take it. Tell Mr. Milburn that I never heard Mr. Wesley preach but my mother has a[?] many times he used to come to [my?] grandfathers before there was any meeting house in Manchester when he preached in the open air. You may tell her I used to hear Benson, Clarke[66] Lessey Dawson, Newton Atmore and most of the good preachers, they all preached good old fashioned religion.

Bishop Janes[67] dedicated our new church he preached an excellent sermon, and collections were taken up to defray all the expense and we have now a beautiful house well furnished, and a good preacher to preach in it, and all are praying for a revival.

Mr. Pitner[68] is our preacher Peter Cartwright's son in law, we like him very much and he will do his part towards a revival if the members will only do theirs, for my own part I am resolved to live nearer and closer to God every day that I live, and my prayer is for Eppy's conversion and that Jemima will hold fast to old fashioned religion, and I pray, for John Lirsy and all. Give my love to Mr.& Mrs. Stribling - tell them I fulfil my promise [to] them and pray that they may be kept safe to the end so that we may spend a blissful eternity together. My love to Mr. & Mrs. Lurton, I sympathise with them in the affliction of their children I hope it will have a sanctified effect to bring them nearer God "for whom the Lord loveth he chastens."

Give my love to Mrs. Milburn and to William[69] if you see them, tell him I wish him to preach Christ's gospel faithfully until he is crowned. Give my love to all enquiring friends. Major Burke has been away nearly thirteen weeks and I dont expect him home for three weeks more. His sister, Mrs. Creamer, her son daughter in law, and baby have been with us two weeks and will stay with us until the Major comes home.[70] So no more at present, Your affectionate Mother

Ann Dumville

PS Miss Birks wants you to send word when last half year commences she expects to go to college then; do not know when I can come to see you.

4. 1856–1857

Political Awareness

During the 1850s the abolition of slavery was the inescapable issue in American politics, and it was, of course, a moral, a religious, and an economic issue as well as a political one. It split the Methodist Church, it was largely responsible for the creation of the Republican Party, and it was the defining issue in the presidential elections of 1856 and 1860. But, as we have seen, the early letters focused on matters close to home. Even the brief mentions of abolition arose in the context of the Pitner case, a controversy within the local Methodist community. As the 1856 presidential election approached, however, the character of the letters changed.

As noted in chapter 1, in 1856 Hephzibah favored the candidacy of Millard Fillmore.[1] As president, Fillmore had been a pro-Southern Whig, but in 1856 he was the candidate of the American Party or, as more popularly known, the "Know-Nothings," a third party that was anti-immigrant[2] and supported the Kansas-Nebraska Act, a pro-Southern stance. James Buchanan, the Democratic candidate, also endorsed the Kansas-Nebraska Act and noninterference with slavery. John C. Fremont of California, a military hero, was the candidate of the new Republican Party, and he supported abolition. The Buchanan ticket carried the Southern states and was elected with a minority of the popular vote. Fremont won eleven of the sixteen free states, while Fillmore carried only Maryland.

In Illinois, Buchanan received 44 percent of the popular vote, Fremont 40 percent, and Fillmore 15.7 percent. There were strong regional differences within the state. In the northern counties, Fremont received almost 64 percent of the vote; in the southern tier, Buchanan received 66 percent.[3] The middle third of the state was more evenly divided, with relatively narrow margins between the two major candidates. Fillmore's greatest support came from areas near St. Louis, where rapid immigration had disturbed the local residents. Morgan, Macoupin, and Sangamon Counties, in the west central part of the state (see figure 4), gave Fillmore and the Know-Nothings more support than did the state as a whole. Many settlers of the southern and middle parts of the state had come from the South.

Unlike the northern counties, which relied on shipping through the Great Lakes to the East, the southern and western sections depended on the Mississippi River for trade and immigration. Richard Steckel's study of antebellum voting in the Old Northwest provides suggestive evidence that the geographic origin of citizens and the direction of commercial ties influenced voting patterns in the 1850s.[4] Religious affiliation and European birth had more tenuous effects.[5] The religious effect was, perhaps, lessened by the fact that many churches avoided partisan politics.[6] *The Ladies' Repository*, the Methodist magazine, made no mention of the Know-Nothings and gave little or no coverage to the elections of 1856 and 1860.[7]

Given Hephzibah's abolitionist views, her support for the Know-Nothings is perhaps surprising. She may have been experimenting with her political identity, differentiating herself from the Democratic allegiance of such acquaintances as the Lurtons and Peter Cartwright.[8] Party identification was strengthened by mobilization efforts such as parades, newspapers, flyers, and political clubs, which encouraged the local population to participate in political discourse and to vote.[9] Jacksonville was indeed a place where there was a wide range of views, but the divisions ran deeper in other parts of the Midwest. Kansas had rival governments in the mid-1850s, one supporting slavery and another opposing it. In 1856, pro-slavery and anti-slavery forces fought armed battles in eastern Kansas, and partisans of both sides sent guns and combatants into the territory.[10] A letter written by Hephzibah in September of 1856 commented on the violence in Kansas and, at the same time, deplored "Utah and its polygamey and other abominations; the Southern states with their African slavery, . . . and the Papel hierarchey, seeking as it does to rule all these things combined." Her anti-Catholic views were a salient part of the politics of the day, and her sentiments regarding Utah were consistent with the antipathy toward Mormons by leaders of other religious groups.[11] Joseph Smith, founder of the Mormon Church, had been murdered by a mob at Carthage, Illinois, in 1844 while he was a prisoner in the jail there.

As is often the case, political tensions were exacerbated by economic hardship. In the debates of the 1850s, and especially during the financial panic of 1857, immigrants were blamed for taking jobs from residents who, in many cases, had not been in the country much longer. The newer immigrants, both

Irish and German, largely supported the Democratic Party. In a letter written in November 1856, after the election of Buchanan, Hephzibah comments, "I believe that Irish is the cause of his election. They nearly all voted for him and there is enough of them to elect old Satan if he was brought out as a candidate." Hephzibah was an immigrant, but she was English, decidedly not Irish, and she had lived in the United States for sixteen years, since childhood. Like many of those who arrived before the great influx that began at the end of the 1840s, she thought of herself as American, and her endorsement of the Know-Nothings in the 1856 election was consistent not only with her disapproval of more recent immigrants but with her Protestant identity, her agrarian values, and her opposition to industrialization and urbanization.

Despite her expressed choice among the candidates, in September 1856 Hephzibah said that she did not want "the privilege of voting." Her attitude toward women's suffrage was typical of women at the time.[12] The ideology of domesticity and "true womanhood"[13] held sway, and the campaign for the right to vote did not gain momentum among middle-class women until after the Civil War.[14] Hephzibah's views were clear, however—she expressed her support for Fillmore forcefully. Motz's study of the letters and diaries of Michigan women from 1820 to 1920 concluded that they "usually avoided discussions of political issues and national events."[15] Hephzibah's letters do not fit this pattern. She was attuned to and commented on both national politics and issues within her local church. Because the true woman had a special office as guardian of morality, she had an acceptable reason to comment on public issues.[16]

In the second half of the 1850s, Hephzibah and Jemima increasingly corresponded with Elizabeth and John Williams, their sister and brother-in-law. The Williams family was then living in Poweshiek County, Iowa, where they had located in the midst of a large migration from the farms of Illinois and Indiana. According to one report, "During the fall and early winter of 1854 there was an almost uninterrupted procession of immigrants crossing the ferries at Prairie du Chien, McGregor, Dubuque, Burlington, Davenport, and Keokuk. Sometimes they had to wait in camp two or three days for their turn to cross. It was estimated that twenty thousand people crossed the ferry at Burlington in thirty days."[17] From 1854 to 1856, the Iowa population increased by 190,000, an increase almost equal to the entire population of the state in 1850.[18] Iowa was attractive not only because of the availability of inexpensive land but because there was a severe drought in the Ohio River valley and an epidemic of cholera in Illinois.[19]

But the Williams family did not find Iowa an unmixed blessing. A January 1856 letter from John said that a new settler would confront "harder times than he ever saw." John was unable to pay his taxes. Nonetheless, the land was fertile. He said that his wheat crop was good and that he had six hogs. In general, Iowa settlers appear to have prospered. Economic historians Galenson and Pope examined the fortunes of Iowa farmers using U.S. Census data from 1850, 1860, and 1870. Their small sample included forty-nine men, twenty-eight of whom each held real estate in 1850 that did not differ significantly in value from the national average for individual real estate holdings then. Of those twenty-eight men, however, all were above the national average ten years later. Their land had appreciated at a rate of 20 percent per year, net of inflation.[20] But the settlers seldom remained settled. They usually arrived in Iowa, bought land, farmed it for a time, and then sold out and moved on, often several times.[21] Galenson and Pope found, however, that those who arrived early fared better—they had been able to choose the more productive land.[22]

The character of the relationship between the Dumvilles and Ann's employer, Major Burke, is not entirely clear. Ann's letters to him, written in the mid-1850s when he was traveling, appear to be cordial, as well as businesslike and professional.[23] He clearly gave her responsibility for supervision of some of his employees and for minor financial matters. But Hephzibah's letters suggest that Burke was stingy and that he did not spend enough time with his children. Her letter of June 9, 1856, includes a sarcastic passage about him, quite bitter in tone; and, in May of 1857, "As for Major Burke, I neither know what to think or say of him"; in October of that year, further sarcasm: "You will feel under neverending obligation to the Major for his unbounded kindness surely." These passages show Hephzibah at her most feisty. The specifics of her complaints about Burke are unstated for the most part, but she pretty clearly felt that Ann's compensation was insufficient. Since Hephzibah was in Jacksonville, her information about this no doubt came from either Jemima or Ann. Such feelings, of course, are not uncommon in the employer-employee relationship, and they are not unlike Hephzibah's feelings toward the Striblings.

From: Hephzibah
Envelope address: Miss Jemima Dumville, Carlinville, Illinois

Monday March 24th 1856

Dear Mima,
After leaving the rail-road I went to work on my dress and worked very industerously all day.... The next day I washed and the next day it being Thursday

I thought I would iron so that I would have the rest of the week to sew on my dress. But [-] aboute ten o clock we looked up the lane and saw a lady and boy and little baby waggon coming down the lane which upon investigation proved to be Sarah Brown and George bringing out the babies. She met Grandma and informed her that she might expect company . . . Soon after sure enough Mrs. [?] Lina and Mary, Mrs. Buckingham and Mary McElfresh soon made their appearance and soone after Greenberry and Bro. Curiosity. The gentlemen left soone after dinner but the ladies remained until five. . . .

April 1st The exhbition will take place tomorrow night from the appearance of the weather I fear we will not have a nice time, And what do you think? Last Saturday I was at the house of Mr. Easy,[24] and Modern Refinement requested one of my old compositions for Watche keeper to put in her paper. I granted the request, and yesterday Watch keeper came to get it in company with Mrs. Green, and while here she told me that [her?] brother [?] and [?] Green had written to Bro Curiosity to write a piece for her paper but he has not sent it on yet. And I thoughtlessly said you need not fret aboute it for I don't expect it would be much if you was to get it Was not that a <u>blunder</u>? I would have given some to have unsiad it if I could have done it. I have finished two letters today. I filled one sheet and half of another to Sister Mary, and nearly one to Iowa, I think that is pretty good business for me. But if I keep writing I wont have room to write aboute the exhibition.

April 3rd Well! That noted exhibition is over at last. I was there and the result is I have the head ach[e] today for being out so late.

The house was not full owing probably to the unfavorableness of the night as wind blew hard and there was some appearance of rain. The exercises was opened with a prayer by Bro. J. A. Palmer. The sing[l]e speeches was pretty good but the dialogues was rather silly. The one in which you was asked to take part was drop[p]ed because the little ones would not do right. The scholars all did well, better than I expected, four of the little boys did fine namely, H. Walter, E. March, L. Buttler, and Oliver Green. Of the two last I scarce know which was best. The other little boys was all either Kerrs or Richersones. They did so so. There was only four large boys and they performed their parts very well. Their names are J. Kerr, J. Walter, O. Green, C. [?]. The two last were the best speakers. Now for the girls. Two little girls sung, "lightly row" and three others spoke and performed a dialogue. They all did passable. The large girls read their paper. . . . Their was four Editors. (as they call themselves). E. Green, J. Walter, B. Kerr, A. Kerr. We did not know that Belle was going to read untill we got there. . . . Elmira and Julia did as well as could be expected, for the first time. But B. and A. beat them all to peaces it would have been a shame if they had not, they have so much better a chance. Their papers was the best. . . . Solitude was the composition Julia selected from my book and it was the poorest thing they had. I was really ashamed of it. . . . My sheet is full & must stop. Yours, Heppa,

From: Hephzibah
To: Jemima

Home. June 9th 1856

Dear Mima. I cant half express my gratitude to you, for writing so <u>very often</u> and sending such <u>long</u> letters. I recieved your last, last Tusday after-wating at least a month longer than I expected. So Mother is not coming to see me? I was affraid something would happen to prevent her coming, but I will try and waite untill fall yet I should have been glad to see her now.

Tell her I do not doubt one instant, that she loves me, for I am sure she does. Why how in the world could Mother help returning to Burks? Such a good home and such kind people: and then his past conduct has proven so clearly that, "dollars and cents are nothing in his eye," Yes <u>we know</u> that he is a very <u>liberal man</u>. His purse must be of immence depth and breadth, and well filled too, to sustain such a heavy draft as has been made upon it lately. Oh! how I do sympathise with him in his distress, poor man! Well I must try and restrain myself and rite about other things.

Little Mary[25] is the sweetest little dolly you almost ever saw, she is walking now, it would really make you laugh to see her open her little plump arms while her bright eys sparkle with delight when grandma goes to see them. She thinks her pa and grandma are the graitest people oute. The day I went to town to post the last letter I sent to you the first object that met my eye was Henry walking to the gate to meet us, O he was pleased because he could walk again. I never saw a child more glad in my life he has been improving ever since, he is now fat and hearty and able to ride his poney all aboute (such ponies as little boys ride you know) when mounted with a whip in his hand he no doubt feels almost as consequental as black Sam did when seated in Aunt Chloes kitchen feasting on the fragments, and delivering his oration to his friend and "bredern."[26]

Grandma has been pretty well this spring rather better than comon, though we are neither of us as fleshy as when you left, we have had work enoug to do too if work ever made any body fat. I will try and give you an idea what we have done though I cant begin to tell you half. Grandma said the other day, "Jemima thinks we are so nasty, I wish she could come to see us now." Well we do feel right nice that's a fact.

Well in the first place grandma and Mr. Hamilton, (the man that is living here) made the garden I have done very little this year in it and I sweept the yard. Then we went and fixed Mary's yard,[27] after that we made our soap, we made more than a barrel full, in the mean time we would take a cart load of litter out of the yard where they had thrown the bricks when cutting the door in the wall, when they finished the new room which they did early in May we got Mr Evens to come and white wash the ceiling down stairs, and paper the three front rooms, and paint the wood work in the house from pa[r]lor to kitchen and also the portico. I took it upon myself to paint the poarch. We have made a new carpet for the pa[r]lor, ripped a seam in the old one and sewed it up again, and put in the new room. We had our old Venitian blinds[28] painted, and made them over and now they look as well as they did at first. I varnished the dressing bureau the bed-stead in the west room and the stant [stand?], also the safe suggar desk[29] and the book-case, that made you jump so once, do you remember? Then we took up the carpets, shook them, washed the floors upstairs and down, and put them down again, beside a hoste of other things to numerous to mention. Now if you dont think we are smart folks up here, I dont know what other proof you would ask to convince you of the fact.

I went to the Belles letter's[30] paper reading the last night in May, in company with C—y M—B—W—K and Fidelity, it was passable but not to be compared with the one before. Mary Prentice and Mat Newman sung and the first readr is unknown to me, the next was Miss King, Alice Cleanland and Vic. Vane, they all did well. I saw Phi Nu[31] at Salem a short time since she wish to be rememberd to you. Mr. and Mrs. Dellzell[32] send their respects also Fidelity. I have not heard from Iowa since I wrote to you. Give my love to all, write soone, will you? Ben [?] was to be married this morning to Miss Route so I heard yesterday. I have much more to write but cant to it now no more.

Yours Heppa.

I am reading Uncle Toms Cabbin, or Life Among the Lowly. I will tell you what I thin[k] aboute when I write again.

From: Hephzibah
To: Jemima

Jacksonville   June 1856[33]

Dear Mima

Your last letter reached me last week. I wrote to you a short time before but I supose you had not received it. I ought to have told you in my last that Mr. P Horrell sent two and half in gold and a half dollar in silver to me for you but I forgot when I wrote do they owe you any more now?

We are all well at present. I came to town this morning with grandma to get her dress fitted. Miss Smith has made one for me already. As you are a daughter or sis (as may be) of temperance you will laugh to hear of the procedings here. Week before last a paddy[34] took it into his head to build a grog shop close to the second rail-road crosing, which he did or began to do. He brought five barrels of the "good creation" oute to his establishment to begin operation, when lo! last Wednesday night a party of men in town disguised themselves went out the grog-shop caught the fellow and held him or tied him I dont know which, while they tore the building intirely down and cutting the timbers so that he could not make use of them again, and to crown the whole they drove in the heads of the barrels and let out the contents. The fellow is trying to put it up again but even if he does it will not be permitted to stay so long I think and so think others. We do not know who tore it down nor shall we be able to find out as those that were ingaged in it think best to keep it to themselves. I assure you we have a rejoycing time in our neighborhood, in consequence of the distruction of the grog-shop.

I went to the male college commencement last Thursday, there were 14 graduates, I was very pleased, but should have been more pleased if I could have had a seat as it was I had to stand some time. Our commencement will take place three weeks from Wednesday next. There will be ten graduates I am told, can you come? I have not heard a word from Iowa cant you write and ask them what they are doing I would like to hear. I am progressing very slowly with my reformation.[35] I have not read any in it since you left. When we had the Repository down I had to read them you know and since then I have read some in a book entitled Select London Lectures which were the best ever delivered in London so you know they must be good. I have read Life Among the Lowly.[36] It is a very diferent work to what I thought it to be before I read it.

I have laughed and cried and admired alternately as the different persons or caracters passed under review.

I think it a well drawn picture highly colored to be sure but not more so than the real. I have also read a book entitled Female life Among the Mormans. It is aboute the size of Bascoms life, really sister if this book be true, the condition of women in Utah is as bad as that of the slave in New Orleans market.[37]

When I began the letter I thought I should have time to fill this sheet but now I must stop and go up town.

Give my love to all, . . . write soon.

Yours Heppa

P. S. I shall send this to you with oute even giveing it a second reading so you must look over all mistakes.

From: Hephzibah, Jacksonville
Envelope address: Miss J. Dumville   Carlynnville

Satturday, September 27, 1856

Woes cluster; rare are solidary woes;

Deare Sister, the truth of this saying of Young has been verified in Mr. Keers family in the past two weeks.

Two weeks ago today Douglas made a speach in town and as the Buchannanites desired to out do anything that had been done this fall, they must needs prepare the day before, by hoisting their polls and unfurling their flags, of which they had quite a number. Mr. Keer[38] was helping to rais the poll when some part of it fell and struck him on the forehead, for a time he was thought to be killed, but soon recoverd a little. The Dr. said if he had been struck an inch from the place where he was he would never have known what hurt him.

He was taken home on a bed in Mr. Anderson's furniture carriage, Isabell had been complaining of a pain in her head for some weeks previous and when her father was brought home; the shock was to much for her to indure, she threw herself on the bed, and never rose again except to change from one bed to an other, she lingered two weeks, and died yesterday morning at four o clock. Mr. Cloude preached her funeral sermon today on Remember now thy Creator in the days of thy youth, while the evil days come not, nor the years drawing when thou shalt say, I have no pleasure in thine, There was a great many present, a waggon load of the [?] came oute. her disease was congestion of the brain. For three days before her death she was unable to speak at all.

Dear Bell, I hope she is free from suffering now. I do not feel as well satisfied in referance to her departure as I would like to feel, one remark which she made three days before her exit gives us encouragement to believe she is at rest, she said: "how sweet it is to die." She has been a profesor of religion and a member of the church for four or five years.

Mr. Kerr is now aboute well. Last Sabbath one of his little girls fell of[f] the lowest step of the rock brige and put her wrist oute of place, but is now getting well.

. . .

I went to camp meeting Sunday before last, it was Mr. Houte's and Jane's in connecttion, When we arrived Mr. W. Rutledge was preaching, you know he can't preach a poor sermon [-]. Mr. Steavenson took for a text; I reckon, the suffering of the present time, are not to be compared, with glory that shall be revealed in us" fifteen minuits after he finished Mr. Wilson[39] preached on "I will prais the Lord; for He has heard my prayer, and the voice of my supplication" I am not sure that I have written the text correctly as I have done entirely by the aid of memory. At night Mr. Bristow preached. I have forgotten his text, there was a multitude in attendance. [?] that I was highly pleased. Kate King was there. I spoke to her, and don't you think she pretended not to know me. I can't think it was fact. her [?] would not look at me, I was dit[t]o,[40] you had better believe.

The county fare was held near town last week, I was there on Tuesday the 15th which was the first day. The ladies shewed their articles on that day, there was not much pleasure for little folks. There was such a croude I could not see anything well. I was tired enough when I left, there was no shack or seats to sit on or anything els much, but dust and people. [?] neighbour south recieved the second premium on his hog, and Consequentiality obtained the first on his colt.

Mr. McCoy[41] is the president of our College for the present year, there are quite a number of girls here now and many coming.

I will tell you sometime next November who is to be the president of the Union, one thing I can tell you now if a good president has ever been needed since the day the declaration of independence, one is needed now, for Utah and its polygamey and other abominations; the Southern states with their African slavery, the desire of some to extend it and determination of others abolish it, and to cap the line [?] the Papel hierarchey seeking as it does, to rule all these thing combined, must and will create a clashing in the political and religious eliments, of which Kansas has had a foretaste. It seems Mima that with all your Quaker like sobriety of appearance, you have had to dip into the political whirlpool. I am not at all surprised at it, it seems to be the order of the day, "all men and maidens, young men and children" all seem to be affected by the prevailing sentiment. On a "big day" here the town is vocal with [little?] Buchannan Fremont and Filmore <u>men</u>. You may tell Mary that I am Descidedly a <u>Know Nothing</u>, and if I had the privelige of voting[42] (which I do not desire) I should vote for Filmore though I know my vote would be of no avail, I would have the consolation of knowing that I had voted for the best man, and all parties seem ready to pronounce <u>him soo</u>. I presume by this time you have a very poor opinion of Mankind in general and of F. and B. in perticular. Well they are rather uncertain animals I believe. but as we have to stay in the world with them we must get along with our disaggreeable situation as well as we can.

It does seem to me that any one who thinks me either pritty or remarkably inteligent must err greatly. I often complain of my ignorance and want of atainment feeling that between what I know and what I desire to know there is no comparison.

Sarah has been at home ever since her school was oute, she has been talking of going to Baltimore but has given it out for the present. Mary has not returned yet but I expect she will soon.

Write soon, I must seace now. My love to Mother and every body els.

Yours Heppa

From: L. P. Horrell

Oct 24th 1856
State of Illinois Scott County

Dear Sister Jemima with pleasure I now take my pen in hand to address you a few liness we are all reasonably well at present for which we are thankful to God, the season has been uncommonly dry both literally and spiritually. Stock has suffered for want of water, but it has rained al most incessantly now for 24 hours and I hope water will be more plenty. We do not appreciate the common blessings of lif until deprived of them! how ungrateful.

There was a religious interest manifested at Lynnville sometime since, but I was lame with rheumatism in one knee and could not attend; there seems to be some fruit of their labor, we have had some good class metings lately.

Charles B says he wishes Jemima was here so he could go to school, he sometimes wants to learn.

Lewis says he wants to see you. He & Charley hollows [hollers?] hurrah for Fillmore & Donalson.

Our respects to your Mother. Hope she enjoys a good share of the comforts of religion.

John Adkisson has sold out and will soon leave.

. . . Tyrrel Headen, on his return from the State fair at Alton met with a railroad accident which soon caused his death.

Charles Schola has been away so that I have not been able to collect your money from him . . . ; he deceived me several times about paying, finally, I got a summons for him but found he was in Cass County and I could not come at him without a great-deal of trouble and expence but as he is now close by I hope soon to get it for you.

Annis wishes you to remember her, would like to hear you sing again. Come and see us when you can.

Farewell

L.P. Horrell

From: Visiting Committee, Robert W. Glass, George R. Hughes

Copy
Extract from report of Visiting Committee for Month of October

"We are pleased to express our Satisfaction generally at the good order maintained and the apparent progress, of the Pupils. A proficiency creditable alike to Teachers, and Pupils, was manifested at Several of the Schools, and without intending any invidious distinction, the desire to note the class of young Ladies[43] in history of U.S. at Miss Dumville's School, as officially meriting our Commendation"
"Signed"

	Robert W. Glass
Nov 4th 1856	George R. Hughes
	Committee

From: Hephzibah
To: Jemima

At Home   November 13th 1856

Yes, Mima, I profess to know some what aboute the reporte, that George Woods and Nette Kerr was going to be married, On the 14 of last month. I was invited to a sewing at Mr. Kerrs, which was to take place on the day following. I had a half mind to be contrary; and not go; but Maggie Walter came by and wanted me to go and be company for her so I went, I thought too as I had gone to see Belle, while she was sick I ought to go perhaps. There were fourteen ladies present, I enjoyed myself very much, Mary Rues and myself entertained our selves by <u>pretending</u> to try to convert Maggie to Filmoreitism.[44] Just one week from that day was the day of Nette's wedding. Though I had no such thought at the time, the curent reporte here was that "Anna was going to head in town and go to College and Nette was going to take music and drawing lessons. but [later] on a note was handed to me which ran as follows; Miss Nittie Kerrs compliments, Oct 22, 7 oclock P. M. accordingly I went in company with the three Miss Poesys [Poseys] and the two Miss Walters and Master C——. I suppose there was a hundred persons present that evening, Netti was dressed in white low neck and short sleves, a white reath of roses around her head and a white vail[45] over her face, she wore no jewelry whatever but had a white rose on each shoulder and another in place of a [?], the two brides-maides Anna and Miss Staley was dressed nearly like her. I presume she never looked better & prettyer in her life. I did not enjoy myself much, not half so well as I did at the sewing, we left quite early only half past ten. I think the rest of the company was in the same predicament at least part of them was, with myself. I presume such a place or party is not designed as much for comfort as show, therefore as I am not a very showy-bred, you may imagine that I appeared somewhat like a chicken among a crowde of Peacocks, after all I suppose it may be well enough for me to go to such a place once in a while, for if there is not much pleasure to be experienced, they may at least if they will keep their eyes open learn a "thing or two."

Mr. Woods and Nette was ingaged, some years ago, but the ingagement was not consumated in consequence of a very ugley reporte being circulated aboute him, wheather it was true or not, I know not, some say it is, others that it is not. You know that a wedding [in] this neighborhood, is such a rare occurance, that of course it created quite an excitement, curiosity is on tip-toe, every lady wants to know if she has "done well" and "what kinde of man is he" "if he has any things" and so forth, and so on—for my own part I know nothing at all aboute the matter, and if you know anything good bad or indifferent just send it on, I'd like to know too.

I heard today that he reached Mr. R.—last night, and they expect to starte to Carlinville next week.

One week from the wedding Mrs Dellzell invited the bride and Anna myself and Maggie and Julia to spend the afternoon with her the two last mentioned was not there, so you see had a <u>little</u> party to our three selves which I enjoyed very well.

Saturday, 15

Since writing to you last, I have succeeded by the most unheard of perseverance, for me, in filling two sheets, of the most interesting matter of which I am capable, one of which was designed for Mr. Carr the other for sister Mary,[46]

. . . I have reserved a copy so that you can have the benefit of a reading when you come to see me. Among other things, I gave her to understand that she might expect a letter from you. Now you be sure and make my word good, if you have not already.

I promised to tell you in November who was to be the President, well James Buchannon is said to be the man, though he is by no means my man, I believe that Irish is the cause of his election. They nearly all voted for him and there is enough of them to elect old Satan if he was brought out as a candidate, well let them go, Pope says; "Partial evil, is universal good",[47] so we will hope this is for the best.

Mrs. Mibourn, has returned home and so [?] Mary, Mrs. McElfresh[48] but I have not seen either of them. Wiliam Milbourn has published a book entitled, The Axe, Rifle and Saddlebags[49] I have not seen it yet but if I ever do, I shall be apt to make use of my eyes.

. . .

Four or five weeks ago I called to see Miss Palmer[50] at the college, she roomes with Maria Cummings, the girls was not in their room when I went so i walked in and waited until they had come from their recitations, as soon as Miss P caught a glimpse of me she exclaimed, "I know that is Miss Dumville because she looks so much like Miss Jemima." she then went on to say that you and mother had sent me five bushels of love but she had kept it so long it had nearly all evaporated, and she kept a large share of it herself. I had an idea before I went that I should see a very sedate young lady, but wasn't I mistaken. An hour in her company convinced me of my error.

Our good bretheron Curiosity and Punctuality, tarried all night with us two weeks ago last Monday. They have both been sent as P. said "to do their first work over," in the course of the evening bro C. asked the usual question, "When did you hear from sister Mima & is she well?" And sometimes adds, "married yet?" that evening however he did not ask the last question, but brother P. asked "where is she now?" of course I answered as well as I could, but I assure you the question and answer both was expressed with so much indifference that a person would have had to be previously initiated to have suspected that there was anything behind the curtain.

I should be delighted to visit you but don't see any way of doing so at present. Grandma and myself are quite well, but grandpa is very much in the background, he has too much to do, we have no one to help him at present.

Did you know [Alsia?] Goodrich, well she died a few days after Bell, she was only sick three or four days. she suffered the most excruciating pain, and in the first part of her sickness she was very unhappy, but a short time before her death she expressed herself as being able to leave everything to the Lord.

I have heard too this week that Charley [Sheef?] is dead also, poor Charley! Is not Mrs. Tiller[51] passing through the straits? I think she is sure, poor woman, I thing she is to be pittyed.

Maggie Walter is going to subscribe for the Repository, can not you do <u>likewise</u>. If I was as young <u>lady</u>, I would.

Give my best love to mother, and my next best to all my friends. . . .

Write soone, and don't look at these straight lines, and this good writing too closely for fear it might injure your eyes. If you want to subscribe for the Ladies Repository, your preacher in charg can tell you all you need to know, if you will ask him. I want you to be sure and do so. Yours, Heppe.

P. S. The folks in Iowa dont think enough of me to write to me, I have not received a letter since mother was here.

From: Hephzibah
Envelope address: Miss Jemima Dumville, Carlinville, Illinois

December 16th 1856

My Dear Sister Mima,

I will write to you, indeed I will, though it is a sad mistake if you suppose that I nod after going to bed. You talk of having so much work to do, I'll venture you have leasure compared to us, I will just let you into the secrete of our matters and then see if we don't have work to do by wholesale. Last week we killed twelve of the largest hogs we had had for many a year, the week before that we disposed of thirteen turkey, the week before that we colored our carpet rags and the week before that we covered over our rose bushes and flowers and mended our old carpet that we had on the sitting room floor last winter. You would hardly recognize the old servant now it looks so well, we cut the part under the bed out and put it in the middle of the floor. We thought we would have one bright spot at least. . . . We intend next week to kill twelve male turkeys, and then our <u>hard</u> work will be done for this winter, I hope, though we have a multitude of minor things to[o] numerous to mention.

While writing to you the volume of William Milburn's is on the table, of which I spoke in my last, I have read part of it. Of course I like it how could I do otherwise? I wish there was not so much truth in his: "hours talk aboute woman"[52] I will give you a few sentences: "Our scheme of common and high school education is adapted to the exigencies of the female as well as the masculine intellect As large a proportion of girls of the country are to be found in school as boys. As much money is expended, and I am led to believe, from such information as I have been able to collect, more, for their training and accomplishment than for those of the boys. There are abundant opportunities for our young women between the time they leave school and that when they are married, to improve and cultivate themselves for the general pursuits of literiture; and yet, for the most part, what are the results? Fashon and folly.

Can it be said with fairness that our young [women] have literary culture, artistic taste, or any of that refinement and elevation of manner, sentiment, and mind, which their advantages justify us in demanding of them? . . . I do not believe I exaggerate when I say that you can find half a dozen or half a score of creditable performers on the piano, for one who can read properly, and with the power of interpreting her author to the listener, among the graduates of our female academies and seminaries. . . .["]

"A space of two years is by courtesy supposed to intervene between the damsel's leaving school and her entrance upon the duties of married life; yet how much substantial reading is done within one of those years?"[53]

I think I have read books before that was, perhaps, as interesting, but my own slight acquaintance with the author gives the book charm which it would not otherwise possess. You will have to read it yourself before you can appreciate it as you ought.[54]

It would seem as though I am not to write to you again withoute my letters conveying the intelligence of the death of someone. I heard some time ago that Mrs. Eli Williams had departed this life. I did not hear the particulars. . . . We are enjoying our usual health. I saw little Dolly today and she is as sweet and smart as ever. . . .

The reason of your not getting my letter <u>sooner</u> was this, on Monday the 17th of Nov. I gave my letter to Willie telling him to be sure and post it that day so that it would go in the next mail, he promised to do so and I thought perhaps he would not forget it as it is something unusual for him to have an opportunity of posting a letter, and it pleases him to do it. But the next Saturday I asked him if he had posted my letter, he blushed and replied that he had not thought of it since I gave it to him, so i had the privelege of posting it myself. . . . Have you sent for the Repository? Grandma sends her love to you and mother, my love to you all. . . . No news from Iowa yet. Write soon, Yours. Heppe. Come to see me els!

From: Hephzibah
Envelope address: Miss Jemima Dumville, Carlinville, Ill

Monday Jan 26th 1857

Dear Mima

I presume you think it is high time that I endeavour to answer you consequential billet which you sent to me a few weeks since. Perhaps it is, but really I have not time to spare today, but for fear the Post Office may suffer seriously by my delaying, and that you know would be a material loss to the comm wealth—and as I don't wish to injur the public in any way whatever I will try to write a few words on the topics which are attracting general attention, which are Matrimony Cold Weather and Small Pocks, I speak of them in regular order, first we have had quite a matrimonial revival in our midst. I will not stop to give you the names of those who have become Mrs as Nette can no doubt give you a correct history of the various personages that have performed a conspicious part in the different weddings. Sufice it to say that, the excitement is subciding, and I have not been in the least affected by it. Next we have had some very cold weather,. . . . I am glad you live South, and would like to think you have not had such cold weather, as me. . . . if you have you will know the better how to sympathise with us.

Now for the last—the small pocks are pretty well scattered over the country. It was discovered Sunday before last that Bob Landers had them or what would have been the small pocks had he not been vaccinated.[55] He had been sick for some time and every young man in town had been to see him before it was known what was the matter with him. His room was full every night and even now they will run up stairs to his room door [to] talk to him.

I have been told that if a person has once been inoculated with the real small pox that there was no danger of their taking them again. I would like for you to ask mother if there is any danger of my taking them I was vaccinated some years ago and it had no affect so i thought I need not try again, write me what mothers says aboute it.

I wrote a letter to John and Lizzie new Years day. I don't know wheather he wil deign to send me an answer or not, I have not had a letter since last July.

I was very much conserned last fall aboute the maner in which I should spend my time this winter, as I had no sewing on hand, I however consoled my self with the idea that I would spend the time quite profitably by leasurely reviewing my last winters studies, and reading good books and finishing my quilt, well what do you suppose is the result of all my calculations? why I have not seen the inside of one of my books except my Arithmatic and perhaps marked out a dozzen exampels . . . and have sewed the first stitch on my quilt and I have more sewing to do than I shall finish this side of April, now there are you not sorry for me?

I have read some and I intend to read more too wheather my sewing gets done or not, dont you think I'm right sis. I do. I have been visiting or going abroad whichever you like to call it. I only went oute five times week befor last, twice last week and once this. I must tell you all about the [roads?] I took week before last. On Sunday went to Salem, on Monday staid at home, Tuesday we all took dinner with Mr and Mrs Dellzell. Wednesday evening called on Nette and took the book which you desired, I presume you have it by this time, Thursday night went to hear the reading of the [Iris?] or the Phi Nu paper reading. The papers were good and the girls read well but the music was poor as usual, Friday night was the best of all, I went in company with Margret Mayberry and Julia Walters, Horatio Austin, Elvira and Marchel Green and William Simpson five or six miles south east of here to a paper reading. O, but we had a capital sleigh ride. We started a little after five and I reached home half past eleven oclock.

The paper was very good considering it was published in the country. I will give you a few remark that was made on Fashon "There is one thing more powerful than the steam engine that is fashon, Fashon rules the women, the women rule the men [who] rule the world therefore Fashon is omnipotent.

Fashon would make a man over eighteen pair of breeches at one time, and have his bootes so sharp at the toes that they would serve as a tooth pic, Fashon restrains all our actions and even regulates the rites of the sepulcher," I have not given the exact words, but as much like them as I could.

We are in a sad delima at present. Last Thursday morning our pump brok in consequence of the freeze, since which time we are obliged to go East when we want a bucket of water. Our cistern proves to be a good friend in time of need. We are very much troubled by colds at this time, and Grandma has been afflicted by a pain in her, why her leg if I must write it, but she is getting well now.

Have I ever written anything to you aboute our young preacher? if I have not I will now say that he is a very nice little man, he has light hair blue eyes and is quite fair and delicate, we are all vastly pleased with him, I do believe that Grandpa and ma think as much of him as they do of our noted Brother Curiosity. . . . You will pleas reread a few of my past letters and answer a few of the questions I have tried to propound. My love to all, Heppe

. . .

From: Hephzibah
Envelope address: Miss Jemima Dumville, Carlinville, Illinois

Wednesday May 20th 1857

My Dear Sister Mima

I will venture to say you begin to think I am paying you in coin from your own mint. Well sis I am sure when I received your last I had no thought that it would be so long before I should write to you, but really we have had so much to do, and had so much company lately that I have not had time to write—Not a day has passed for two weeks or more but we have had company and last Monday twenty five persons were at our house during the day which will do for a begining for this week. You gave me a brief history of the maner in which you spend your time during one week, and I think you have enough to do. I will give you a short account of my performance one day last week, on the 12 ins Mr. McCoy announce to the young ladies of our College that a Pick Nick[56] would be held in Stribling Grove the following day. The morning of the appointed day was rather unpromising but aboute ten o clock the woods was alive with boys and girls, a clap of thunder soon after caused them to mak a general rush for the house, we opened our doors and in [a] few moments the rooms were full to overflowing the weather not permiting them to be oute much so we gathered all the tables we could muster and spread them in the porch, they plased there nick nack on them, and tried to enjoy themselvs as best they could under the sircumstances upon the whole I presume they had a nice time as could have been expected, at four in the evening the word was given to move home ward and at six the last one took her leave, and we had the house to ourselves again. After a day of comotion such as these old walls never witnessed before and perhaps never will again, there must have been at least two hundred present.

    I attended the Belles Letters paper reading the second night of this month. The readers were Misses Davis sister of the teachers, Willson Kenedy and [?]. It passed off pretty well but I did not enjoy it as much as I have done sometimes.

    I heard a sermon last Sunday which I enjoyed very much indeed delivered by the Rev Mr Eddy[57] Editor of the North Western Christian Advocate I have seldom if ever heard a better sermon. The text was 1 Thes 2 chap and 4 verse.[58] Over two hundred dollars Misonary money was obtained at the close. I fear you will find my letter rather dull this time if you do don't be surprised at all for I am at Mrs Lurton's this evening and the children keep such a fuss that I can't half the time tell what I am aboute.

    As for your going to school next term I don't know what to say to you aboute it. . . . Wheather you had better start untill you can see your way through is a question which I don't know how to . . . answer to my liking, so I will guest [just] hand you over to mother, feeling sure that she can tell you better than I can. It would be the hight of my ambition to take a thorough course, but my prospects for it are exceedingly dark at present. The first of July will be commencement day. The Phi Nus will have their anniversary the night before I would like very much for you to be hear. . . .

    I will tell you what I have been reading that will perhaps pleas you as well as any thing els. Last week I finished reading a little book entitled "Captain Vicars" it gives an account of the life of a young British soldier who was killed in the late Russian war[59] also a number of letters which he sent home to his friends, and I have been reading this week every little minuite I could get a book which Mrs. [?] Lurton brought from Chicago to grandpa. She leaves this week so I fear that I shall not get through, the book is written by Rev Professor J. H. Ingraham and is entitled "The Prince of the House of David or three Years in the Holy City the author represents [?] rich Jew of Alexandria of Egypt sending his daughter Adina to Jerusalem to [be] educated in a maner suited to one of her rank and the sole inheritor of his welth, it would seem that she reached there aboute the time that John the Baptist began his ministry. She writes letters to her father giving her impressions of the different sights which she saw, of the preaching of "John of Jordan" and also of "Jesus of Nazareth" She gives a very pretty acount of His baptism by John, in fact all the noted caracters that figure in the New Testament she brings in in the course of the letters, to one who has read the scriptures there is nothing very new. . . . It is interesting in so much as it is in rather a diffrrant style to the Testament, and then too you have matters more minutely detailed.

I finished a letter to brother this morning, for my own part I think they will stand as good a chance in Kansas as where they are. Mr. L B. Denis P. E. [Presiding Elder] at Laurance Kansas gives a very pleasing account of the brightening prospects there.

So sis you are taking music lessons are you? Of course you succeed admyrably & I hope you do full as well as you expected to.

I have not seen Curiosity lately, I fear it would flatter his vanity to know that you would like to see him or write to him either so I had better not tell him so.

I must close this poor thing for it is getting late . . . Kiss mother for me. I hope to have the pleasure of kissing her my self soon. Mr. Walters family have been very much afflicted lately almost all the family have been sick, Mr. W is sick now himself . . . Forgive me dear sister for not writing, before now, write soon, my love to all.

Good Night   Epper

Lucy Williams is married, did you know it?

From: Hephzibah
Envelope address: Miss Mima Dumville, Carlinville Illinois

At Home   August 7th 1857

Dear Mima

When I last wrote to you it was my intention to start for Carlinville next week, or at least towards the last of this month, but the day before I received your last I obtained one from John in which he stated that I might "look oute for them the 10 or 20 of September and if I did see them to look in again"

I assure it was with reluctance that I gave up my visit, for the present, . . . and then to think that I have to wait 60 days or 1440 hour or 86,400 minutes, now does not that seem like a little eternity? . . . Had it not been for the thought that sister would be disapointed, . . . and I knew to[o] that [mother] would want to see al her children together once more. Taking these things in to consideration, with a little coaxing from grandma, for she want me to wait untill Sister comes, I concluded to postpone my visit untill they come. It makes me feel quite serious to hear that any one expects to see much when they see me, knowing as I do how far I am from what I would like to be . . . I am by no means satisfied with my self.

Dr. Akers[60] preached in town yesterday perhaps for the last time as he starts for Minnesota to-morrow, I got ready to go and hear him but the rain prevented, I presume you have heard that William Milbourn is now in England, attracting attention wherever he goes, and receiveing the homage of the great and learned of that greatest of all cities, London perhaps we shall have a notice of him in the next London Litterary Correspondence. I will close my letter now not quite so formally as . . . my last, and reserve everything els that I may have to say untill I see you. My love to all my friends I shall try to appear to the best advantage when I come, we shall [see] what that will be, I fancy I shall cut quite figure in the presence of Mrs S. I do hope she may not be looking for a great wonder.

look for me when you see me coming and then you will not be disapointed. Yours Heppe.

A P.S. I don't know that you will be able to read this pencil writing. I could not carry pen and ink with me well if you cant just wait till I come and I will tell you what I have written.

From: Charles B. Horrell [young son of H. P. Horrell]
Envelope address: Miss Jemima Dumville, Carlinville Illinois

Sep 7 1857

Dear Aunt Jemima

I sit down to write you a few lines to tell you that I am well at present. I was up to Jacksonville [?] since and saw Heppy and she was well then & I have been going to schol I read in the third reader and spell in the sanders speling book[61] and cipher in the Rays arithmetic[62] and study, Mitchells new primary geography,[63] I went to school to Mrs todd this summer and am going to school to Mrs Bernam this winter [?] So, as it is getting late I will close by saying good by

Charles B. Horrell
to Jemima Dumville

From: John Williams
To: Ann

Oct 18, /57

Deare Mother, From Carlinville we reached Mr. Striblings late in the evening safe. The next morning started weste. Done some buoisness in Jacksonvill, dined at Mr. Hucksteps, called at L. P. Horrells. C. C. Coats, took super at Josiah Williams,[64] called at G. Wardewicks & so on to Winchester. Got theire at 9. or 10 o clock at Night on Sunday. Hearde the beste sermon that I have hearde for four years. Monday was rainy, Tuesday we started for Waggoners made some hasty preparations & Wednesday started for home [Iowa].

Got one mile weste of Versales late in the eavening. Saw a boy 8 or 9 years olde fall out of a wagon. The wheels run over him. The team started to run but was soon stopt. As soon as my teame & wagon was safe I ran to the boy, picked him up and brought him to my wagon. Bathe him in camphor. Just then a young man rode up. I ordered him to go for the doctor & the Parents of the boy. Another brother 10 or 12 run to a house harde by for some helpe & none being at hande returned while the bathing was going on I took the boy & caried him to the house. On a closer examination founde his rite arme broken. He was injured in the breste & lefte hip by the wheels the doctor & parents soon arived & took charge of him.

Next day we got to my uncles founde another little boy with a broken arme the next day we got to Carthage. The nexte crossed the [Mississippi] river at Keokuck.[65] about 12 oclock night found us fifteen miles out on the roade & as the weather was threatening we started Sunday morning about 12. The raine comenced to come in earnest I drove five miles to an olde friende & took up untill the next morning when it was cleare. We had mud & watter holesale & retail. Monday we traveled 18 miles to Birmingham, the next Dalonega, the next to South Skunk. Stayed with a quaker. Next morning we started fasing a northwest wind & raine. Reached home wet & chilled. Founde Elias[66] well & everything moderately straite. The clouds broke away in the evening & we saw the first frost in this part of the state which come the 15th night of Oct. This day has been raining & at 5 oclock snow came thick & fast for a while.

We are all well except Martha has the chills.

As it is geting late I must close. Adue

J.W. Williams

From: Hephzibah
To: Jemima and Ann

At home   Oct 29th 1857

Dear Mother and Mima

We are rather on the complaining order today, but able to be up a little. grandpa has been quite unwell for some time, and grandma is almost sick from sympathy.

If the idea of sending Elizabeths likeness and those paterns by Mrs. W. had not occured to me before receiveing your letter it would not have profited either of us much as she had been at home two weeks before your letter reached me. I shall expect to learn how you are pleased with them in your next. I was glad to learn that you did not grieve long after our departure. I am surprised at Sophia and George, some would have been pleased at such an occurrance, I had no idea that the fatal day was so near at hand when I spoke to you aboute it.

Oct. 30

Yes Mima we felt the earthquake, the quivering of my bed must have waked me. I heard the window ratling but felt no fear. It waked them over at Mrs. Poseys and Sarah was so frightened that she could not sleep after it. Mr. Walters family knew nothing of it. Mrs. Milbourn has been oute since I returned home and passed a night with us, she sent her love to mother. Sarah Brown and Lina have reached home again we expect her oute tomorrow with Mary McElfresh.

There seems to be no danger of our being deserted, last Wednesday Mr and Mrs. McCoy came out and dined with us and the evening they with Mr James and Lady, Mr. Sinnock[67] and his Bride, and Will Haines took tea. Mr. Sinnock was married on the 15th inst, to a lady who resided near his fathers. We were a little surprised to hear it, as we had no intimation of it when he left us. They started for his station yesterday.

Even Aunt Milley gave us a call yesterday, we tried to keep her with us hoping some one would come for her but she thought she could not stay as she was in a hurry. so I walked back to the poor house[68] with her, she was bare headed and had nothing on her feet, poor aunt Milley!

Since I came home grandma has made a visit to Beardstown, they left home on Saturday the 17 and returned on Wednesday the 21. I keept house through the day and the neighbour girls came and staid with me at night. There has been quite a social revival among the young folks here, they had had three parties when I returned home and have had three since. I attended two and was invited to the other but would not go. I expect there will be more soon.

I have not heard from Iowa yet but think it time they were writing. We went to hear uncle Peter last Sunday of course his sermon was after the Cartwright style, and in the evening we went to Salem to hear our young preacher Mr. Harmantroute, how do you like the name? and if I am any judge I will say the evening sermon was the better of the two.

I finished the Reformation two weeks since, is not that wonderful?

Mima I am surprised at our lack of ready wit in conversation. I think our wit might be compared as a certain writer likens the wit of the Germans, to an "old rusty gun that never goes off till after the game is gone"[69]

I was thinking somtime ago why did you not ask Mr. Plain what the Almighty did with Saten before the Christian Era if he had no hell to stay in? now I think we might have argued on this wise, Saten and his angels fell from heaven before or aboute the time that man was created for so the Bible teaches and if there had been no devil how could Eve have been tempted to sin, read in 25 chapter and 41 verse of Matthew we read: Depart from me, ye cursed, into everlasting fire, prepared for the devil and his angels.

From this I conclude that hell was not made expressly for sinners, but was "prepared" for the devil and his angels" and the men that serve him in this life will of course go to him in the next, if this reasoning be correct, why was there not as much need of a hell before the Christian Era as since.

This is my humble opinion of the matter roughly expressed so you can make any disposition of it you see proper.

Have you noticed that there is to be war in Utah?[70] I saw a notice of it today for the first time. This is a very long letter you see, now I shall expect a long one in return. You will feel under <u>neverending</u> obligation to the Major [Burke] for his <u>unbounded</u> kindness, surely. My best love to all and mother beside. Write <u>soon</u> do you hear. . . .

Yours Heppa

From: Hephzibah
Envelope address: Miss Jemima Dumville, Carlinville, Illinois

Nov 25th 1857

Dear Mima,

I heartily agree with your sentiment, that early rising is delightful, and to be smart quite as much so, though both are strangers here, for my own part I don't feel smart and fear I never shall but I wish I was though.

If you are not moved yet, well, if you are as long moving after you begin as you have been talking aboute it I shall feel sorrey for you indeed. As it is, I try to console my self by thinking that you will get moved sometime and I suppose you do the same.[71]

I rejoyce at Mr. Van Meeters and trust that it will be the means of relieving many poor sufferers, that there will be an abundance of persons needing assistance in the large cities is painfully certain, many more in consequence of the hard times,[72] so many having been thrown oute of employment, and always enough even when times are good. I have heard that thirty thousand persons have been turned off because of the factorys and other establishments having to be closed for want of means to go on, the greater part of the thirty thousand being young girls. A Boston merchant in Jacksonville some weeks since showed a letter to Mr. Lurton which he received from his wife in which she stated that girls were applying constantly for employment offering to work for anything even their board, and not able to get that. O how much suffering in this world who can conscience, we sometimes think that we have very hard times, and we do to what some have, but we have not the faintest idea of the privations with [which] others endure.

Did it not make your heart ache to read the last "London Correspondents" really that in connection with other notices of the Indian outrages[73] makes me heartsick, then on the other hand there is Mormons with their hateful notions enough to make Saten himself ashamed. I presume you have seen notices of the United States troops having started for Utah and of Brigham Young and Co. being determined to resist, all attempts that may be made against them, they surely have a good chance to defend themselves surrounded by mountains as they are, to think that hundreds of brave hearts may perish in the mountains and other places in consequence of their abominations is horrible. But let us turn from these dark objects and see if we cannot find some sunshiny spot in which to bask awhile.

Our town will present quite a changed appearance when you come again if you should happen to come at night as they are having all the principle streets and all the large buildings lit with gas.[74] Can't you make araingments to come to see us Christmas or New Years. Try. Will you?

Tomorrow is Thanksgiving Day. You will have holliday.[75] Won't that be a treat. I hope you may have a nice time if I can't. We will have to begin hog killing next week and how I dread it. We have 14 to kill as we can't sell any of them times being so hard.

Thursday, 26th

What a delightful morning we had, the first thing of note that I did was to saw a wheelbarrow load of wood, grandpa being tired down and Willie not at home. We have a baked turkey and minced pies for dinner,[76] and after we have eaten I shall go to washing we have no one to help us yet but there is a man here now that will stay with us I expect and go to school, he came about noone to day.[77]

. . .

I am sure you all would feel obliged for the miniature if you knew what an efort it cost me to part with it. I thought it was good though I did not tell you so before. Sister thought hers was not as good as the other, but I am sure it is better.

How eloquent you become in writing to your old <u>lovers</u>! What an <u>inspiring</u> theam it must be! Do write an essay on the subject and send to me won't you? I am in ernest, you may sure. Who would have thought that Curiosity would be the last one married of those that joined the conference at the same time that he did. He tries to do for others what he does not do for himself. Get a helpmeet.

Mrs. Milbourn is sick at present and Mr. James' family have the Scarlet fever. They have burried one childe.

You surely did not get my last letter before you wrote your last. You did not notice the first item in my letter if you had. I thought I was writing quite a letter, and did not know but what you would be surprised at the clearness of my Theology.[78] . . . My best love to all. Write soon. It is very late now so good night. Heppa

From: Hephzibah
Envelope address: Miss Mima Dumville, Carlinville Illinois

Jacksonville, December 15th 1857

Dear Mima,

I declare if you do not stop dating your letters so strangely I shall begin to think you are getting absent minded, perhaps, in consequence of an old beau, and I shall not know but as he sails away on the smooth and pleasureable sea of matrimony, that your heart may glide after. I hope it may not get drownded!

Dear Mima the year is now almost gone and the time to renew your subscription for the Repository is at hand, if the hard times prevent your coming to see me <u>dont</u> let it keep you from sending for the Ladies Repository. Margret Walter will send for it and if she can I know you are able to do it. Dont be behind the times aboute it. if you dont get the value of your money in every number you will in the volume surely, and then the money goes to a good purpose beside, I hardly expect it is necessary for me to say so much, but I thought for fear you would give it up I would say all I could to prevent it, in time.

I am happy to hear that your are moved at last, I think with you that extravagance has been the cause of much suffering, for my own part I have never thought so much aboute economy in my whole life as I have this year, so it seames to me, and yet my expenses will not be much short of sixty dollars, the most I have ever spent in one year. It shall not be so much next year I think.

The news which I have heard from the Mormons is not very cheering and the prospects of Kansas are darkening again. I fear much blood will be shed before pease will be restored to North America.

I answered the letter which I received from Iowa, a short time ago.

I have no news to tell you I believe. Matters in this region keep on the even tenor of their way.

I have taken a notion to read Uncle Peters Autobiography.[79] Grandpa has read it and likes it very well. it has not the polish of Finleys Autobiography. We could not expect a polished production from an unpolished source. Nevertheless I like it very well so far it is <u>rather</u> amusing as well as instructive, to my notion the most innocent and yet amusing anacdotes that I have read are those of the gentelman's trying to bring him into contempt in company, on account of this ignorance, by addressing him in Greek and uncle Peters replying in Dutch, an Irish man could not have been more ready,[80] and his useing up the Halcyon brother so compleatly is the other.[81]

I have also begun to read Paradise Lost, I did not like it much at first, but persevered untill I did like it, now I think it is equal to what it has been represented to be as far as I am able to judge.

Miss. J. Palmer is going home [to Carlinville] soone. I called to see her last Saturday and should have had a nice "tete a tete" had it not been for the girls passing in so much, and you know I am to <u>timid</u> to talk in much company.

Dear Sister you write as though your heart is filled with bitterness towards grandma, dont think so heard [hard] of her, I hope matters will not terminate as badly as you anticipate.

. . . I hope you will be promt in answering my letters and I will do the same. Your devoted Sister Heppa

I am glad you are getting along so well with your school, I should be glad to hear you sing. Perhaps I will stop in some evening when you are not looking for me. Who knows.

I fear you will find this letter rather dull entertainment, but it is as good as I can give this time.

The fire company had a supper last night, I have not heard how it came off.

I don't know how I shall spend Christmass, I have no arangements made for the ocasion, I suppose I can do as I usually do, stay at home, and mind my own buisness.

Let me hear from you soon Mima. . . .

Heppa

5. 1858–1860

The Lincoln-Douglas Elections

In 1858 Lincoln sought the Senate seat held by Stephen Douglas. Both were local heroes—Lincoln practiced law in Springfield and had previously represented the district in Congress, and Douglas had been the county prosecutor in Jacksonville. Although U.S. Senators were then elected by the state legislatures, Lincoln and Douglas campaigned throughout Illinois to generate public support for their candidacies, and the two met in several locations for a famous series of debates. The debates gave Lincoln national prominence, but a majority of the Illinois legislators chose to return Douglas to the Senate. In a letter to Jemima dated November 10, 1858, Hephzibah comments on the election of Douglas, ". . . and to think too that he should be elected after all, is not that a shame!"[1]

In 1860, Lincoln and Douglas squared off again, this time as candidates for the presidency, but there were two other presidential candidates as well. After the Democrats nominated Douglas, Southern Democrats held another convention and selected the sitting vice president, John Breckenridge, a Kentuckian, as their presidential candidate, and a coalition of conservative Whigs and Know-Nothings, known as the Constitutional Union party, ran John Bell of Tennessee for president. Lincoln was elected with less than 40 percent of the popular vote. Douglas had the second-largest share, but he ran fourth in the Electoral College—there were 180 votes for Lincoln, 72 for Breckenridge, 39 for Bell, and only 12 for Douglas. Lincoln and Douglas divided the vote in the North, but Douglas carried only Missouri.

In Illinois, Lincoln received 51 percent of the vote, Douglas 47 percent, Breckenridge 0.7 percent, and Bell 1.4 percent. As in 1856, regional differences were pronounced, with Lincoln receiving his strongest support in the northern third of the state, Douglas in the southern third, and a closely divided vote in the middle. Douglas carried Morgan, where he had practiced law, by 107 votes (2,419 to 2,313) and carried Lincoln's home county, Sangamon, by 42 votes (3,598 to 3,556). In Macoupin County, Douglas had 52 percent of the vote.

The correspondence of this period closes with an important letter written by Hephzibah in late October 1860, a few weeks before the presidential election. The letter begins by deploring the fact that it was necessary for Ann to travel on the train to Springfield with a group of Douglas partisans. Hephzibah, however, had arranged for a male member of the church, also traveling to Springfield, "to take charge of Mother." In the 1850s women seldom traveled alone, especially on public conveyances.

Ann and Jemima had recently visited Hephzibah in Jacksonville to attend the county fair and the Methodist conference—the conference at which Ann made her remarkable speech to the assembly, with which this book began. Despite the letters' attention to events at the conference, however, including a dinner party of church leaders at which Ann and Hephzibah were present, there is no reference to Ann's speech. This seems odd. Surely it was a topic of conversation. Perhaps the speech had already been so thoroughly discussed within the family that no further comment was necessary. The letter does mention other conflict within the church. At the dinner, there was an argument between two Jacksonville preachers concerning the allocation of local Methodists to their two congregations. According to Hephzibah, one preacher wanted "to pick his men and take the most influential talented and rich among them for his end of the town, you know that is the Aristocratic part of the city." Hephzibah was, thus, attuned to the socioeconomic hierarchy in the community and its consequences within the church. The two preachers "had some words about it" until one of them "picked up his hat and left." Hephzibah noted that the preacher who ministered to the more elite congregation was permitted to "have his own way." Hephzibah's letters of this period, thus, devote increasing attention to politics and demonstrate greater sophistication about political alignments. Some of this political awareness may well have been generated by local debates concerning slavery. At the college's graduation exercises in 1854, a graduating senior had inserted in her speech a few sentences advocating abolition. This caused a furor, resulting in heated argument both within the college and in the community.[2] Hephzibah surely knew about the controversy.

The education of women, although advocated by some of the religious leaders who endorsed domesticity, such as Catherine Beecher,[3] furthered the greater involvement of women in public issues. Political historian Paula Baker has observed that "abolitionism taught women how to turn women's rights into a political movement."[4] But women's roles were being shaped by contradictory norms—religiosity was in competition with the emphasis on fashion and the growth of consumer markets, the desire for social and material advancement was at odds with the quiet enjoyment of life, and the boosterism that sought to attract settlers and promote the cultivation of open lands threatened the established hierarchy.[5] Women had an especially difficult time balancing the competing values. They often had to choose among them without appearing to do so.

Politics was, of course, not the sole focus of Hephzibah's interests during these years. The letters began to discuss romance when Jemima and Hephzibah were in their mid- to late twenties. They were then beyond the age at which most women married, and the letters had already reported the weddings of several of their friends. On November 10, 1858, Hephzibah wrote "who knows but one or other of us may be the President's lady before we die," but the same letter says that she had decided not "to bestow one serious thought on Mr. H." because "prospects are not very flattering at present." The letters are circumspect. They include few details about their relationships, relying instead on veiled references: "the gentleman who wished me to correspond with him" (November 10, 1858); "an old beau" (December 15, 1857); "my last year's correspondent—Now so no longer" (November 2, 1859); "my Virginia friend" and "when I see you I will tell you all" (January 8, 185[9]). There were some things that one did not put in a letter. It simply was not done. It is, therefore, necessary to read between the lines. We infer, for example, that Jemima had a romantic interest in a young preacher consistently referred to as "Brother Curiosity." In a letter dated November 13, 1856, Hephzibah says that he had inquired about Jemima, and she then comments: "A person would have had to be previously initiated to have suspected that there was anything behind the curtain." This letter was written after the marriage of Curiosity, but he seems to have had some prior relationship with Jemima. A December 1857 letter refers to an old beau who "sails away on the smooth and pleasurable sea of matrimony," but the next year Hephzibah wrote to Jemima, regarding Brother Curiosity: "I am as unfavorably disposed towards him as yourself. I do think he is a man of very little principal to say the least." But if 1857 closed with hard feelings, 1858 began with fresh news of parties and marriages. Mr. Walter was reported to have become "a popular ladies man."

From: Hephzibah
To: Jemima

Jacksonville Jan. 7th 1858

Why sister, what is the reason you have not written to me before this time? . . .

I need scarsely tell you that I was at the Phi Nu paper reading and thought it very good, as I have no doubt that you have heard an extended detail of the whole matter from Julia P[almer]. . . .

I must tell you however, for fear it has slipped her memory that the marriage of Miss Jenny Duston and Mr I dont know who. Miss Jenny Haryz and Mr. J. Shaw and Mr. Punctuality and so forth, was announced.

. . . As I see no prospect of hearing how you spent Christmas and New Year days, I will tell you how I past part of the time. On Christmass day Mr and Mrs Dellzell dined with us and in the evening I went to a *small* party and you will think it was little sure enough when I tell you who all was there. Well the three Miss Poesy's [Posey], Miss J. Walter and my self constituted the ladies of our party and Messers O Pelt, W. Hains, J. Kerr, J. Warner and M. Walter the jentelmen, but what we lacked in numbers we made up in fun.

New Years day we all dined at Mr. Dellzell's and spent the day pleasantly. I must not forget to tell you that I had the <u>exquisit</u> pleasure of seeing our <u>dear</u> old friend Bailey again, last Saturday. . . . He passed the night with us and yet I was impolite enough to go to church with a parcel of young folks, and leave him with the old folks at home.

There has been a protracted meeting going on at the West charge - for aboute a month, but Saturday night is the only time that I have been there. The meeting must have been good, or they surely would not have protracted it so long. Still I canot tell you anything aboute their success as I have not heard much aboute it.

I have not heard from Iowa since I wrote you last but I intend to write to them again soon, I thought of writing to them New Years night and was only prevented from doing so by the thought that by wa[i]ting untill l should get a letter from you I might make <u>my</u> letter more interesting.

I went to another [?] party the other night at Mr Reeve's. There was between forty and fifty present, but although there was so many I did not enjoy my self, but I was not alone in that respect. I intend it shall be the last one I go to for a few nights at least, Mr. M. Walter is quite a leader in getting up our parties. I assure you he is getting to be quite a <u>popular</u> ladies man. Listen sis and I will give you an item of news, but now dont breath it for I only surmise, you need not be astonished to hear of him and Sarah Posey getting married. It would be taxing your imagination considerably to conceive how very friendly the two familys are at present. How we all, the young folks I mean, shall miss Mr. W's family when they move away in the spring. We will then have to say good bye, to parties, and pleasure trips as well. Perhaps we will be none the wors for it.

Jan 12th

I have finished uncle Peters book, and like it very well. When reading Rifle Ax and Saddle bags [by William Milburn], one felt, at least I did, that the author was writing on a subject of which he was totally ignorant. In fact, how could a man that had been born in an eastern city, and raised in our modern Athen's,[6] know anything aboute back woods life it was entirely oute of the question. But when you read father Cartwright life it is another thing altogether. One feels that he knows by his own something of the trials and hardship of frontier life experience. Yes indeed he can tell of nights passed <u>pleasantly</u> on a straw bed made of the bark of trees p[l]aced on funchion[7] bedcords, and covered with the scin of the wild beasts whos flesh served them for food which was eaten off funchion tables and scharpened sticks and pocket knives were used for want of more suitable implements. Also of traveling through unbroken forests and trackless prairies s[w]im[m]ing swolen streams and rivers. And performing labor that would frighten the timid delicate man of our time to think of[8] . . . and [Cartwright should] finaly receive a crown of unfaiding glory, in return for his sufferings here.

I see in our last paper that civil war has really broken oute in Kansas, between the pro slavery and free state men. The United States Marchal with 80 troupes orderd the free state men to surrender and they returned as answer a voley of musket ball. I wish them all possible success. I see by the same paper that the afairs in India are still very distressing. They have determined in England to double the number of Missionaries to India which number eleven now but at a meeting at Leeds several speakers proposed to send 20 more which was received with aplaus by the people present and a callection was lifted amounting to 10,750 dolars was not that doing things up aboute the right way?[9] I know it will pleas mother to hear it. Give my love to all my friends. I shall expect an answer to this soon. Good night to all

I wish you a happy new year. Heppa

From: John Williams
To: Jemima

Jan 17, /58

Deare Sister we received yours a fiew days ago altho unlooked for. We was glad to heare from you. Oure health is only moderate. Coles is very common & severe here. Martha has sick the past week. . . . The winter has been very moderate & open with rain often the coldest wether we had in Novem. Times is distressing harde. Money is not to be had for nothing. I have not colected any that is due me so my debts is unpaide. I have been looking for the officer to be employed to force colection but so fare they have gave me lenity. I have turned my way in vaine for means to pay my tax which is $27.85 cts. Wheat is

40 to 50 cts in goods, corne 20 to 30 cts, pork 3.00 to 3.50. Pork was taken on last years account. Stock is very harde sale at low prices. If times kepes as they are mutch longar it looks like evry thing will go by the boarde.

We & the quakers have concluded to builde a schoolhouse in 1 1/4 miles of us.[10]

Theire is nothing special transpired since we came home corne is badly frostbiten. Seed corne will be an object in the spring. George[11] says he will abdicate his property . . . for youre special benifit as you may neede them . . . soon if not sooner as his hole time is taken up with the pet goose . . . Tell J. McLure if he wants to keep cleare of harder times than he ever saw stay away from Iowa.

J. W. Williams

Dear Sister and Mother I wd like to Se you once more. George sends a kiss Elizabeth Williams

Deare Mother as theire is a little space I will rite a fiew lines to you but the barinness of the times theire is nothing left to rite so we will have to look else where for a subject. The harde times in England will cause distress among the poore. We often think of Mary & hur children but what can we do destitute & peniless oure selvs, altho through the blessing of the great giver we have bread enough & to spare. I have 200 bushels of wheat but no market or demand & six hogs yet in the pen. One I shall give to oure minister.

. . .

J. W. Williams

From: Hephzibah
To: Jemima

At Home   February 20th 1858

Dear Mother and Sister

Was not my letter as satisfactory as you desired? Well perhaps it was not as much so as it ought to have been, but the fact is I am always afraid to express my feelings for fear I shall say more than I really feel, and rather than say more than i feel, I would not say as much. Still I cannot help thinking that I said volums, in my last, not in size to be sure but in meaning. But if you are not satisfied I will try to give the perticulars as well as I can.

The meeting begun at Salem on the 25 of January I think. When I first heard of it I had little or no hope attending it and not much desire, however the third night of the meeting being Wednesday night I went Mayberry having told me they were going our way as the lane by their house was very bad traveling, and from that to the end of the meeting I missed only three nights, besides going sometimes in the day (the meeting lasted three weeks). But to return, the two first nights that I was there after the sermon the members were called round the alter, with a view to get <u>them stired up</u>. On Friday night an invitation was given for seekers of religion to come forward for the prayers of the church but no one presented themselves. I had as I thought determined never to go to the alter again not that I was either afraid or ashamed, but becaus I thought it was not the place for me to be blest, that there was to[o] much confusion and so on. Well as no one went forward Mr Harmantroute requested if any one present desired religion to rise. I had no objection . . . so I rose. The next night Mag Walters was there and when the invitation was given again Mrs Richardson urged me to go but I said no I don't think it is worth while. While she was speaking Mag turned to Julia and me and said "Hep, Julia let's go let's all go," and I said, well, and we started, I did not get to Salem the next day but went to town to preaching at eleven and to general class in the afternoon. The next night I went to Salem again but did not obtain any peace of mind, the next night Tuesday when meeting was over I told Mag that I was almost happy she replied "I am glad of it but I feel awful" I felt that I ought to have acknowledged that the Lord had blessed me, but I did not. I determined that if the Lord would bless me the next night I would confess it, and I did, and I thank the Lord that I did. Now to say that I felt the raptures that you Mima sometimes enjoy, I cant do it, for I did not feel like shouting, but I felt all condemnation removed, and a feeling of peace in stead. And I was enabled to say in the sincerity of my heart "I <u>do</u> believe. I <u>will</u> believe that Jesus <u>died for me</u>."

I can say truly I never enjoyed a meeting so much in my life the three past weeks have been the happiest of my life I do think. During the meeting Maggie, Julia, and Mayberry professed religion and others amounting in all to twenty I believe—

You wil be surprised when I tell you that one or two of Mrs Posey's girls went with us almost every evening during the meeting, their mother seemed more than willing for them to go and you will perhaps be still more surprised when you learn that Sarah went forward to the alter several nights, I regret exceedingly that she did not obtain the blessing, she became discouraged and as she said "all that went at the time I started have been blessed and I am left, and I cant go.

Now dear mother and sister you must not expect to see a real saint when you see me again for I feel that I am not one, but I hope through the all prevailing merits of Christ to be one by and bye. I feel assured that I have an interst in your prayers, let me now ask you to pray for all that have professed religion at Salem during our meeting. You may not know them yourselves but the Lord knows them, and I do hope that when He comes to take the faithful to Himself we may be among that number. The meeting still continues at the East charg.[12] Aboute a hundred have joined the church - some of the very hardest cases in town have been converted. The number at the West charge that have professed is 170 and several have professed the blessing of sanctification.

The meeting stopped a short time since. . . . Grandma sends her love to you and says "I still try to hope, but it is like hoping against hope, while others are rejoyceing to see their children and friend turning to Christ, mine seem to be as h[e]ard hearted as ever I still desire an intrest in your prayrs"

I have not yet written to Iowa since receiving their last, but intend doing so soon. I have done little els lately beside go to church, and was very sorry when the time came to stop going. I will now have to be "diligent in business" and I desire to be "fervent in spirit, serving the Lord." Give my best love to all my friends and write soon. Have you bought a Piano? You need not look for us at your house this season as Surprise parties are not the order of the night any longer but rather prayer meeting, I would like to think [it] will now be the exercise that will attract our attention. Yours Heppy

From: Hephzibah
To: Jemima

June 22nd 1858

Dear Mima,

I had not thought when I received your last well filled sheet, that it would be so long before I should attempt an answer . . . I have been kept busy all the time this Spring and Summer so far and yet I can scarely see anything that I have done.

We are all able to get aboute, though grandpa is quite in the order of mederation and grandma has been complaing of her right hand a day or too so she can hardly [?] I hope [?] that it will not [?] to[o] seriously.

I received a letter from iowa in the early part of this month. Brother gives rather a dreary account of his prospects for a crop, his letter was dated May 30th . . . To the 20th they had had frost and rain in succession and a great deal of the latter sinc that time. He added that some had to break up their ground waiting knee deep in mud, and that he almost mired trying to finish his. They were all well except Maggie and Mattie, they had had the chills for two weeks.

He concluded his letter by . . . [requesting] me to get a copy of the school law for this State and forward to him he would be obliged to me, I don't know anything about school law or any other law, but thought that as you are a school "Marm" perhaps you could accomodate him. Do if you can.

I hope you had a nice time in Springfield, you must tell me aboute it when you write. It is well enough that I concluded not to go . . . on account of the rain that fell the night before. The Mauvaise [Creek][13] was higher than it had been for years before.

The commencement of the female academy came off on the 10th and that of the Illinois college on the 17th. I heard that the exercises were very interesting but had not the pleasure of being there myself. The commencement of our college takes place next week. I think I am not sure that I should be able to go though I intend to try. I in[t]imated to you that Miss Martha Spaulding[14] was married so it was reported that she was to have been on a certain night, but the thing did not take place, though I think it will before long.

Mr. Delzell's two daughters have come to see him from Keokuk Iowa—they have been here aboute two weeks. I think them very pleasant ladies, we have spent a little time together. I presume they will start home in a few days.

I succeeded in disposing of your saddle. Mr. Rapp sent me word that he had sold it, and that I could come and get the money. when they asked me what price they should put upon it I proposed ten dollars, but the young man said he thought it was worth [more?] that he would be willing to ask if it were his, but he would get it if he could. I then said that I did not want more than it was worth. but I did want that it was worth, and if he thought he could get nine for it to ask that much for it. he said he would and did so. But when I went to get the money Mr Rapp said he would have to charge me a dollar for his trouble so you onely get eight for it after all. I thought he need not ask so much but did not tell him so.

I would send the money to you in this letter were it not that I have a thought of writing to you soon, that is if you or mother do not intend coming to see me this summer and it will be a safer plan to take it myself than it will be to send it by mail.

I can't tell you exactly when you may look for me. I don't want to come before your school is oute, though I think that it will be soon after, which will be aboute the last of July, I suppose. I think I can leave home then more conveniently than at any other time, as we have had two young men living with us all the season and then or aboute that time they will be oute harvesting so that there will be no one at home but grandpa and me.

. . .

This evening is prayr meeting evening at Salem. How I should like to go, but I fear that I shall not have the chance. I have not been to pray meeting for three months I think. However I will try to be resigned to my lot and believe that everying will work for my good if I only trust in the Lord and do my duty which I very often find rather hard to do and I fear I don't always do it. My love to all my friends, my time is short, so I must close. Pray for me still.

I remain your devoted sister Heppy

From: Hephzibah
To: Ann and Jemima

Jacksonville Sep 11 1858

My Dear Mother and Sister

At last I am nearly home. I reached Springfield with very little difficulty I suppose it was aboute one oclock. I remained at the American House trying to pass the time away as best I could, but feeling very lonely as there was not one person there that I had ever seen befor, untill after five in the evening, I then went to the Depot in company with two ladies and gentelmen, who were returning from St Louis from attending the fair, they lived in *Virginia*, so I thought I could have a little company down to Jacksonville. I entered in to conversation with the oldest of the ladies and found that she knew a few persons whith whom I had a slight acquaintance.

When we arrived at the Depot we found that we had to wait two hours or mor in consequence of a collission that took place on that road that day. I cant tell you all aboute it, but as near as I can tell it was a freight train and wood train that came in contact a few miles from Springfield, smashing up I dont know how many cars and seriously injuring three men one poor fellow had both his legs taken off and another one had his broken, or one of them broken and the other cut off, I am not sure which, bad enough though you may be sure.

While I was sitting with the lady afore named I thought I heard a voice that sounded familiar so I went in quest of its possesser, I found him it was Mr. Becraft, he seemed surprised to see me, told me he was not going my way, but said he would try to find some one that was, he called Tom McElfresh to him. Mr. Mc lives in Springfield and requested him to see me safe on the cars, he said that he would do so with pleasure. Soon after Mr Blodget came along and said he was going to Jacksonville and I was then placed in his care, so then there was three gentlemen to help me off safely. As soon as I got on the cars whom should I see but Mr. Greenberry McElfresh he recognized me at once I seated self befor him, and Mr. Blodget beside me, when we reached the Junction Mr. B got off to attend to his trunk and while he was gone Mr. James our preacher step[p]ed on the cars and seeing me took posession of me at once, I told Mr. Blodget that Mr. James was going my way and I would not trouble him when we reached our destination to see me home. I enjoyed myself very well listning to those around me talking politics and as soon as I steped foot on the platform Mr. Lurton took me by the arm, and he and Mr. James gallanted me to Mr. Lurtons, so you see I was well provided for in the way of beaux. I feel thankful that I am this near home with oute any accident befaling me. I found the folks all well, as usual. Grandpa has not come for me yet but I am looking for him every moment it is now about nine I think.

I know you will want to hear how I got along so I take this early opportunity to write to you. I should not be surprised if we have company this evening. Mary and Sarah and Lou was talking of coming oute to stay all night. Mr. Lurton said, I saw Sarah a little while ago and she thought they would not come as Greenberry was down but I think very likely they will and he with them.

As I expected a letter was waiting for me when I aome [come?] here last night, my friend has been sick again. I told Mr. L[urton] what mother said I must tell him as near as I could remember, he had not a word to say. My love to all. Write soon, Yours sincerely Eppie,

Grandpa is coming and I will run to meet him goodbye.

You did not know Mima that when you spoke of my looking pale that I was so sick that I could hardly conceal it. I tried very hard not to appear well and this morn feel as well as usual, I was really afraid that I should be sick on the way but I got along.

From: Hephzibah
Envelope address: Miss Jemima Dumville, Carlinville, Illinois

Sunny Dell   Nov 10th 1858

Darling Mima

I had been premeditating action in bring a cogent reprimand but as you ask me so humbly not to scold I will give you one more chance to redeem your caracter for punctuality, and I hope you will make good use of the privilege, especially as I am setting so good an example. I suppose you have not yet written to England, now—Mime, don't neglect that whatever you do. I dare say you do feel very little like writing after being in school all day but you must rally your energies and it will not hurt you but prove beneficial to you and pleasing to them. I think you have as much time to write as I have, and to stimulate you, I will tell you how much I have written since I came home, besides what I have sent you, I wrote one long letter to Grace Gathwell that used to be which filled two sheets that as I wrote on four sides of one sheet and on three of another, I am not disposed to brag, but, I wish to tell you that it was done up in my best style, also five to my Verginia correspondent and I have kept a copy of the whole so when you come to see me I can treat you to the pleasure of them if you wish.

How I managed to write so much, I can hardly say, true we have not done very much els but dry some apples, besides the house work. Mima I have not yet heard from iowa and feel quite uneasy about it. I have a half mind to write to Sarah Williams [Kimmbo?] I dont know whether this is the right way to spell the name or not in Winchester to know if she has heard from them lately, unless you will undertake to do it in my place, it would suit me very well if you would and I think you could do the matter much nicer than I would be able to do it.

You did not mistake my meaning in reference to Bro Curiosity and I am as unfavorably disposed towards him as yourself. i do think he is a man of a very little principal to say the least, but I presume he can well dispence with our good will or opinion since he has obtained the hand and purse of Miss [?]. I dont know but Mr. Belt is a gentleman by the look of him, after all, I suppose. Jo starts to Maryland this week. Yes sis I think it would be folly in the superlative degree to bestow one serious thought on Mr. H. not that I think him so superior to the rest of mankind, but simply because prospects are not very flattering at present. I can, however, give him up with out a sigh, for he did not make a very deep impression on my heart as you so thought, we do not know what will befall us, who knows but one or the other of us may be the President's lady before we die. So you think [Beck?] would sympathise with you? . . . I'd make her more anxious still or try for it. I think I would test the strength of her attraction for once ah yes I would put on my best looks and my best <u>dress</u> too, and then would not I be irresistible. I admit Beck has more <u>heart</u> and <u>brain</u> than I can boast, but if I was there she would have to sharpen her wits, considerably or she would be apt to lose some of her laurels.

I must not forget to tell you that my friend Will was here last Friday three weeks ago and brought with him the gentleman who wished me to correspond with him. He was quite social but did not mention that subject and I did not so there the matter rests. You had better believe I was astonished to see them for I had not the least intimation of their coming till I opened the door they stood before me. No sister you need not write to grandma for it was not Sarah that told her. I was one day speaking about the matter and she said that she was not aware that Sarah and you had ever spoken aboute it. Theres another to whom she has told the matter" said grandma. I could not get her to hint who her informant could be, but I rather guess that it came from the neighborhood of Linnville through the medium of Bro Curiosity.

Our folks have never found out that we was [?] when we went to hear Douglas, though I told them I went to hear him, and to think too that he should be elected after all is not that a shame!

. . . My love to all, let me hear from you soon. I have been to see Mrs. Moore, she has had a child but was well yesterday the little boy said. Yours in love Eppie

From: Hephzibah
Envelope address: Miss Mima Dumville, Carlinville Illinois

Sunny Dell   Jan 8th [1859]

Dear Sister

. . .

You wish to know what I have done with my Virginia[15] friend. Well we have been corresponding quite as often as grandma thinks prudent for a young gentleman and lady to do unless they had very serious intentions, and she is sure that I should be stooping very much to take him as a partner for life. She has opposed me all the time, and grandpa now has joined his opposition to hers, and gives it as his opinion that I shall "throw myself away entirely if I ever take him." I received a letter from him a week ago today but have not yet answered it. and I dont think I shall. Though it will cause me an effort to give it up still i think it best to do so, not because my friend are opposed to it, but I think he does not do just as he ought. I mean he does not write to pleas me, though I could not tell you just what it is that I dont like. I have not told any one that I

am going to quit writing and dont expect to but your self, and when I see you I wll tell you all. My love to all pray for me. Write soon and believe me as ever
   Your devoted Eppie B. Dumville

   P.S. I thought I was done but it seems not. Now Mima I dont want you to think that anything very serious passed between Will and my self. but our folks seemed to think that matters began to wear a very grave aspect when, I would write say on Monday and get an answer by the next Thursday or Friday, which I often did, and they wished to give me timely warning. They were the more suspicious because they remained in blissful ignorance of the contents of our letters, I say blissful because I am sure if they knew some of the remarks that have passed it would not add much to their enjoyments.
   I must tell you a joke Mr. Lurton had on me Monday. Sarah spent the day there and Mr. L. was telling her she ought to buy a lot of him and turning to me remarke and "you ought to have one two, but you would rather have a man," to which I replyed I would rather have both, whereupon he was so amused that he exclaimed "give us your hand. It is the first time that I ever got you to tell the truth on this subject." Do Mima write to me often.
   Yours truly Eppie

From: Hephzibah
To: Ann and Jemima

Sunny Dell   July 4th 1859

Dear Mother and Sister
   I have been to town today to witness the celebration of the return of the day in which the American colonies "were born into the family of Nations." And a grand and imposing sight it was. Aboute eleven o clock the procession passed in front of Mr. Lurton's,[16] first came three or four men drawing the canon next to that the old sections that remain who had fought in the war of twelve [War of 1812], after them the standard bearer then the band of music, after which the first fire company, dressed in their red flanel shirts and embroidered collars drawing their engine turned off and picture of Washington in front and three little boys dressed like them standing on it. After them followed the next fire company dressed like the first only they wore glazed caps with the name of the company on the front.
   Then came a band of Odd Fellows some of them drawing a wagon or something of the kind in which was a lady dressed all in black surrounded by a group of children. The conveyance was covered with pink cambric and on the side the words were printed in large letters "The Orphans of Lodge No 4" after which cam another band of Odd Fellows, and then a chariot with a parosol like top decorated with sedar and round the pillars that supported the top sedar also was

entwined and in it with one hand on a water [?] or pitcher stood a young girl, dressed in a white scirt [skirt] and red waist with a pink sash tied round the top of her head, her curls just reaching to her chin. This was designed to represent Rebecca at the well giving to the stranger a drink of cold water, little thinking as you know that he came seeking a wife for his master. Well another band of Odd Fellows followed this chariot, and last of all came another chariot, with a purple velvet top trimed with fringe and long black velvet curtains sweeping almost to the ground, in front of which stood three young men with masks on, this I am told is the Temple of Honor. Upon the whole it was a handsome sight, but I fear my attempt to tell you aboute it will fail to convey anything like an idea of it to you. I wish you could have seen it. As soon as the prossesion passed, Mr. Lurton and my self hop[p]ed in the carriage and rode oute to the Fair ground to hear a celebrated orator deliver an adress to the Odd Fellows with additional remarks in honor of the day and the Patriots of seventy six [1776]. The exercise opened by the band playing, next a hymn was sung then prayer then the Declarations of Indipendance was read by Mr. Bristow, music by the band and then came the crowning of the whole, A splendid speach by a splendid orator Mr Colfax[17], a member of the House of Representatives, and a strong Republican.

. . .

I must close. Write soon my love to all. Willie want me to say fifty things to you for him but I have not time now. Good bye sis,

Eppie

From: Ann, Carlinville
To: Jemima and Hephzibah

Augst 31st [year unknown]

My Dear Daughters

I received your letter to day, and was sorry to her Jemima was sick, but I hope she will soon be well. . . . I have such good meetings, particularly the last two class meetings; we are all well, there is not much sickness in town.

The Macoupin Co. school convention meets here next week; they are making quite a preparation. Old Mr. Williams was to see me, and said he should like for you to be here if you could. I promised to take two young ladies to keep during the session.

Mary has been round, but she has not collected the first cent, they say they will pay just as soon as they can get it.

Our preacher is gone to camp meeting at Chatham [a town near Springfield]. he has been gone a week. He will return before Sunday

I begin to feel like I want to see you, but if you get well and can enjoy yourself I want you to stay until after the Fair. Give my love to Eppy and tell her I cannot say any thing about conference yet. I hope Providence will open the way for me to do so.

I have got the interest of my money from Major Burke, and enclosed you will find a [?] in the bank 20$. Give my love to Mr and Mrs Stribling Mr and Mrs Lurton and Willie and Mr and Mrs Moore. Tell them I want them all [?] near God that we may spend eternity together in glory.

I remain you affectionate mother.
Ann Dumville

Write immediately on the receipt of this and let me know the worst.[18]

From: Hephzibah
[Based on internal evidence, addressee was a Dumville cousin in England]

Sept, 1859
Jacksonville

Dear cousin[19]

You will no doubt be very much surprised to receive these lines, coming as they do, from one who has not the least recollection of ever having seen you. I suppose that I have seen you, but so many years have intervened, that not the slightest trace of your appearance runs in my memory. I have no apology to give for the liberty I have taken in addressing you. The fact that we are cousins is in my opinion, reason enough of it self. that we have lived [as] strangers so long is no reason why we should continue so longer. True we may never meet again on earth; very likely we never shall, but the facilities for transmitting inteligence from one place to another, which we enjoy in this age of telagraphs and rail-roads give us ample opportunity to be come acquainted by means of written corespondence.

Many are the changes which have take place in our family since we parted, the death of father which took place two years after we came to America left us friendless indeed so far as human aid was concerned but he consoled himself during his sickness by thinking that the God in whom he trusted would take care of the wife and children that he would leave behind.

We certainly have no reason to complain, for goodness and mercy has followd us all our days, the promis, "I will be a father to the father less and a husband to the widow"[20] has been verified in our behalf.

I being the youngest of the family, perhaps, did not feel the changes in our affairs as much as the other members of our family, I will therefore leave sister[21] to tell you of those things as "They best can tell them, that can feel them most."

I have been making my home in the family of a methodist preacher William C. Stribling for twelve years past. He lives aboute two miles East of Jacksonville. I am very well satisfied with my home.

94 CHAPTER 5

I went to see mother and sister a short time since and enjoyd my visit very much.

Now dear cousin if these lines prove acceptable to you; which I hope they will, pleas favor me with an answer as soon as possible and oblige your

Affectionate cousin

Eppie B. Dumville

From: John Williams
To: Ann and Jemima

Sept 7 1859   Powshiek Co Iowa

Deare Mother & Sister. In due time we Received youres & was glad to hear of youre good health & also of Mary & heire family.

Oure health is but moderate Elis has the ague the past week. Theire is some prospect of geting it broke soone. This season is very Sickly, chills & fever is the prevaling complaint we had frost on the 2 & 5 inst. Corne will be damaged. Some vines & tender plants is all killed. Corne looked well. The frost was very light on my farme on the botoms[22] [?] and everything is drying up. Wheat crops is good & I has [?] acres. I have done the most of my harvisting & haying myself. I put up near twenty bushels of hay. I am diging a [?] ft have a lot of capenting work to do on my hous & stable, brick laying & plastering & some corne to cut up besides a lot of little [clovering?] this fall. I have but little news to rite as times is very dull & but little buiosness doing [?] is some work doing on the Railroade in the County & some prospect of it being completed to Grinnell in a year.[23]

Elis wants you to sende some [large?] wilde grape seed. I keep up the [?] school. The [Quaker?] let [their?] school go down.... Miss Williams... taught [?] for us this season & done well for the [pupils?]. All of my corespondances is very clamorous for me to Rite. I have not time to Rite but little. This is rote because I am not able to work this morning.

You may send a endlis verity of f[l]ower seed & all the pinks to boot.[24] While riting I have been to see a sick childe. Sickness all around us.

Elis went to town & ran [?] in debt for a new stove 28, 00. I am afraid when payday comes I will be behind hand all tho I have neare two hundred on intrest. I have the finest boy & spoilt so he stinks. We think some of sending Sarah to Westfield to School this winter if we can make the arrangements to suit. She is nearly as large as hur Mother. If you think of comeing to see us you could go to Iowa Cty on the cars & to Montezuma on the Stage I shoulde like to have a boy like Jack next spring to drive my oxen to harow in wheat & oats. We send oure love to all

J.W. Williams

to A & J D

From: Hephzibah
Envelope address: Miss Mima Dumville   Carlinville Illinois

Jacksonvill Ill Sep 12th [unknown date]

Dear Mima
   . . . Ma can tell you that grandpa lookd very badly when she was here, but he looks worse now. He is aboute as lifeless a creature to be moving around as I ever saw, and I never want to see the like again. They would not want to take as short a trip as Carlinvill, and so thought they would go to Chicago and perhaps come by Carlinvill on their way home, but now you need not look for them for I think they will never come. . . .
   My dress is made and I intend to have my likeness taken soon.
   Aboute the children's musical abilities, I will just say they both have a great ear for music and if Will did not play well it would be a shame for he has had the best teachers in the place for four or five years. As for Joe, she succeeds with anything she undertakes, she applyes herself so diligently that she cant help getting along well, and then both Instruments playd to gether sound much better. While I write this they are singing "The Old Cabin Home." But to take the piano alone I would <u>rather here my sister play than any one els</u>.
   I am very glad that Ma enjoyed her visit. I know I did my best to make the time pass pleasantly. I should have liked to have taken her aboute more but I could not, I had expected from what Br. More had said that he would have taken her in the country to see some good people but he did not say anything aboute it to her when she came, and I would not ask him of course. I left her there one night expecting nothing els but he would take her oute the next day but he did not, it was just before the Celebration and I suppose he had not time. He preache his Missionary sermon at Salem yesterday, and raised twelve dollars beside what we paid him. Was not that great encouragement.
   . . . Enclosed I send you some White Cyprus seed. My love to all.
   Good by

From: John Williams[25]
To: Hephzibah

Sept 28, 1859

Dear Sister how often I have rote to you that had been complaining of some pain or slite alement which was only the prelude of what we have now felt.
   The dred monster has visited us in the form of Tyfoid & taken away oure first parental care & love. She was taken on the 11th inst & departed this life the 25.th two weeks did she sufer patiently all that a childe coulde her place is vacant in the family & we have to say Sarah is not as Jacob did of Joseph.[26] She was very anxious to get well to go to Sabbath School again. & to finish a quilt

& some other wair before colde wether so as to go to School at Westfielde this winter. A few moments before she died I went to the bed she looked at [me] very earnest & asked why Ma cried. Before I coulde compose myself to speak she said do you think I am going to die, how earnest she spoke. She said I might get the Bible & read a pray for hur which was about the last she spoke. Elisabeth took the chills [?] got them broke in a week she is very sick & complaining yet. my health is very poore the past two months George is complaining of diarea & sore throat. theire has been a great many children died with sore throat this season. This is as sickly season as I ever new. The olde & young alike has falln like leaves in autom. I do not feele like riting about other things. If you want the particulars I will give them at another time you will please forward this to Mother or rite us imediately. Remember us

J.W. Williams / To H. B. D.

From: Hephzibah
To: Ann and Jemima

Oct 10th 1859[27]

Dear Mother and Sister

It makes my heart sad to send this letter to you knowing how sad it will make you to receive it. Poor Lizzie how desolate she must feel now little Sarah was so much help to her[28] and so kind to the little children. I have often felt bad when thinking what a poor chance she had to get an education, but she is gone now where she can learn better things than she could have done at Westfield. Dear little Sarah how we shall miss her when John and Lizzie come to see us again if they are spared to come again.

But she is better off now than we, she has not lived to wish she had died when a child as we have often done.

We will not mourn for her as one that is lost but remember that she is only gone before and we may soon join her sooner than we think.

How I wish it was so that we could go to see them. Sister must feel so lonly sick and away from us all.

I received this letter Saturday evening. I have written a letter to them. Do you write too as soon as you get this. That will perhaps give them some comfort, to think that we sympathise with them.

. . . Tell Ma that Mrs. Seyes started to Baltimore last Tuesday night. Her daughter went with her to Baltimore and will return when her mother sails. She leaves her son with Mr Vanwinkle.

I don't suppose she ever expects to see her children on earth again and they never expect to see her.[29]

We are all aboute write soon

Your affectionate Eppie.

From: Hephzibah
Envelope address: Miss Mima Dumville, Carlinville, Illinois

Sunny Dell Nov 2nd 1859

My Dear Sister,

    I received your last the day after mine was posted, and have been trying for the last two weeks to get time to answer it, but I have been so busy. Last week washing bed cloths and this week taking up our verbenas and getting up our stores and cleaning the leaves oute of the yard. that I could not get leasure enough to do so. I have been at work at the yard all day to day, and to night I feel to[o] tired to write but I am afraid if I don't write now I'll not get a chance to morrow and write to you this week I must.

    Grandma and my self are as well as usual but Grandpa has been more complaining lately than common. Indeed for some weeks past he has not been able to be off the bed a third of the time. . . . When he lays abed all day as he some times does grandma lookes almost as desolate as if she were already a widow. But he is not so poorly to day and she hopes he will be better.

    I did not send my likeness to you . . . I have not had it taken befor this because I have been waiting for grandpa and grandma to go at the same time. They want to have there likenesses taken also. . . . I hope you did not feel hurt at what I said in my last letter or think that I did not want to see you. You must know, Mima that was not the case.

    I hope you will enjoy your preacher more this year than you did last.[30] I don't expect we shall like ours as well though we may before the year closes. Mr. Trotter is our preacher in charge and Jemima Harris's brother is the junior. He is not as tallented by a long way as Mr. Phillips though I think he is more religious and that as you know is more needful in a preacher. This is brother Harris first year I believ. He is spoken of as being a young man of promis. If you have seen a list of the appointments you will perhaps have noticed the name of my last year's correspondent. Now so no longer. When I see you I will tell you aboute the matter.

    I must tell you I saw Joanna Wall a short time ago. You remember her sister. She went to school the first time we ever went to the College. She is going again to the College. She looks as natural as though it had only been a few months since we went to school together, though it has been some years. Dear me how time does fly, how many changes have taken place then, I presume I don't looke much changed, but I feel very much changed I assure you. Sometimes when I look back to those times I feel as though I am hardly the same being. I have not the faith in people now that I then had. I think I had too much confidence in persons then perhaps I have not enough now. I don't know. One thing it sure is very hard to be just right always.

    Mr. Jaquess was in town last week and promised to come oute and spend the night with us but he did not come. I think matters are comming to such a pass that preachers promises are getting below parr.[31]

Mima, I don't want to write to England. That is, I don't want to do it all. You know, I wrote once and never received any answer. I want however when you write to send a few lines also. I think you need not answer their letter before the middle of next month. I have saved a few verbena seed that I wish to send. There are very few indeed but all that I could get at the time. I intended to try and get more but the frost came not long after and I did not get them. I had as many more as I now have but Mrs. Seyes wanted some to take to Africa and I divided with her. Grandpa subscribed for the paper and I am sorry that Ma did not send me her name. I was in hopes she would before Mrs. S. went away but I suppose she forgot it when she went home.

Dear Mima, you was no doubt sho[c]ked by the intelligence of little Sarah's death but I trust you Ma have become reconciled to it. We ought not to grieve to[o] much when we feel that our loss is as I hope her gain. I feel more for Elizabeth than any one els. Now don't wait for the news before you write again but write immediatly. My love to all my friends beginning at home. Write soon and oblige your devoted Eppie.

From: Hephzibah
Envelope address: Miss Jemima Dumville, Carlinville Illinois

Sunny Dell   Nov 28th 1859

My Dear Mima

I was begining to think you was becoming very negligent in answering my letters, to be sure I tried to excuse you when others expressed the same opinion by saying that you was busy in school and had your sewing and practiseing to perform when school was oute, . . . however since you tell me that you have had a convention and I suppose was preparing for your concert I think you are excusible—only dont do so any more.

How I should have enjoyed being with you. I think that I am a dear lover of music. The children in town have given two concerts this fall but of course I could not go. Mr Lurton pronounce them grand, magnificent & Willie said I ought to have been there, but that I was to stingy to spend twenty five cents, thats all he knows about it. I sometimes tell Willie something that you write in your letters. The other day I was telling him aboute your musical convention and so on, and always when I tell him anything aboute you the first thing that seems to occur to him is that it has been a long time since he saw you and that he would like to see you again—so as usual he remarked, when I told him, "Why don't she come to see us; when is she coming; is she never going to come any more?" I replied that you was in school now, "Tell her to stop school a month and come down. Christmas will be here, tell her to stop school and come then and we'll have a pancake for her." I could not but laugh at his earnest way of talking for he said it almost in a breath so I told him I would tell you just what he said. He exclaimed "Will you? will she get mad if you do.

Now sis I suppose you will have holliday Christmass. do come to see us. I should be delighted. I have been secretly cherishing the thought that perhaps I might be able to visit you at that time. I have not spoken of it but my judgment tells me that my hope is in vain. Grandpa continues so poorly that we scarsely leave home at all. We have not spent a day in town for a long time we go in part of a day aboute once a week and that is nearly all the going we do. Grandpa keep his bed two thirds of the time, and when oute of bed is unable to attend to anything. I think it is the Eresipelas[32] and the reumatism that is the matter with him.

You speak as though the letter containing the news of Sarahs death is the last you received. I wrote two weeks after. Did you not get that letter also. I do not think you need feel the least uneasy abut little Sarah I think she could hardly have come to the years of accountability. I think that some children are accountable earlier than others and perhaps Sarah might have been if she had been surrounded by different circumstances, but you know the circumstances which surrounded her were not calculated to rapidly develop the mental powers and I believe that a person is accountable to his Maker in proportion as he is capable of understanding his responsibility to his Maker. Sarah was not surrounded by the temptations and alurements of this world and I am unwilling to believe that as kind and simple honest hearted a little creature as she is unfit for heaven. What does Ma think aboute it? I requested John to give me the particulars when he wrote again. I have not heard from him yet. . . .

I have not any news to tell you except that there was a fire in town last Friday night which destroyed a two story brick three rooms front which was between the ME Church and Squair. I dont know how it took fire unless someone set fire to it that was opposed to the Morgan Journal. The Journal office was in the building. A great many things that was carried out of the houses to keep them from the fire was stolen which is not saying much for the morals of some . . .

I must close now and send my letter as usual with oute reading it over Your affectionate Eppie

From: Jemima
To: Hephzibah

Carlinville Dec, 20th, 1859

My Dear sister I hope you do not think me cruel. I do not mean to be so. Although I do not write to you as often as I ought nevertheless I think of you just as often. Amid all my toils by day and night at home and abroad (My Dear Hep & Eliza) often pass before my minds eye, my mind is with you. I have been waiting for an opportunity to write to you for some time but have concluded to write any way although it is now half passed eleven and since dark we entertained three visitors untill after 9 and then Ma & I went to washing and have prepared the close [clothes] for the boil and while I write all is quiet. The children are snoreing Jack also (that is Ma's pet dog), and Ma's well fat & rosy sitting right here smoking her pipe. We are very busy here in town preparing for a supper to be made by the Methodists for the benefit of the Sabbath school library to be held on Thursday evening we expect Bro. More here to deliver an address. How much I wish you could come with him. If you could come I would make an effort to go but as you cannot be here I do not much expect to go. It is almost impossible to get money. I expect there is fully $150. due for teaching previous to the present term besid interest on $120, which should have been paid last summer and here I am without enough to take me to the supper let alone any thing else. I might perhaps come to see you if I had the means by me but as it, it is impossible.

We received a letter from Iowa. We have received all your letters & I received your last at the time that we obtained one from John. He gave us all the particulars conserning little Sarah which relieved us to some extent & I think your ideas about an individuals association & advantages are correct. We with you hope dear Sarah is singing among the angels. Let us prepare for that glorious company. Mr. Plain is recovering. Sophia has been confined and has a fine girl but I suppose he is not reconsiled and I should not be surprised if he should leave her. Tell William that I was not vexed to hear of his remarks but I was somewhat amused that he should talk so fast as to give utterance to all those words is one breath. Tell him I should like to see him very much for it appears to me a very long time since I saw him. We like Bro Bargar very much. We are looking foreward with joeyful anticipations. I hope we may realiz all that we hope for. They appointed Ma as one of the commitee to beg for the poor again this winter and she has a subscription for over $100, We do not know what the others have, and I am appointed to go with Mrs. Chestnut to collect for the Missionary this is the fourth year that I have been appointed as a beggar. Dear Sis as the clock says 12 & as I fear of nodding in school tomorrow I will retire as dear Ma has gone to bed and left me requesting that I should follow her example, so good night and you will hear from me again in the morning if nothing happens out of the common course of events.

Good morning Sister it is a very pleasant morning. I am rather ashamed of my writing but you must excuse it this time. I think you have improved greatly of late and I am glad to see it.

My school is rather small at present but those who are attending are learning as fast as I could expect considering our conserts and Christmas times.

I kept Thanksgiving day by going to church to hear Brother Barger preach and one of my friends in town had invited me to come and dine with them and as it rained Bro Keeler (for it was sister K who had invited me) came with an umbrella to take me home with him. Ma went & spent the day with Sister Grubs, sewing on Jacks pants. Sister Grubbs is going home to Father Hampers and her husband is going to Kentucky. It must be very humiliating to be compelled to break up house-keeping after raising children to be men almost. I feel sorry for them because they do not know to work on marriage. I suppose you know that for improper conduct Bro Grubbs withdrew from Conference to keep from having a trial and being turned out.

Sis what do you think of poor [John] Brown who was taken at Harpers Ferry I suppose you have heard of the awful events in Virginia.

I have not written to England yet but I hope to do so before long and then I will send it to you, on your way write one to me for Sister and I will post it here. I shall try to write next week for then I shall be out of school a week.

I planted the tulips and dafodils as soon as Ma came home, Have I done wrightly to let them remain in the ground, I believe I have sent you all the news that I can think of at present. I suppose it is not necessary to send my love to all inquiring friends as my friends up there are almost as scarce as hens teeth or werse. I think it is unjust but I will try to submit to it. Mother sends her love to all her friends and especially to Grandma and Grandpa and [?]

From: Hephzibah
To: Jemima

Sunny Dell   Feb 15th 1860

My Dear Mima

I intended to have written this letter last Monday but did not get time, and if I had written it you would not have received it any sooner because none of us have been to town this week and there is not much appearance of our getting there soon if it keeps on snowing at this rate. The deepest snow we have had this winter is on the ground now, did I tell you that I had had one invitation to go sleigh ride this winter. I have forgotten whether I told you or not. Any way I did not go, it was so cold was one reason and another reason was that that company was going to Mr Walters. I have never been to see them since they moved and grandma does not want me to go. I would like to see Magg but I dont expect she will ever come to see me again till I go to see her, so I see no chance of my seeing her soon.[33]

I have been hearing that Margret and Mayberry and Julia were going to be married but I expect it was all talk. Julia is going to school this winter I am told, perhaps, she is preparing herself to teach. I think she ought to try and do something for her self. Mrs Epler is married. Mima, had you heard it? I don't suppose you have although she is now living not many miles this side of you. She and Mr. Dean of Virden were married at Mr Lurtons the 18th of last month. Mr D. is a fine looking man aboute fifty I should think as his hair is quite grey, he was a widower and had one daughter and she is a widow. Her name is Rose. Mr. Rose has been dead now aboute five months, I believe Mr Dean is said to be quite well of[f] though I believe he in deabt at present in consequence of having gave security for some of his friends. Mrs. Dean wrote home, I mean to

Mr Lurton that she was very well pleased and that everything was in fine style. She had not been acquainted with Mr. D. more than three months when they were married, and not more than two weeks when they were engaged. I was at her wedding but did not enjoy my self. There was not more than twenty there, and Mary McElfresh was one. She and my self were the only girls there, there was two young widows present, Mrs Rose and Meenava [Minerva?] Dunlap-Bibb at supper. I sat between Mary and Menerva. They were talking aboute old school mates and Menurva remarked that she had received a letter from Hattie Cliffe a few weeks before, Mary enquired if she was still living to which Menurva replied yes and that she had married a lawyer some three years ago," Mary said she either heard that Hattie was dead or married she was not sure which it was something solomn any way "I have not heard any thing more aboute her since. I think I have told you enough aboute Mrs Es wedding if you want to hear anything more, just say so.

There was a robbery committed in town last Monday night week. Eight hundred dollars worth of the very best of Mr. Smiths goods was taken such as silks and the like. It is a positive shame for if there ever was an honest merchant Mr Smith is one. A number of stors was broken into besid but not much taken, the theif has not been discovered that I know of.

You say that you sent an interesting letter to Mary. Unless your part was better than mine, I think it hardly deserves the appelation, I thought mine was not fit to send but it was the best I could do at the time. You know by this time that I did not send my likeness by Nette,—she never came to see me and I never went to see her,—I dont mean to do all the visiting—and if I dont visit I dont want to ask favors of her, so that is the reason I did'nt send my likeness. It is on the parlor table and I think it is a very good one, but I am afraid Ma wont like the way I was dressed. If she don't, why I'll have another one taken that s all.

I have not received or written a letter to John this year. If I am not to tired when I finish this I will write to them I almost allways write two letters to his one.

When you write again dont forget to send some of your and mothers hair. I am making hair flowers and I want some. There has been a great deal of sickness and a number of deaths. Mrs Saunderson and Miss Gearson both died week before last the first had the consumption the other lung fever. Grandpas health is no better or worse. He is very low spirited and not one of the preachers has been to see him except Harris now and then called to see him as he went the rounds of his circuit, untill last Monday. Bro Moore came to see him, he has been promising all winter to come but did not make the trip till then....

Jane Posey came home a week ago to day. She has been over to [McDoneaughs?] to visit her brother, the past three months. His wife was not expected to live when she went, but she is now able to be up a little. The gerls often ask aboute you and so does Mr and Mrs Delzell. Also Mary and

Sarah, so you see you have a few friends in Morgan. I have not written near all I want, but I dont feel like writing two more pages, so Ill stop.... Give my best love to Mother and the children. Is not the picture of the Lords prayer in the Repository beautiful.

Your Eppie

Figure 10: "The Lord's Prayer" from *The Ladies' Repository*, 1860.

From: John Williams
To: Jemima and Ann

March 4th 1860

Deare Mother & Sister it is a long time since we have heard from you. I rote to you twice in the fall months & as yet no answer has come to hand to the last one. There has been Some protracted eforts put fourth here the past winter & 5 have been added to the little number here & others feels it theire duty to come forward but have not [?] courage to take a desided Stand. & another woulde come if he coulde come with hatred males [malice] & Reveng against a brother & a load of guilt & infamy on his guilty Sole. Oure health is tolerable good except colds which is very comon at this time. Theire has been some sickness this winter & about half of the cases was fatal. Winter fever & sore throat is the jeneral complaint. Luck still strikes at my horses, I have had to bye one latly to make out a team & as olde Sal is taken in the calculation I may be oblige to bye again I have directed one hundred Dollars to be sent to you by Josiah Williams it must be nearly or quite pay the not[e] you have against me you will send the note in youre next & then we can settle any balance in some satisfactory way. Times keeps hard money scarse & buoisness dull with but little prospect of a change soon. The children has gon to school some this winter. Theire is nothing more that I now think of that would be of intrest
  give oure love to all enquireing friends
  J. W. Williams

From: Hephzibah
To: Jemima

Sunny Dell April 5th [1860][34]

Dear Sister,
  You see I don't follow your example and wait a month or more before I take time to answer your letters. . . . Go to the Convention if you can get suitable company. Dont stop and think that you are a stranger, and that you cant render your self as interesting and agreeable as some people, and make as grand a display as somebody els in the world might perhaps do. Any one can do that best which they are most in the habite of doing, and if you just stick at home all the time how can you expect to appear at ease when you go abroad.
  Now sis you must not give way to the blues so much but be determined to go in company and enjoy your self, and you'll get over that feeling of embaresment, and it will be a benefit to you. I know Mima it is much easier to tell others what they ought to do than it is to do that which we feel to be our own duty, but it does seem to me if I had so much encouragement to go oute as you have I certainly would go. So take my advise and go whenever you can. . . .

Grandma sometimes tells me that I am extravagant. I dont know whether I am or not but I must confess that I never could see any use for money unless it was to spend for the purpose of making ones self comfortable. Now dont think that I am in favor of your giving up you school though I think it would be best for you to rest this Summer. Still unless you could secure it for the Winter it would be best for you to continue teaching if your health will admit of it. I did not see any signs of your being insane when you wrote to me though I confess it did look a little cross grained.

You may just tell Mary that if she does not succeed in getting a cat at Mr. Rameys that if she will call here in morning we will give her a sack'sfull as we have more than we have any need for

April 6th

Grandpa got very much hurt this morning falling from a horse. It seems that he was getting on to start home when the horse started to[o] soon and he fell. I hope however that he will soon be well again. There are a great many old people dying this Spring. Mr. Tucker is not expected to live. I do not know whether you know him or not. I should like to say more but I must close for I have a chance to send the letter to town now, and I am afraid I shall not have another soon. My love to all. Write soon.

From: Hephzibah
To: Jemima

Sunny Dell April 22nd 1860.

Dear Mima

I have but a little while ago returned home from the funeral of our nearest neighbour Mrs. Posey[35] who departed this life on the afternoon of Friday last, after a protracted illness of over four weeks. Her disease in the first place was Lung fever which changed into the Typhoid but the affliction which caused her death was what is called "Typhoid sores," what causes these sores is more than I can tell but I rather think it is Calomel.[36] Dr. Reace, Margrets husband tended on her during her illness and was with her evry night except one and the cause of his not being with her then was that he thought her to be in a fair way of recovery and had gone home. He certainly gave her all the attention he was capable of giving and if he erred at all it was in judgement not in intention.

I was there almost every day sometimes oftener, and although she suffered greatly no word of complaining or murmering escaped her lips. Her patience was a subject of remark by all that saw her. The Dr. thought evry morning that she could not last till night and evry night that she could not live till morning and thus she lingered for more than a week after all hope of her recovery had left the hearts of her loved ones. You will have some idea of her sufferings when I tell you that almost the whole of her right cheek was taken oute it haveing become so diseazed, the Dr. pronounced it mortifyed but I always thought a person could not live more than a few hours if any part of the system was mortifyed, however I dont know. During all her sickness her girls were as kind and devoted as daughters could be tending every wish or want with all the promptness that affection could suggest. Poor girls I feel sorry for them they will feel so desolate. <u>Home</u> will not seem <u>like home with oute a Mother</u>. Mrs. Posey was buried in the Town grave yard. The bodies of those that were burried in the garden will be taken up and placed beside her. I suppose the girls and John will continue there this year perhap longer I cannot tell as I have not heard them say. I hope they may.

I was told that from the first of her sickness Mrs. Posey did not expect to recover but was entirely resigned to the will of God. She and her husband with ten others were the first organized church of their order in Jacksonville or perhaps in the County and I am not sure that there was any other denomination here before them, for I believe the Presbyterians are aboute as energetic in advancing the interests of their church as any other denomination, and I think they are generally to be found in the van[guard] of population as it swells on Westwards.

How rapidly the old people are passing away, not long since old Mr. Saunderson went oute with one of his sons a short distance from home to put up some fence and after being there a short time remarked that he did not feel well and thought he would go home. His son told him he had better wait a little while and go with him, he said no he would go now" turned to go home, exclaimed O! fell and with a gasp all was over, his spirit had gone to join the wife who had preceeded aboute two months before. Although death came suddenly it no doubt found him ready, he had remarked only a short time befor that if he had his choice "he would rather die suddenly and not linger as his poor wife had done" in the morning of the day on which he died he had complained a little but his daughter prepared something for him to take after which he seemed better than usual that is more cheerful. His family take his death very hard I heard that one of his sones said their "home seemed like a world with oute a Sun" none of the boys are members of the church and they no doubt miss the religious exercises to which they have been accustomed.

You missed it by not taking the Repository this year if for nothing els but to get the engraving in the Febuary number. I think it is the prettiest picture I ever saw.

I have received a letter from John and answered it since I wrote to you last. They were well when he wrote, he said he expected to commence digging for gold on a certain particular spot of ground where he has dug evry year since he has been there and see what he could make by it. I hope he may succeed to his satisfaction and ours.

. . .

I am glad you sent the hair. I intended sending you a specimen of my work in this letter but as I have none ready to send, and I want to post this tomorrow I must wait till another time. if you have any of fathers hair I should like to have some.

I have heard that there has been a terible Tornado in Carlinville.[37] Write soon and let me know the particulars. . . .

Give best love to Mother how glad I should be to see her. My love to all enquiring friends. . . .

Now goodbye, sis, Believe your devoted

Eppie

What a pity that Martha Woods should have been so meanly deserted, but if he is so trifling she is better off withoute him than with him. I am glad that George and Sophia have parted friends. I hope he is not going to give her the slip. I suppose Benny[38] will correspond with you. It would be nice to get letters from such a wild region.

From: Josiah Williams
To: Jemima

Geneva, Scott Co. Ills.
May the 4th 1860

Belove Sister in the Lord—

I recieve your kind letter of Feb 8th 60. I should of answered sooner only for carlesness and the press of business which has crowded me sorely this spring. You kned make no apolagy for writing to me - for I was truly glad to recieve a letter from you and to hear from you and of your dooing well and glad was I to hear of your good success as a teacher for the fact or your continueing in one school for four years speaks highly of your success - your calling is one in which more good can bee accomplished than allmost any other. You have the care of training the young mind and making impressions that will last during life. Yours is a high calling and I wish you abundant success. You all most startle me when you speak of the years of 1853. It seems hardly possible that so much time has whirled a way since that good meeting was held at the school house. Oh - that was a good time but it has passed away and with it many of our friends have gone - we have abandoned the school house for church purposes - and have built a fine Brick Church[39] - further west - but I am sorry to say that we are not getting along as a society as well spiritually as I could desire yet I live in hopes of better times pray for us. My children you want to hear from - Jane is living with us. Frances Reed is living a mile or two south of Striblings - Lucinda Hornbeak is living four miles south of Jacksonville. Elias is maryed and lives in Mcdonough Co Ills. Anderson is maryed and on the

Hornell farm. Luiza Marian Mineare lives in Charlestown Coles County Ills. They are Pilgrims and sojourners and are sent by the Conferance from place to place year after year. Peter is at home and is nearly grone. Sarah is a large girl. I am old and gray headed and wife and I have to ware <u>specks</u> as they are called - uncle Ely and Aunt Sarah and Armilaa and one of his girls have gon to inherit a portion amongst the blest. Elizabeth and Sarah Kimble lives in Winchester. I hear from John [?] a short time since - all well I suppose. You heard that they lost their Sarah last fall. Huckstep lives on the king farm. Katharin is maryed. Perry Horrell lives at the same place. Coots sold Johns farm to Wm Barrows. Elizabeth Ballinger is not maryed. Clinton is at home. Hugh is expected home this spring. I believe this all that I recolect of that would interest you. I think you mite make us a visit this summer and while a way a few weeks pleasantly. Jane is going on a visit to [Minearas?] next week. I know not how long she will stay - tho not long I guess. Dinner is about reddy so I must close by subscribing my self your brother in the Lord and well wishes

Josiah Williams

Ps- please write again as I should be happy to heare from you give my love to Mother Dumville.

From: Hephzibah
To: Ann and Jemima

Desolate Dell, May 8th 1860

Dear Mother and Sister

Fearing that you might hear terible tidings from this region through the news papers, as we did from your a few weeks since,[40] and knowing if you did that you would be very anxious aboute us, as we were aboute you when we heard that a Tornado passed through Carlinville. I thought I would give you the facts as they came under my own observation. We have been expecting rain for some days, and fearing when it did come we should have a storm, so to day between one and two o clock it began to rain and hail very hard the wind blowing a perfect storm. I went up stairs' to shut the windows in the west room grandpa was lyeing on the bed in that room. I then went into my room shut the window there, and then went down stair it being so unpleasant up stairs. I could hear nothing but a constant roar. When I reached the sitting room the rain was pouring in like a flood in at the window and door, the floors nearly covered and the window glass was flying aboute like hail. I snatched something off the bed and went into the parlor and there was grandma and Willie they had deserted the sitting room, and was pretty badly scared. She asked where grandpa was. I told her he was up stairs she said he must come down so I ran back to help him down stairs and by the time he got down the storm began to subside, so you may know it did not last long. But if the storm did not last long I assure you it left destruction and desolation in its path. The best of our apple trees are either blown up by the roots or broken to peices six or more of the locust trees are blown down in the grove and the same number in the front lot, and it is the same all over the timber. That large tree by the pump you remember was blown up by the roots and fell on the milk house and nocked it in two. It has not fallen yet but it will as soon as the tree is taken off if not before the top fell on the middle room and kitchen but did not hurt. The currants was striped of the bushes and our onions and beans was served the same way we cant find a single tomato though we have had them for sometime. The fence round the yard and garden and on the place was blown flat, and the corn is gone to parts unknown. We have been busy almost ever since puting up fence to keep the stock from running all over the place. Mr. Lurton came out with some other men to help put up fence.

Our neighbours faired no better than we. The Posey girls poor things were scared almost to death. Fanny told me they were all children together, and that she thought of her Mother all the time and thought they would all soon be with her. You will see that it was bad enough but we all felt glad that we had escaped with our lives and limbs unbroken. I must go to bed now as it is very late and I shall have to be up by times in the morning as a number of men are to be here to put up fence, good night.

May 9th

Another day with its cares and toils is gone, but before placing my self under the refreshing influence of sleep, I will tell you a little more aboute how we and times are getting on togeather. I have not heard much more aboute the storm, there was very little harm done in town a few chimneys blown down and a stable or so and some fence and that was mostly in the South Easte part of town.

We have been out replanting our beans beets and radishes this afternoon. I could get along very well were it not that all our fruit is destroyed. Other things can be replanted but we will have to wait till next year for fruit. There has been seven men out to day getting things in order. They had some trouble getting the tree off of the house. I dare say the little milk house was all that save the dwelling.

Mrs. Dean came up to see Mr. Lurton and family week before last she spent the first of May with us. Joe went with her to Chicago last Wednesday, she is to return home with her to Virden. . . . I hope now that you will write some time this Spring. . . . But, Oh! how much better to see you.

How did you make the dress abute which you wished my advice. Give my love to all enquiring friends, if there are any such and what they dont want you may keep for your self sis.

Don't you think I have improved in writing. Good night.

Eppie

From: Hephzibah
To: Jemima

Sunny Dell   July 11th 1860

My Dear Mima
    ... I have not received those letters of which you spoke. Perhaps I never shall. I think strange of it for I dont remember to have ever failed getting letters sent me before.
    Perhaps you will not be much surprised, when I tell you that grand pa and grand ma have not gone yet, I hear less talk aboute it now then when I wrote to you last, though I believe they have not entirely given up the notion of taking a trip perhaps one reason of thier saying less aboute it is that grandpas health is not quite so bad as at that time.
    Sarah is still with us as she came the morning I wrote to you last. Her presence makes the time pass more pleasantly, but that does not make me any the less anxious to see you, Mima. I tell Sarah every day that I want to see my sister and last night I dreamed I was with you. But I woke to finde it only a dream. I was really disapointed sis that you did not make your arrangements to come sooner after school. . . . if you are going to take the matter so liesurly as all that I should think the people would give you the money to get you to stop.
    I suppose Mother is by this time rejuvinating at Harris Point and vicinity, how many battles she will fight over again while revisiting the places once so familiar to us all, I wonder which have changed the most they or we?
    By the way sis how did you spend the Fourth? I expected to spend it quietly at home and was thinking what a nice easy time Sarah and I would have together, but lo, and behold aboute eight or a little after Mr Lurton came for a carriage to go to a Sunday School celebration aboute six miles from town and wanted me to go with him and Joe so I made ready as soon as possible and went. The morning was cool and bright and we enjoyed the ride very much when we reached the place the Declaration of Independence had already been read and Mr Collins was delivering the Oration, "The Union Saved" was the subject. Mr. C. is a Congregational preacher so withoute further information you may suppose he is rather a dry speaker. Anyway there was no cheering when he finished. I heard that there was an abundant supply of good thing for the accomodation of the people, and was fortunate enough to be invited to go to the table, but as Joe was unwilling to go I couldn't so we refreshed ourselves with the contents of our own basket, after which we conversed with those present whom we knew and commented on those we did not know untill the people were called together again to listen to the address to the Sabbath Schools. By this time the place had become so extreemly warm that Mr Lurton proposed going. We started and on our way home stopped at the Diamond Grove where Mr L had been especially invited to attend. There they had music and dancing swearing and drinking and fighting and such things as are common on the Celebration of a day of which the American people are so proude.

For my own part I thought it would be no credit to my self or my mother to remain on the ground so I went to Mr. Becrafts house which was a few yards off and on whose ground the people were assembled and remained there untill Mr Lurton came for me to go home. Sue had just returned from Ohio, a short time before. I think I told you she had gone there to school. We returned to town aboute six o clock. I took tea there after which Dolly and I drove out home.

Upon the whole I believe . . . aboute Lizzie's I had not heard from them for so long. I hope nothing serious has befalen them.

Dear Sister I hoped that this letter would have been in your possession before this time but here it is yet unfinished, well it does seem to me that the time does pass away very unaccountably. I am busy all the time and for the life of me I can hardly tell what I have done. You wished to know if I had read the speeches on slavery. I read that came in my way, which was likely all that was delivered, as it has been some weeks since I read them my ideas of them are getting rather indistinct. At a venture, however, I will say the Mr. Moody's was the most soule stiring of any, though at the same time it seemed strangely oute of place, there and then as all present professed to be antaslavery, some say that Sewall[41] speach was the best and I rather think grandpa is one of them, but that will be easily accounted for, he rather favored the Minority, but I am not with him there, I [am] desidely with the Majority, and I think that C. Kingsly and E. Thomson's[42] speaches were the point and the best, did you notice that expression in Thomson's speach, the abolitionists are blaimed for the agitation on slavery, as well the Declaration of Independance for the blood of the Revolution? I have often been puzzled when I have heard that remark, I feel now that I have an answer. Mima you will begin to think that Thomson is quite a favorite with me, well he is, I feel that he is no stranger to me for I have been familiar with his writings for years and have taken great pleasure in reading them and I certainly think you will do the same. I think the American people ought to feel grateful to old England for giving them such a son.

Was there any notice in your last paper concerning a new paper just started in New York called the "Methodist," in opposition to the Christian Advocate and Journal, if so tell me what you think of the originators, of it. . . . For my own part I think it is a positive shame and I hope they will get the reward they merit.

W. M. Milburn too has to have his finger in the pie, I am not surprised at him, but I am at the others, perhaps it is because I dont know them so well, as I do him. Mrs Milburn and Nick started to visit William last week. I have just looked into the Advocate and finde that it is Dr. McClintoc who is the corresponding editor in place of Stevens as I first thought however Dr. Steveans is associated in the loyal enterprise I fear that I am not interesting you, but you see I am trying so to do.

The weather is opressively hot. I think it will rain soon from appearances . . . It is now almost eleven o clock, so I must go and prepare dinner, if I dont get time to write more this time I will send this sheet as it is only partly filled. . . .

My love to all. Let me know the exact time you expect to be here. Now write soon do.

Your devoted Eppie

From: John Williams
Envelope address: Mrs. Ann Dumvill Carlinville Macoupin Co Ills

July 11 [1860][43]

Deare Mother & Sister after a long silence I againe send you a fiew lines to let you know how we are geting along & the propsect of crops, health in jeneral is good the whooping cough has been spred here to some extent & we have to bare oure part with the Rest The children is getting along well. Mary Ellen is the worst of any. We have no fears about hur doing well as we beleave the worst time is past, the children has gone to school some this season. The School stopt like all the other quaker—teachers has done here.

Corne looks well over an average at this time. Wheat & oats hardly an averag owing to the dry spring. I will have enough to do us & 23 acres of corne with oats + grass. I shall aime to fat 16 head of hogs, with a good stock of Cattle & Sheep. We often wish oure circumstances would admit of a visit to see you this fall but times is to harde to Raise any money to travil on or get a team. I have onley one horse to depend on, olde Sal can do some work yet. I am attending Sabbath School again this season. My time is all taken up in atending to the rounds of duty. We try to have class in two weeks we feel some what nominal in Religion but we hope in the Lord for his promises secures oure hopes of happiness in this life & in the life to come, there is nothing of buoisness transactions worth relating as the cry of harde times continues & but very little doing.

Eliza [Elizabeth Williams] wants to know her exact age.

I know of nothing more that woulde be interesting to rite if I had time.

We heare of storms in diferant places but Iowa seartainly witnessed the full forse of the elements. It passed north some 60 or 70 miles, every thing was destroyed or badly damaged.

Mary E. is 7 weeks olde.

do you keep the children yet[44]

J.W. Williams

From: Hephzibah
Envelope address: Miss Mima Dumvill, Carlinville Illinois

Sunny Dell Oct 23rd 1860

Dear Sister

I can hardly realize now that the Fair and the Conference are both over, and that you and Ma have both been to see me and are gone again, and that now days and weeks and months, will pass according to the common order of things before I may expect to see you again. It seems like a long weary time to look forward too, but September 1861 will not be long in coming and then, well I will not say what then but I'll hope.[45] I felt right bad Thursday when I went with Ma to the Depot to find that the Douglass ites were going to the Capitol if it had been myself I should not have cared so much but for Ma to go in such a crowde was quite another thing. I hope she was comfortable on the way, I tried to get her company and felt pretty sure that I had succeeded for when the cars started I saw her through the window very busy talking to some one I supposed it was Mr. Rucker as I requested him when I step[p]ed of[f] the cars to take charge of Mother he said certainly and then asked if there was not a vacant seat beside her I replied there is, he said he would get it and I suppose did so. I had requested Dr. Knight to take care of her before but I thought he was not as attentive as I wished, and that was the reason of my speaking to Rucker. Tell me when you write all aboute it, and whether Mr. Prents met her at the depot. Sarah and Rebeck Van Wincle[46] came oute last Friday evening and remained untill Sunday evening. Sarah of course had news to tell, I will give you a little sip of it. There was a great deal of fault found aboute the Conference being sent to Jacksonville and I do hope it will never be sent there again. Mrs R[47] says she hopes it never will come here again, she wants the people of Jacksonville to be ready the next time it comes. It was hard work to get places for the preachers to stop, and when one of the members was asked to take preachers he replied send them to the Tavern and let them pay their board." (I hope there was not many such).

There was hard feeling between Rutledge ande Moore. Moore wanted to pick his men and take the most influential talented and rich among them for his end of the town, you know that is the Aristocratic part of the city, Rutledge said he would not stand it, that Moore ought to take the list of names and take every other one but Mr. Moore would not do that, so they had some words aboute it, and finally R—picked up his hat and left, then George Rutledge had to go in between them and quiet the discord. Mr R. at last gave in to M. and let him have his own way. It seems there was a young preacher from Canada Conference visiting there. Mr. R. said well [?] your choice of the others I suppose you will let me take care of him? speaking the young mans name I have a place for him by request said Moore, Well where is it? At my own house, replied Mr. Moore." I then asked Sarah if his name was Smith, she replied, yes. Well said I, I suppose he staid there then for when Ma and I dined there Sallie told me that there was a very nice young man staying with them but he was not there that day, by the name of Smith, and I afterwards saw her at church talking with him. Now if that is not wire-pulling I don't know what you would call it. I want you to show a spirit above that next year.

Ben Newman's case passed too and Moore said he was glad of it. Mr Lurton says it will sink the Conference not a little in the estimation of the people, letting it pass and he is right there. Ma will be sorry to hear that Mr. Fisher, the

Kansas preacher, lost [3?]60 dollars of his own money and 340 for Kansas. . . . He gave his satschel to the porter and the money was in it he has entered suit against Mr. Foy the Hotel Keeper. I hope he may get it. I intend sending three dollars to Kansas cant you and Ma give one apiece. send it to me and I'll send it with mine. Fannie T. told me as a great secret last Saturday that Sarah and Mr. Barrows were to be married next Thursday evening. They are going to Chicago and from there to Delivan Wiss [Wisconsin]. Margret and her husband are to go with them. I have more to tell you but I most close. write soon
  yours, Eppie
  . . . good by, write soon if not before

[*In margin*] I am glad to learn that sophia is cheerful. . . . How do you like your present, they would have been nicer if I had not been in such a buzz when they were made. I like my picture very much. It lookes nicely upstairs, take care of those roses. Ma left her white scirt [skirt] here, she need not wear it . . .

From: John Williams
To: Ann and Jemima

Octe 28, 1860

Dear Mother & Sister after some delay I take up my pen to acknowledge the receipt of youre last which came to hand in due time we was glad to heare of youre returning health & of the general good health. Our health is good except colds we have no reason to complain. There is nothing special worth relating since I rote last. Crops is good better than was expected some two months ago wheat is 50 cts to 67 cts per bu. corne 15 oats 12 to 15 per bu. pork 3.50 gross per hund. Farmers is recovering a little from the hard pressure of the past & can begin to make some calculations for the future if crops do not fail again. I can get along if I can colect what is due me which is over $90,00 I have corne wheat & pork to sell. The two parcels of the papers you sent came to hand. The girls says they woulde like you to send them on[e] dollar each so they coulde send to the gift book establishment they are some what taken with the idea of geting a present of gold.[48]

I am one of the Simon pure Abe supports as I canot go the black African or mulato candidates or the crouching survility of the constutional slavocrat.[49] As news is scars & I have but little inclination to rite you will take this as an apology.
  J. W. Williams

6. 1861–1863

The War

In the early months of the war, Union troops had little success, and Hephzibah's letters at that time express the anxiety of the public in the North. A letter written late in 1861 comments on two battles, one successful and the other a defeat. The victory was a naval assault on Port Royal, located between Savannah, Georgia, and Charleston, South Carolina, where there were two forts, one on each side of the entry to the harbor. Union ships shelled the forts until the Confederate forces retreated. The defeat took place at Ball's Bluff, near Leesburg, Virginia. The Union army was generally thought to have been attempting to take Leesburg, and this assumption is reflected in Hephzibah's letter, but that was probably not the case. The engagement began as a reconnaissance mission and, because of several failures of communication, evolved into a full-scale battle in which the Union troops were routed.[1] Hephzibah celebrated the "brilliant victory" at Port Royal but decried "the miserable blunderings of our officers" in other battles.

Letters from the Williams family during this period reflect continuing concern about economic conditions and about the activity of Copperheads (Southern sympathizers—see chapter 1). Early in 1861, John Williams wrote, "Here we are in the midst of a set of disunion traitors, so that a few gallons of sod corn [that is, corn whiskey] just would set them on."[2] In September, Williams complained about his financial circumstances and asked the Dumvilles for a loan. Because of the war, the Mississippi River was often blockaded, Midwest agricultural commodities and other goods could not reach Southern markets, and there was a severe economic recession in the upper Mississippi River valley. The price of corn was so low that some farmers burned it as fuel, and hog prices were cut by half.[3] Many banks had issued their own banknotes, often backed by bonds issued by Southern states. As the bonds on which the banknotes were based lost value, the money did as well.[4] The result, of course, was that paper money was less often accepted in commercial transactions, trade was disrupted, and bankruptcy was common. Although the financial panic of 1857 had already weeded out weak banks, only seventeen Illinois banks survived 1861–62.[5] The Morrill Tariff Act of 1861, which protected Northeastern manufacturers from competition with imported goods, imposed further costs on the Midwest. Agricultural interests in both the Midwest and the South usually favored free trade, and Democrats used the protective tariffs and the Midwest recession as political ammunition in their attacks on Lincoln's administration.[6]

In late December 1861, Hephzibah reported that, at a gathering of Methodist clergy, she participated in a discussion of the possibility that England might intervene in the war. The Union blockade of Confederate ports had deprived British textile mills of shipments of cotton, and the Confederacy sought to exploit the resulting tension in U.S.-British relations. Since the Dumvilles were English immigrants, they were particularly sensitive to the English position. In November 1861 a Union ship stopped a British packet, the "Trent," which was carrying two Confederate diplomats, Mason and Slidell, who were on their way to London and Paris to seek diplomatic recognition of the Confederacy. The British government then demanded the release of the diplomats. Lincoln defused the situation by complying with that demand, but the United States did not apologize for its action. Hephzibah's letter commented: "I was loude in my condemnation of her [England's] course in case she should go to waring with us because of the capture of Mason and Slidell." At age twenty-eight, Hephzibah clearly had the self-confidence to express her views on public affairs.

In the winter of 1861–62, Union troops under the command of Ulysses S. Grant were assembled at Cairo, Illinois, at the southernmost tip of the state, near the confluence of the Ohio and Mississippi Rivers. Soldiers from both Carlinville and Jacksonville were based there, and the Dumvilles wrote to them. Jemima's letters usually emphasized religious themes, including the evils of slavery. These messages were no doubt heartfelt, but they were sometimes grim. Her letter to a soldier stationed at Cairo, dated January 11, 1862, said, "We see little else but confusion bloodshed tyranny and death" and "surely the powers of darkness are loose." It is hard to imagine that the young man found these thoughts comforting.

Early in 1862, a Carlinville soldier wrote to Jemima about the Union's "march through Kentucky." The federal troops based at Cairo had advanced through Kentucky to northern Tennessee, where they attacked Fort Henry and nearby Fort Donelson. Henry was taken relatively easily, with the aid of a flood that inundated the fort, but Donelson was stoutly defended. The Confederates counterattacked at Donelson and almost broke through the Union lines, but the South then abandoned the attack, leaving its troops with no escape. Twelve thousand Confederate soldiers were captured; it was the Union's first major victory. A few days later, Nashville fell to another Union army.

A letter written by Hephzibah in March 1862 comments on two officers from Carlinville, John Logan and John Palmer. Logan was a physician who served as a field commander rather than as a medical officer.[7] He had been in the Indian wars before taking up the practice of medicine (he had also worked as a carpenter), and in 1861 he volunteered for army duty and was commissioned as a colonel. His regiment, a part of General Grant's army, fought in the battles of Forts Henry and Donelson. As noted in chapter 2, Palmer was a Carlinville lawyer and politician who rose from colonel to major general during the war. In 1861 he served under John C. Fremont in putting down a rebellion in Missouri, and in 1862 he commanded a division of the Army of the Mississippi in Alabama and Tennessee. Hephzibah's letter expresses disbelief that Palmer's forces would be "so far south," and she refers to a report that they "had all been taken prisoners." They were that far south, but they were not captured. In the absence of hard news, rumors were very common. Early in the war, Ann Dumville considered accompanying Palmer's regiment as a sort of chaplain or spiritual advisor, but she decided against it. Women did not serve as military chaplains, at least not officially, until 1864 when Mrs. Ella Gibson Hobart became chaplain of a Wisconsin artillery regiment, and Hobart served in that capacity only until Secretary of War Stanton found out about it.[8]

Hephzibah noted an especially horrific battle in a letter written in April 1862, about six weeks after the battle of Fort Donelson. Grant's troops had been camped at Pittsburg Landing, Tennessee, on the Tennessee River, about twenty miles northeast of Corinth, Mississippi. Confederate troops, eager to avenge the loss of Donelson, attempted a surprise attack on Grant's camp. It became the bloodiest battle in American history up to that time.[9] Much of the fighting took place near a small log church named Shiloh, and the engagement became known as the Battle of Shiloh. The commanding Confederate general, A. S. Johnston, was killed on the first day of the assault, but the Confederate army made substantial progress that day and appeared to be near victory. Union reinforcements arrived overnight, however, and on the second day of the battle the Confederate army was compelled to retreat to Corinth.

After the battle, the Union army regrouped and moved slowly toward Corinth, an important rail center. As of May 6, three weeks after Hephzibah's letter, a Carlinville soldier wrote to Jemima and reported that his company was still located only a few miles from Pittsburg Landing. Their slow progress was attributable to heavy rain. Although he had not been in the battle at Shiloh, he said that "from the marks on the trees and the graves everything goes to show that it was a dreadful battle." Union troops finally reached Corinth in late May, began an artillery barrage on May 25, and captured the city on May 30. The soldier's letter expresses the view (or hope) that "if we whip them out here they can't last long," but the war did not end until April 9, 1865, three years later.

The first sheet of the soldier's letter is on stationery decorated with a portrait of Major General Curtis. The second sheet shows an eagle standing on the dome of the U.S. Capitol. In the eagle's mouth is a ribbon bearing the legend "Our Country." A caption reads "The Eagle's Throne" (see figure 11). Perhaps this stationery was distributed to the Union troops. The dome of the Capitol was still under construction when the letter was written.[10]

In July Hephzibah wrote to Jemima describing a celebration of "the taking of Richmond," the Confederate capital. The celebration was premature. In the spring of 1862, Union forces under the command of Major General George McClellan had mounted a major offensive in Virginia known as the Peninsular Campaign, and its ultimate objective was the capture of Richmond, but the plan failed. Despite some early success in advancing along the Virginia peninsula, Union forces were decisively defeated by a Confederate army led by Robert E. Lee.

In their comments concerning the war, both Hephzibah and Jemima place greater emphasis on the abolition of slavery than do the soldiers.[11] This is consistent with James McPherson's reading of thousands of letters written by Civil War soldiers. He concluded that "few Union soldiers professed to fight for racial equality" or "had any real interest in emancipation *per se.*"[12] The evidence in the Dumville collection is that the men from Carlinville and Jacksonville were motivated by feelings of duty and by the impetus to survive. One expressed distaste for meeting "our fellow man face to face with our guns and weapons to mow them down as a man would go into a slaughter pen to butcher oxen" (letter of May 6, 1862). The women's letters, by contrast, discuss the war in terms of national policy, grand military strategy, and religious destiny, and they articulate support for the war in the phrases that local and national leaders used in public speeches. Hephzibah's letters, especially, express more enthusiasm for the sword and the hangman's noose than do the letters of the soldiers. The men, not surprisingly, saw it more

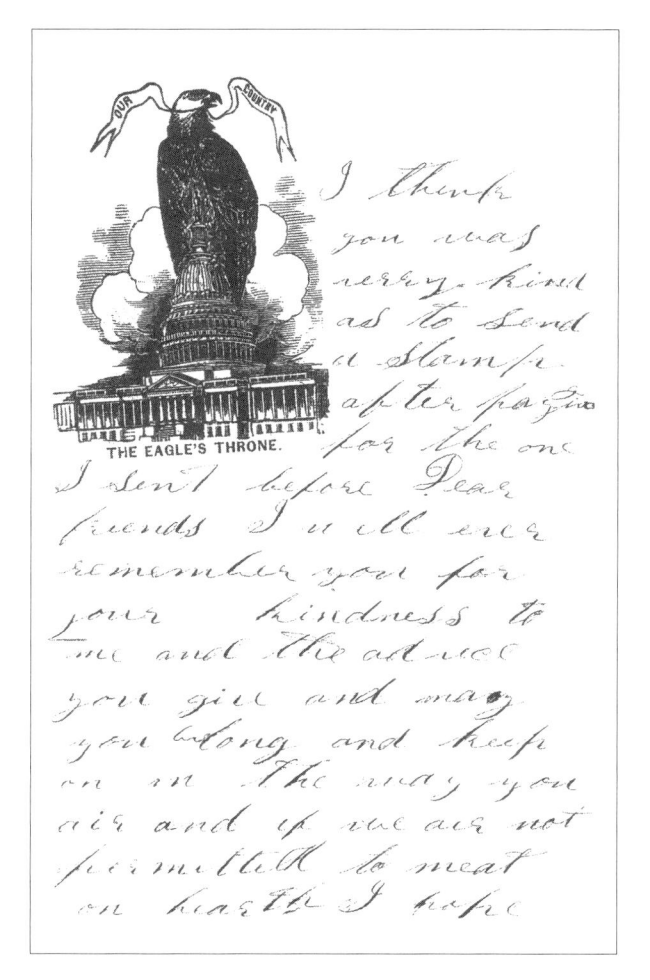

Figure 11: Letter from a soldier, 1862. Courtesy of Abraham Lincoln Presidential Library and Museum.

personally. From the perspective of the battlefield it was difficult to focus on distant goals. The soldiers were confronted with the daily hardships, the squalor, the illness, the drudgery, the mud, and the dying.

The last letter from Hephzibah, dated June 2, 1863, refers to the siege of Vicksburg, fought from May 18 until July 4, 1863. On the same day that Hephzibah wrote, a soldier from the Carlinville area reported casualties suffered by his company. A lieutenant and a private had been killed, and eleven of the company's men had been captured, reducing its strength to only forty. His letter refers to "great movements going on now." On the day before the surrender of Vicksburg, the Confederate army was defeated at Gettysburg, and the combination of the two Confederate defeats is often considered the major turning point of the war.

But, as we might expect, the war, important as it was, was not the only subject dealt with in these letters. Religion, social visits, family matters, and the problems of daily life continued to command their attention. Hephzibah's letters were increasingly concerned with the inability or unwillingness of both her family and the Striblings to resolve the terms of her employment and to plan for her return to Carlinville, and the letters demonstrate her ambivalence about the matter and her reluctance to discuss it with the Striblings. On the one hand, she wanted to return to her mother and sister, "home"; on the other, she felt a duty to the Striblings. She often reported the Striblings' ill health and expressed concern about whether they were able to care for themselves. There was an element of guilt in her feelings. A letter from John Williams in March 1861, however, focused Hephzibah more clearly on whether she had spent her "youth and vigor with out proper remuneration and saving something for the future." After receiving that letter, she gave greater attention to her own welfare. But she was still uncertain. Two months later, she asked her mother and sister: "Tell me again what I had better do."

Stribling was a singular character. An article published in the *New York Times* after his death described him as "a tall, gaunt, long-featured man, of most wonderful gravity, made ludicrous to outsiders by his nasal tone and big words."[13] William Milburn, one of the most prominent Methodist ministers of the day, said that Stribling "afforded me endless entertainment."

> His sermons were most elaborately prepared, and delivered with the greatest fluency and unction. He poured forth his sonorous periods with the most weighty seriousness; yet I confess that I have not always been able to repress a smile when I have heard him utter a periphrase of this kind: "The small particle of the aqueous fluid which trickles from the visual organ over the lineaments of the countenance, betokening grief." . . . A man of quenchless zeal and indefatigable industry, he abounded in labors, preaching constantly while he supported himself by his farm.[14]

In fact, he supported himself quite well. Doyle's history of Jacksonville reports that only ten percent of the town's adult males had wealth in excess of $5,000 in 1860,[15] but Stribling is listed in the 1860 Census as having property valued at $42,000. As early as 1857 the letters noted that he was bedridden, but he survived until 1872 despite continuing complaints.

The last letter in the Dumville file at the Abraham Lincoln Library was written by Stribling to Ann Dumville. It is difficult to interpret, but it makes clear that he was unhappy about Hephzibah's departure. In the spring of 1861 there had been negotiation about the terms of her compensation and about the timing of her return to Carlinville. The negotiations continued, sporadically, for more than two years. In late 1862 or early 1863 she visited her mother and sister, and in 1863 she finally left the Stribling farm with Fred Bechly. This was then followed in December of that year by the letter from Stribling.

His letter is eccentric and agitated. It suggests, among other things, that Hephzibah "wished us not to employ F [Fred] in consequence of his efforts made against her previously." But there is no suggestion in Hephzibah's letters that she was other than pleased with Fred. Her letter to Jemima in April 1862 closes with "Fred sends his respects," and in August 1862 Fred loaned money to John and Elizabeth Williams and was later reimbursed by Hephzibah. So Fred was, a year before their departure from the Stribling farm, treated much like a member of the Dumville family. Two letters written after Hephzibah's visit to Carlinville but before she left the Striblings, letters dated January 27 and June 2, 1863, are silent about her plans for the future. Neither of these 1863 letters mentions her departure from the Stribling farm or marriage to Fred. Perhaps those matters had been dealt with fully during the visit to Carlinville, so that her mother and sister did not need further information about her intentions. Or perhaps the decisions were made quickly in the summer of 1863. In any event, Hephzibah married Fred Bechly in Carlinville in August 1864,[16] and she remained married to him until her death.

The Stribling letter suggests some of the vulnerabilities of serving women. The negotiation regarding Hephzibah's wages, referred to in the letter, took place after the work had been done, and therefore when she had little bargaining power. This was a common practice.[17] There may or may not have been some sort of written agreement before Hephzibah went to live at the Striblings—perhaps only an informal exchange of letters—but that appears to have been of little consequence. Mr. Stribling's letter is revealing about status differences, at least as perceived by him. Although Hephzibah was thirty years old in 1863, his letter was addressed to her mother, and he appears to have felt that Ann was the real party in interest. To the extent that he acknowledges an obligation, it was one owed to the mother. He adopts the stance of Hephzibah's guardian or protector and is at pains to defend himself against any implication that he had failed to care for her properly. This posture emphasizes Stribling's superior position in the social hierarchy. He refers to Hephzibah as "our daughter" and treats her as his subordinate in the household and as inferior to him in age (and, therefore, wisdom), gender, learning, and standing within the church. The letter appears to suggest, moreover, that Hephzibah was departing under a cloud—that she had behaved badly and had, perhaps, fallen from grace. This suggestion, if made more publicly, would threaten her reputation. The Dumvilles, therefore, were on notice that they should not sully his good name, lest theirs also suffer.

Stribling seems to have felt that his role in Hephzibah's life gave him authority to evaluate her suitors, even when she was thirty, and Fred Bechly, apparently, was found wanting. It is possible that Stribling would not have countenanced any romance that lacked his prior approval. Or he may simply have thought that Bechly was an unsuitable match. Hephzibah was the daughter of a pillar of the Methodist church, a family friend of the Striblings, while Bechly was a German immigrant and a laborer, two years younger than Hephzibah.[18] Stribling may have felt that Hephzibah should marry someone more prosperous and substantial, or perhaps a Methodist preacher. This is all speculation, of course. We do know, however, that the Striblings had received the benefit of Hephzibah's labor for sixteen years, that they were reluctant to lose it, and that she wanted to leave.

Hephzibah's departure from the Stribling farm, or at least the timing of that departure, may have been precipitated by the Civil War. John Williams eventually served in the Union army, and Elizabeth then needed help with their farm, the household, and the children. Hephzibah and Fred could provide that help. We do not have letters from Hephzibah or John documenting such a plan, but it seems reasonably clear from the subsequent history and from Stribling's letter that this is what in fact occurred. Without the war's demand for John's services, Hephzibah might, perhaps, have continued to delay her decision and might then have remained at the Stribling farm for yet more months or years. The war altered lives in many ways, direct and indirect.

From: Hephzibah
To: Jemima

Sunny Dell January 4th 1861

My Dear Sister

Eighteen sixty—with all its joys and sorrows, distressing doubts and anxious cares. Its hours of sunshine and hours of shade. Its moments of pleasure and moments of pain. Has past. It has been the last year of earthly life to many, and the first year of earthly life to many more.

Among the former is the name of one that will shock you, to hear Julia C. Walter died the 24th of Dec. I tried to go to her burying the 25th but did not get there in time. I hoped to see the family but as they were just starting another way we did not meet them. She was buried at Mr. Mortons grave yard which is about a quarter of a mile from his house. I went with Jane and Fannie. Who would have thought when we saw her at the Fair that she would have been called so soon. She certainly appeared more like living than either you or I. But Julia is gone and we remain. I should dearly love to visit the family but how to get there is a problem. Poor Magg. I feel for her, she lookes so poorly. She appears to me like one who had a heart full of trouble. And I do not doubt that it is the case. The whole family have been sick I hear. They were all at the burying except Harvey who was too unwell to be out. Typhoid fever, was the disease of which she died. The Tody girls and myself have talked of going to see the family but I dont know how it will be. For grandma dont seem any more willing for me to go than she did before. But if I get a chance, I think I shall risk her displeasure and go. She seems to think if anything will bring Mrs. W. down it is this. I heard that she took Julias death very hard indeed. I have heard very little concerning the way she died. She was not conscious at the time but a few days before she told them she thought that she would die and that she was willing.[19] Julia professed religion and joined the church at Salem during the protracted meeting three winters since. She is the third of those that then united with the church that have gone hence. And I trust they are all resting in pease.

 I hoped to have written to you Christmass day but after finishing a letter to brother John I had not time and I have been busy ever since. Sarah and Mary came out the Thursday after Christemass and spent the night and part of the next day with us. Sarah wished to stay untill the next Tuesday, but Mary would have her go back to town as she expected to starte to Griggsville the next morning and she dreaded crossing the [Illinois] river so much. She had such a time getting over when she came, and she wanted Sarah to stay with her and keep her spirits up untill she started. Sarah, however came out Monday evening and went back Tuesday. Mary wrote a letter last month and directed it to your sister, though the contents were addressed mostly to Mr. and Mrs S—[Stribling]. I was not dispose[d] to find fault with the arrangement. As it was designed for all, I was willing the most should apply to them. For I know that old people are apt to be sensitive at least they are and feel a little lack of attention more than a young person. Mary writes well. I think a few sentences will pleas you and also give you an idea of her style: "I have a very interesting school of about 45 boys, A perfect little army, all to teach to fight for "The Right." I sometimes fancy that among them, perhaps, are Ministers, Authors, and Statesmen and maybe, a President, Most certainly, they are destined soon to take responsible places in life, and this makes me feel my responsibility as a teacher and I would naturlly shrink from it, were it not for the consoling thought that I claim to be in the wake of Providence. . . ." Many times have we gone oute there with our hearts burdened with care, and our spirits almost crushed by the bluntings and trials of life, and felt that we had found a quiet resting place, a tempting harbor into which we could gently moor and cast anchor in sweet composure for a few days. And, after disburdening our frail barque of its surplus burden, we would float oute on Monday Morning into heigh sea, with our sails all straightened for another week's steering against the breakers and among the rocks, and quicksands, in the sea of a teachers life."[20] When here she urged me to write to her, I should like to do it if I thought myself capable of doing such a thing. But I can tell you that I dont relish the idea of writing to her in the blundering way that I am in the habit of doing. Mary is a quick observer, and I dont like to expose my ignorance. I think it is quite bad enough that I should know it with oute making it a public matter.

I can tell you Sis that a few moments thinking of the deficiency of my education makes me anything but happy. It does not make me feel very kindly towards people in general and a few in particular. I have been foolish enough to imagin that while I have been trying to serve others and make them comfortable, often to the forgetfulness of self, that sometime in the bright future there was a <u>good time coming for me</u>. But weeks months and years pass restlessly on. And Hope defered makes the heart sick. You are taking music lessons and in other ways trying to improve. I am glad you are. I used to think my advantages were as good as yours. I dont think so now. For while you have gone from good to better, I have stopped . . . or if I advance at all—it is backwards.

You think of writing to Mr. Jaquess [former president of the College]. I hope you may derive pleasure and profit therefrom. I think if you write for Mrs J-[21] it will be an unpardonable slight to neglect Miss Olin[22] as she is in the same institution. I move therefore that Miss Olin be invited.

Three Saturdays since the Misses Seeman, Stribling and Colwell came oute to engage Cedar to adorn the Chapel for the paper reading to come off the next Friday night. I was invited but did not go as we were in the midst of hog killing.[23] Miss C—is a sister of Grace's, she graduates this year. Annie Seyes [daughter of missionaries to Liberia] and Sarah B was oute when the girls came. Annie is boarding in the building—taking music and French lessons. She is not yet out of her term and has graduated in the classicall course more than a year since. This thought started me on a not very pleasing track. She expects her Mother home in the Spring, or rather hopes she will come.

So Mima . . . did not tell me whether your tooth had been extracted or broken off. Do you expect to have one put in its place?

While you were here you once spoke of Mr. P—having said that the Protestants' had persecuted the Catholics or something of that sort. I thought they had but grandpa did not seem to know, I believe. Well, we have a borrowed book here. It is a magaziene which has been bound, entitled "Monthly Literary Miscellany." I have read a piece there in entitled "A Walk in Westminster Abbey." The name of the author is not given. . . . I have read the sermon, you sent and like it very well. I could almost tell when I came to the places where Mother with a nod of the head would say "<u>Yes Yes</u>" bless her: There was one text of scripture that he quoted, that I should like to have his authority for saying that it ment that it was the law not the slavery that was to be perpetual. I asked grandpa. He refered me to Clark and Benson,[24] but they are silent. You see how long a letter I have written and yet there are many things I wish to say. Give my love to the children. Grandma joins me in sending love to all. A happy New Year to you all. Write soon will you? I remain your devoted. Eppie

From: L. P. Horrell
Envelope Address: Miss Jemima Dumville, Carlinville, Illinois

Scott County   Jan 6th 1861

Dear Sister Jemima

. . .

You spoke of money; and religion as being very scarce, and not looking for much better until Lincoln was elected; well Lincoln is elected! but religion has not become very flourishing, money is scarce—enough yet we have no cause for complaint.

. . .

Religious matters are not very flattering here; but we hear that it is not so dull some other places. Brother Huckstep received a letter from Stephen yesterday; from Rushville; stating he was in a glorious revival; there had been over 60 convertions, at one appointment and 70 or more accessions; at another place 12 or 14 accessions and about as many convertions and the altar crouded with penitents;

. . .

L. P. Horrell

From: Hephzibah
To: Jemima

Jacksonville   Feb 3th 1861

My dear sister . . . I should dearly love to go to school but, such a thing is oute of the question this year. If I could make it convenient to go next year at the beginning of the term I dont know but I should like it. though I feel a little ashamed to go now I used to think I never should feel so, but I often think of and feel the force of an [?] which you made while here.
We are now only where we should have been ten years ago.
Last winter I hoped to get through my Arithmatic but did not quite do it. I should like to have begun this winter where I left off but have not had the chance as yet.
Since Mrs Lurton has had an addation to her family.[25] Dollie [4 years old] and Robbie [3 years old] have been there with us all the time, we brought Dollie home today and expect her to stay. Robbie will go back, Joe [Johanna, 12 years

old] staid with us a week and Willie [aged 17] comes oute at night and home again in the morning to school. So you can guess what chance I have had lately to study . . .

You must be sure to send this letter back to me. There was twelve little papers of flower seed in their letter done up very nicely with the name written on. I will divide them between you and Lizzie, but will not send them this time as the two letters will be enough.

Mary Hannah, the youngest of Mary's[26] girls as she notes, sent me a note to let me see how good she writes, and she writes well I assure you, also a nice little Valentine with two pretty verses on it entitled "A Blessing." She wants my likeness. I should like to send it. I am glad that Mary seems so alive to the education of her children.

There has been a very good meeting at Salem but it is closed now. There was over twenty joined, but I did not go at all. The roades was bad and I had no way to go. Certainly we have [?] trouble to compare with those girls of which you wrote! Trust me, never may you doubt the men get the most pity and the girls the most blame, but it is not right. "The serpant is carressed and the victems cast oute."[27] To steal a horse is a penitentiary act. but to destroy a female caracter is gentalmanly. I think tarring and feathering is too good. They ought to be hung or whipped half to death.

. . . I hear that William Milburn and father Cartwright are going to Europe to deliver lectures. Uncle Peter has been lecturing in New York and has given $500 to the College that he made by it. I guess he will make a [-] little sum by his lectures in the old World. You know that anything from America takes there. We see the truth of this in the number of people that go from there to watch.

. . . Fred [Bechly] has made a bow for your fiddle. I told him he would have the use of it if he wished to.

I have written a letter to Mary such as it is. . . . I must close now [-] What I think of the war and the south. I shall greatly oblige you. Write soon now and you will tell you at some other time. devoted sister Eppie

My love to Ma and all.

If you write to Iowa tell them aboute the letter and let me know you have done so, or perhaps I shall them the same story if I ever write to them again.

From: John Williams
To: Ann and Jemima

Feb 3 1861 Powshiek Co Iowa

Deare Mother & Sister we received youres thee last day in the yeare. Was glad to heare of youre good health & prospects in the future. We enjoy moderate good health & feel thankful to the giver of all good for his care & providence extended to us. Altho we feel the pressure of the times we hope for the beter as soon as the Political horison is settled but when will that be? The dark future must tell. The Sword will have to do its work first if the sines of the times dos not deseave me. Treason stalk abroad in open day & the storme gathers blackness & darkness & if not arested must break in awfull reality to the weal or wo[e] of one or the other party. Oure hole land is filled with Torys & Traitors preaching peacible secession.[28] Such men would pitch & straw in a hurican & say peace be still. Who canot say the north is not a slumbering volcano gathering slow but sure strength & if once breaks fourth whoo will be able to stand before the violence & fury of the storme & if the main of the Northren war horse gets up may not the Lion tremble in his lair. I have a friend in Canada who says England will not be an idle spectator in the contest. Perhaps I have said enough on the all absorbing question of the day but here we are in the midst of a set of disunion traitors so that a fiew gallons of sod corne juse woulde set them on but they may expect the grit for their mettal,

We have no meetings this winter so we are quite nominal [minimal?], we had a fine fall up to Nov 20 when the first snow came. Theire has been sleding ever since. We have two big snows, the first a fiew days before Chrismas which was 11 inches deep. The other some two weeks ago that made it Some 3. It is very harde geting about as the snow is drifting & shifting about. I am doing nothing but geting wood & feeding. Theire is very little going about as the roads is to break every time the wind blows. . . .

The cars is runing in the next Co east of us & the probability is that the road will be in Grinell by the midle of summer. We will look for our friends to visit us then as they have been waiting its completion. I do not now think of athing more that woulde be of interest to rite. The Sermon you spoke of sending has not come to hand yet. The girls is going to school when the wether will admit of it. Give oure love to all enquireing friends.

 Adue

 J. W. Williams

 Inhast [In haste?] you two com and seus [see us?]

 Elizabeth Williams

From: Hephzibah
Envelope address: Miss Mima Dumville, Carlinville Illinois

Sunny Dell March 8th 1861[29]

Dear Sister

 I have not often had my sympathy so fully aroused as I had one moonlight night a few weeks since, It was on this wise—I was sleeping in the trundle bed with Robin and was awakened a little after twelve by hearing some one in the room say "who is there?" and the reply "It is Fannie." Grandma asked me to open the door. I did not wait for a second bidding. When the door was opened there stood Fannie P[osey][30] almost in disabille.[31] she had on her dress an[d] a shawl thrown around her head as though she had not had time for getting anything els. Why Fannie I began, what is the matter? "Ah we got frightened" Come in what frightened you? and how did it happen? She went on to tell us that she and Jane were alone and at twelve some one nocked at the kitchen door they supposing it to [be] John [their younger brother]. Jane jumped up and ran down stairs to let him in. before opening the door, however, she had the prudence to ask, "John is that you?" No reply was given. She called again, again, again, but still no answer, she became so frightened that she went back up stairs and told Fan—It could not be John or he would speak. She looked out at the windows to see if she could see anything of him, but she could not. At last she felt so badly that she told Fannie to get up and they would come here. Fannie hesitated. When Jane remarked if you felt as frightened as I do you would go, F—then got up they sliped out at the front door locked it after them and ran over here. I proposed taking them right to bed, but Jane seemed as though she wanted to go back home saying if Fred or Willie would go with her she would not be afraid, so I went to call Fred but before he could get down stairs and ready to start Fannie was streached out on the floor in a fit. As soon as she recovered a little we put her on the bed I had been sleeping in. Fred went over East but did not see any one though he heard a noise as though some one was passing through the gate towards the [house?]. John did not come home till four in the morning, so we know it was not him. Jane and I went to bed but not to sleep as neighther of us slept at all. She then told me that it was not for her self she feared so much as Fannie but the idea of their being alone and a man trying to get in the house, Fannie liable at any moment to take a fit, and then the impossibility of getting away all together made her feel like getting away while she could. And I thought they were wise in doing so. I know I was glad they did come. And we made them promis not to stay alone again. They came over last night and Sarah with them.

I have always been inclined to take Johns part and thought he had not been treated right. I have changed my mind some. . . . He has left those girls night after night alone not returning till twelve and any time after that or perhaps not at all. Knowing at the same time that they were staying to accomodate him with a home as much as any thing els. [Their mother had died the year before, see April 22, 1860 letter.] They have determined now to leave, the place is to [be] sold the 16 inst. they will leave then if not before.[32] They are both going to live at Margrets.[33] . . . I shall feel lonly then but I dont blame them for going.

What I think about the affairs of the Nation it will be rather hard to tell. When I first heard talk of S. C. leaving the Union I did not know but she could do so without leave or license. I felt sorry to think that she had any notion of going out but thought it could not be helped. I soon saw, however, that she had no right to go with out consent from the other States and also that this is not the first time that she has threatened to leave. Then I concluded that she was trying some of her old tricks and would cool down presently as she had done aforetime. But as the secession fever seemed rather to gain instead of loosing ground and State after State declared herself out of the Union,[34] I felt right badly and I would try to get all the news hoping to hear something encouraging but not one ray of hope could I find. I really began to dispare, then came a lull in the storm and hope began to revive. I have all along thought if Lincoln could get to Washington and the fourth of March could pass without blood-shed there would be great cause to think that the greatest danger had passed for the present. Those two events have passed. Lincoln has been peaceably Inaugurated at Washington, which you know some said should never be.

When I heard the boom of the Canon on the evening of the fourth and learned what it was for I was glad indeed. But right along with it came the news that [John M.] Palmer had returned and said there was <u>no hope</u>. The Union would be divided, and that Virginia had gone too or would before he could get home.[35] I thought that was worse than ever. All I can say is that if after reading the Presidents address the South will presist in disobeying the laws of the United States hand them over to the tender mercies of the soward [sword], and give the leaders the same treatment that John Brown received. I am very much pleased with the conduct of Mr Lincoln, his silence before starting to the Capitol and his speeches since.[36] I think with others that he is the man for the hour.

He has the prayors of the good in this and other lands and the good wishes of all lovers of right and liberty with the blessing of the Almightly he must succeed. I have read S[e]wards speach[37] and like it well. Dont you?

You think I am a long time getting to the subject which has been on your mind and mine ever since I began this letter. Well I first thought when reading that part of your letter that you thought of marrying someone whom you thought I should object to, [-] or two and I knew it was not that. Then I thought sis is going to write a piece for the Advocate and wants to know what I think of it. Wrong again I soon found. Then I thought I would let you tell me your self which you were rather slow in doing and for which I was not particularltly greatful. I was frightened before finding out what it was and surprised afterwards. You are waiting to hear what I think.[38] It is not a wild undertaking. There are dangers and difficulties on the way and when you get there, dangers and difficulties and privations will not deminish.

But they will not be greater than thousands have endured in going to California to make a fortune. Should you go I shall hardly hope to see you again in this world. Still others have gone there and have lived many years and you might be one more that could bear the climate. Along the coast it is not healthy, though some say it is not more unhealthy than the Atlantic of South Carolina, at least parts of it. The interior of Africa is not so unhealthy, indeed some say it is healthy, but whether it is so for a white man I cannot say. I heard Mr. Seyes when he was here . . . that Africa is emphatically the black mans country as it is rarely that a white man can long exist there. Yet he has been there thirteen years or more, and his wife has not been dangerously sick that I have heard since being there. The last time though she had been away eighteen years.[39] Africa is eminently the country that is at the present time attracting the notice of explorers and scientific men.

If you could get the works of Livingston[40] it might give you some valubel information. Monrovia is the name of the town where Mr. Seyes has been, and from the ammount of its exports I should think it a place of importance. In [18]59 the exports were $190,369,22; imports, $143,858; excess of exports over imports, $46,515.22; And I expect it was greater last year. As for the costume, white is mostly worn light lawns or calicos are worn a little. They need no winter clothing as they have no winter . . .

Now Sister I have written all this and yet I dont expect you to go. If you think the path of duty leads that way I shall not object to your walking in it though it takes you to "Africas sunny fountain."[41] But I think it well for us both to remember that it is one thing to contemplate the dangers and privations of such a course . . ., here at home with the comforts of life aboute us and altogether another thing to go forth and hear them. I rather think when the time for parting comes we will both shrink. Still if the Lord has called you to the work surely So will prepare you for it and sustain you in it. . . . Should you determine to go and after suffering much should die in a far off foreign land it would be consoling to think that you fell at your post and in a glorious cause.

I have not spoken of this to any one. Write soon and let me know if you still feel like going. Should [you] do so I want it understood that I am to come and live with Ma so she need not make other arangments. Perhaps I may come any way if you encourage me a little.

From: Hephzibah
To: Jemima

Monday March 11th [1861][42]

Dear Mima

Tell Ma that I sent the letter to Mr. Mathers. . . . Grandpa did not sign his name or try to get any one els to do so. They generally think they have enough to do to make them selves comfortable with out trying to attend to the wants of any thing or any body els and after all is done they are not comfortable. Perhaps I ought not to say this as they sent ten dollars to Kansas.[43] I received a letter from John [Williams] lately . . . he was in fine spirits apparently, after being silent so long, one thing he mentioned which always gives me the blues to think aboute. These are his words. "I do not like to meddle with family affairs but I will ask what you are doing for your self. Are you making any thing for a rainy day after you spend youth and vigor with out proper renumeration and saving something for the future to look to what are we living for but to be dependent on some one els as long as we live."

    Now I imagine I shall feel rather like a fool to tell him that I have lived here 14 years and yet do not know what I am to get for it or whether I shall get anything. I used to think when anything was said about these things that it was unnecessary caution. I now think to have had this matter settled long ago would have only been wise prudence. I can hardly think Grandma will be willing that I shall have nothing but how much the good part which she has always promised will amount to is for the future to reveal. Mrs. Tiller promised you a good part and we have long been in possession of inestimable blessings. I used to think that Grandma was almost the embodyment of exelence and of course would do what was right. She often says that she wants you and Mother to be satisfied. I think she ought to tell me just what she does intend to do, and if I had not such an insurmountable dislike to talking of the hateful thing I would know. . . . Send me the letter that Grandpa sent to Ma before I came here[44] and let me see if there is anything worth a cent in that. While writing the quotation from John's letter, Grandma came and stood by me a moment or so. . . . Finally she said "Tell your mother to pray for me—more ardently than ever." I thought if she knew what I was writing she would hardly have said it, after all I can't help feeling sorry for her sometimes. I don't know but it is better to have a light [purse?] than a hard heart. You must write a letter to Mary [their English half-sister] and then send it and her letter to me that I may do so to. Enclosed are some flower seed she sent me. I shall send some to Iowa. I must close though I am not done. Give my love to all and write very soon. I shall feel anxious to hear. Your devoted sister. Eppie

From: L. P. Horrell

Scott County, Ill, March 29th 1861

Dear Sister Jemima

    We received your letter of Feb 25, and was very glad to hear from you, especially as you so generously pardoned my former negligence conditionally. Well as we cannot always do as we wish we must do the best we can in our circumstances. So, as it is very rainy today, I will mak[e] a virtue of necessity and write while I cant be out at work, (which there is plenty of). We are all pretty well at present, and hope when this comes to hand, it may find you all enjoyin the same blessing.

    O how thankful we ought to be, when we think of the goodness of God, in daily ministering to all our returning wants, Annis's youngest sister, (Martha Stagle) has been laboring for 5 or 6 weeks under mental derangement. Although a very exemplary Christian, she seems to have conceived the idea that she is the vilest of the vile. She had been attending a protracted meeting (near Bakers) at Rutledge Chapel, for near 4 weeks, previous to her becoming irrational; she now seems at time to be better; yet she is very flighty. . . .

We have a very good preacher. Brother Sweeny held a protracted meeting which lasted near 2 weeks without any marked effect. Temporaly we have nothing to boast of. We have very little money; cannot collect what is due; yet we have enough to eat and wear without getting much in debt.

. . .

Your brother in Christ
L. P. Horrell

From: Hephzibah
To: Ann and Jemima

Sunny Dell May 6th 1861

Deary Mother and Sister

Both of your letters were received last Thursday and as you will readily guess, have been the cause of a great deal of talk, and overhauling of old events and sayings, that had almost become buried beneath the accumelation of years. Perhaps too, it had been better that some of them had been entirely buried, however it is hard to tell always just what is the best to be done and then again what is best to be left undone.[45] . . . By the way who wrote that letter for Mother? And why did not you do it? . . . Grandma wishes me to say for her that she greaty regrets very much that you and my sisters have had their minds kept in a state of uneasiness on account of no agreement having been made between her and you about what I was to get for staying with them. The reason of it is, that you never spoke of the matter but once and I then did not seem satisfied remarking that I had expected to live as one of the family and was unwilling to remain on any other terms. All she could then do was to request me to keep an account of all my expenses (which I have tried to do)[46] and then when I left she could determine what she could do for me. Now as you desire the matter to be settled, to which she has no objections, she is willing to give me 500, dollars,[47] which is now in bank, and also a bed and some bed cloths, bedstead, and a cow, which I can take now or let them stay here untill I leave, as I see proper. She wishes you to be satisfied and if you are not, to speak your mind freely, that she has always intended to do right, and still intends doing so if I remain with her, though as times are at present she does not feel free to place herself under obligations to any great extent. She still desires an intrest in your preyers and hopes that nothing that may have been said or done will cause you to loose confidence in her, that she wishes very much to see you and have a talk with you then she could say many things that would be hard to make you understand by writing.[48] And I very much wish she could see both you and

Mima together for it is out of the question for me to make her think that Mima is any other than our [her] enemy, and regards her with feelings of unkindness. Though she thinks that Mima got her start in the world here and that what she is enjoying now or may ever enjoy will be to some extent in consequence of her privileges here and I think there is more truth [than] poetry [to] it. You will not deny that, will you? I wish in my heart you could be better friends. I am sorry to think that two persons whom I wish to love so much should not love each other.

    Grandma wishes to know if I will still remain with her. I told her that I had always felt as though I could not remain here only as one of the family; that I knew a girl that had to work for herself away from home was not as much respected as others and on that account I thought I had better go home to Mother when she should get to keeping house to her self. Another reason I gave was that I was not satisfied with my education and you Mima could help me very much in my studies. She replied that she thought with Mother that so long as a girl behaved herself well and kept a regular home she could not see why she was not as much respected as any one els and if I wished to go to school again I could go from here as well now as when you went with me, and if I wished I could start as early in the fall as convenient and go during the winter and she would help me all she could to get off in time, adding you know I [Mrs. Stribling] have often said that if we moved to town I [Mrs. Stribling] intended you [Hephzibah] should go to school more, and I would have been willing for you to have gone from here some years since. It could have been more convenient then than now, still I am willing for you to go now if you wish. I answered I would ask Ma about it. It will be something of a task for me to go now, feeling as I do, that I am so much behind the times. Yet if I do not go I may see the time that I shall wish I had. Tell me what you think I had better do. Grandma wishes to know as soon as possible what I will do. She would rather I would stay if I can feel content to do so. If I do not stay she wishes to know [so] that she may make other arangements. Tell me again what I had better do.

    Of the 500 which I am to get I should like to send 375 to you as you say that you have no trouble in lending it with a good prospect of getting it back with interest and I would like to get interest on that much. The rest I will keep here as I may find use for it before I come to see you. You must not think from the first of this letter that we have had anything like a quarrel, not at all. I think we have kept our tempers admirably, considering that it is no secret that we both have tempers.

    I think you have done the children all the good you will be likely to do them and as soon as they can leave you conveniently let them go with your blessing for if they stay many months or years longer you may have no blessing to give them at parting. Tell me also if you intend building this summer. . . .

    As for war news, six car loads of soldiers came to Jacksonville this morning to remain till called. I fear they will have a stormey time at Ca[i]ro, but if they do have a battle there I do hope and pray that our soldiers may gain a compleat victory and in all other engagements which they may have. Have you heard that the Rebels have possession of Washington? I have not and I trust I never may though they boasted that they would have it by the first of this month and Independance Hall by the fourth of July. They will have to wake up before day light and ketch our men napping before they make either of those boasts good. I read the sermon preached to the Jacksonville volunteers in Strawns hall by Bro Sanders. It was very good. . . . I did not go in to see the soldiers leave because I did not know there would be any parade, but I expect it was quite as solemn as the parting you saw. Two flags was presented by Miss Kirby, one to the Hardin volenteers and the other to the Home Guards.[49] A short speech was made by her and a reply by one of the soldiers. Both was printed. They went away amid the tears, prayers, and well wishes of friends, the booming of cannon, and waving of flags.

. . . There is some talk of Rev William Rutlege going as chaplain. Two of Mr. Delzells sons have volenteered in another state also a soninlaw of Mr.D—. . . . Sarah and Mary came when I had written this much and say those car loads of soilders did not stop in town. They were going under sealed orders to Quincy it was thought. . . . Now Sister dont feel too badly about this letter, write to me soon and tell me just what you think I had best do under these circumstances. I cant help feeling sorry for them when I see how lonely and unhappy they are. I know you pray for us. Still, do so.

Eppie

From: Hephzibah
To: Jemima

Sunny Dell, August 26th [1861][50]

Dear Mima

Have you been expecting to hear from me for a long time? Perhaps I ought to have written but really I have been buisy and am more so at present than ever trying to get ready to come to see you. I should like very much to come a week before Conference begins, but I dont see how I can as the fair will be next week and I want to put some apples out to dry before I leave. I want to grandma to get some one to stay with her while I am away but she wont hear to it. Grandpa, grandma, Willie, and Joe spent week before last visiting near Virginia [about fifteen miles north of Jacksonville]. The two first named did not enjoy themselves much but the two [children] I suppose had a grand time. Sarah staid with me in their absence. She begins teaching next Monday in North East

August 27 [apparently Hephzibah continued the letter the next day]
District where she taught last year. She made a visit to Champaign City [approximately 120 miles northeast of Jacksonville] some time since to Mary

and Greenberry McElfresh. . . . I should like to know who are the preachers that are to stay with you. John M—L—was at our house yesterday with his wife and was wondering if they would do him the favor to send him to Mother Dumvilles. To day Mr. Vickers and lady are spending the day with us. They are both English. She has not been here in the country four months yet. Mr. V. is one of our preachers and a fine one he is too.

. . .

I dou[b]t but General Scot[51] lost a great deal of valubel information by not being here Monday to hear Mr. Lanes plan for taking Richmond. To hear him talk you would think that if he had had charge of military matters the Rebellion would have been crushed out in 6 mo and he would now be marching triumphantly toward Richmond which he thinks can be taken easily enough.

I have not time to write much now and I soon expect to see you. O, how I want the time to come. I shall come down the Saturday before Conference if I can if not on Monday. . . .

My love to all if you want anything write to me before I come.

Your devoted sister

Eppie

From: John Williams
To: Jemima

Sept 1, 1861

Sister J.D, about the first of July I rote to you & have been anxiously waiting an answer. . . . In youre last you said mother had promised to go with Palmers Reg[iment]. In my last I gave my protest against it. I enterain the same opinion yet that she shoulde not go. We . . . are very anxious to [know] if she went or not.

I sent you one of my papers that had the proseedings of the Stump tailed democracy[52] of this Co. The names with a pencil circle around them lives within 6 miles of us & several in the immediate neighborhood & latley they boast of an organization of three hundred. . . . When I tolde you that were ware prepared for the trators you must not think we go with revolver & buoe [bowie?] nife all tho we kneed them badly for we may have serious work before three months passes by. I lack the means to get them is the reason that I am without. The big rifle is all my defence.[53] If the Gard dos not defend us & vindicate the right our hopes are gon & we must be opressed by tyrants but we must use all the means in oure reach to sustain our rights & liberties. My means is small as harde times is closing down on us. G[r]ain produce is low & money scarse & theire apeares nothing but gloom & darkness before us, I had asked you for the lone of some money & I have been looking anxiously for some but suppose you have failed to get any in. If you get it I shall be thankful of the favor. My circumstances is close as I made some trades last winter with the prospect of moderate good times this season. I had 40 1/2 acre broke the past season. The principal part is paid for & bought 5 acres of timber for $120.00. I have paid $62 1/2 on it besides some other debts I have been oblige[d] to make this summer. I have 80 acres inclosed & 23 broke that I want to take in this winter to sow in wheat in the spring I will fat 25 hogs & calulate on 200 bu of wheat, what is only 35 to 45 at Oskaloosa,[54] . . . Will you rite immediately.

J. W. Williams
to J. D.

From: John Williams
Envelope address: Mrs Ann Dumvill, Carlinvill Macoupin Co Ill

Sept 29 1861

Deare Mother & Sister we received yours of Aug 29 in due time containing a check of fify Dollars, which was a favor in need . . . Crops is fare. I have 30 acres of corne that will average 40 or 50 bushels per acre, about 12 of wheat that is fare besides 14 acres of sod corne 2 acres of cane which we want to comence to work up in a day or two. Wm. Fillmer has been drove out of Mo. He is in Polk Co. Iowa. He has been badly treated by the Mo. rabble. We have a great many Jeff Davis sympathizers here & theire is some prospect of them carying the state election which may cause war here on the same ground as it started in Mo & Ky. nearly all that can be induced to volinteer has been taken out of the state & yet theire is a heavy call for more. We are looking for a draft to come on us in a week or ten days. & if it dose come it will be the breaking up of a great many poor families. For my part I do not see how I coulde go without losing a great deal or perhaps all & life to[o]. If I coulde leave here we woulde be off in a short time but I [need to] have the means to meet my debts.[55]

I hope to be able to meet the demands against me if pork is a fare price. I will have 20 hogs to sell & some wheat. . . . Come to see us if you can & we will do the Same.

J.W. Williams

Sister rite Elizabith Williams.

From: Dan Cheney
To: Jemima

Cairo, Ills.[56]   Oct the 18 1861

Miss gemima . . .

Respected Friend, thinking perhaps you would like some inteligence from camp this evening I seat or rather lay myself down in tent to address you a few lines but before proceeding any farther I will ask you to please excuse all mistakes bad writeing but for I have no seat desk or any thing else to write upon but will try however to interest you for a little while but there are so many things here of rather an exciting and interesting nature to write about that I hardly know where to begin.

I will first give you a slight [poem?]or idea of our location. We are located gust back of the citty in the valley camp [Midelenand?], Defiance. Birds, [?] and fors [forest?] [?] are all in cannon shot of each other and pretty well fortified, there is also a knew camp forming a few miles below Cairo on the Ky, shore at which the searchers seem to have a particular spite to judge from the way it seemes to annoy them,

We expect a fight here or some whereelse soon but when the call comes We expect to march on to the battlefield as one man bearing with us the old flag of our country determined it shall never fall while We stand.

Jemima, I should surely love to visit you, see all the folks and have a social talk. my friend Ben Stead received a letter from you yesterday.

I was happy to learn you have not forgotten me. You cannot imagine the pleasure it afford us to heare from you. I must thank you a thousand times for your kind wishes and advice We will take it to our selfs and think of it while on the battlefield.

Now, Jemima, as my time is a bout out will you keep no doubt [?] sending [?] will close [?] you. So please favor me with an immediate answer. Give my love to yourself, sister, and all the folks.

Good bye from your friend

Dan Levi Cheney

Miss Harris[57] [included with the letter to Jemima]

As I have a few leisure moments I will improve them by writing [?] with you a few moments. Mary you will no doubt consider me very bold for taking liberty to address you thus. But considering me a friend I hope you will be generous to me. Mary as I feel rather lonely this evening I would like to write a long letter to you but as the drum is calling us into ranks I can only write enough to convince you that I have not forgotten you.

Now Mary if you consider this little note worthy of an answer I should like very much to heare from you. Good bye Please write soon. Accept the best wishes from your friend.

Dan Levi Cheney

From: Hephzibah
To: Ann and Jemima

Sunny Dell   Nov 25th, 61

Dear Mother and Sister, I know you are looking impatiently for this letter and I had hoped to have been able to have sent it to you last week but I have been so buisy. We have dried a large quantity of apples since I came home, perhaps six or seven bushels, but as we have a peeler and a dry house it was not such a great job.[58] Since we finished that I have been trying to do a little knitting and sewing but precious little I have done yet. I have but one calico dress to my back and that more than a year old and when I get the next one done is more than I can tell though I was trying the most of last week.

You know I must read come what will. I must read the Advocate when it comes and I must read The World when Sarah is kinde enough to send it to me. I spent the time last week which I intended to have occupied in writing to you in reading an account of the briliant victory of our fleet at Port Royal, which some what revived my drooping hope. For I had read of the miserable blundering of our officers at Leesburg and other places untill I was almost in dispair. By a great deal of perseverance I succeeded in getting through Louis Napoleon. I liked some parts very well. Sarah has it now and when she gets through Beck. Van Wincle wants it I hope they will take care of it. I charged them to do so. I intend if I can ever get a dollar and a quarter to spare to send it to Mr. Poe and Hitchchock publishers of the Advocate for them to send to some of the soldiers. They will send it for that amount and I think it will gladden the heart of some poor fellow. I am not particular who though I think I shall request it to be sent to Western Virginia as I think they are most needy. I wish you would join me in this. Can't you sis. I have to pay Dr. S—thirty dollars yet which I am anxious to do right soon.

Grandma and myself were in town some weeks since and chanced to meet Dem Rosson. Poor girl she seemed glad to see us and I felt sorry for her. Her husband is as strong and helthy a man as you will find but actually to[o] lazy to breath[e] if it required an effort to do so. If ever I marry I do hope I may not be cursed with a lazy husband for I do think it is enough to torment the life out of any woman who has a spark of spirit. Dem works hard I know. She begins to look old, had no hoops on and her dress was faded. Grandma gave her ten yards of calico. I hope to do as much soon.

Ah! was not that a mysterious dispensation of providence I refer to the death of James Barger.[59] We called to see Mrs. B. a few days before it happened. She seemed very anxious aboute her boys in the army, remarking that the[y] weighed on her mind all the time and that she was continually praying for them, but that she did not feel so about James. When to be the first taken. I hope he was prepared to go but I should have felt better had he said so. We called again to see them last Monday, but Mrs B- had gone with her husband to his appointment and there was no one at home but Mattie [James's wife]. She is a very pleasant woman I think. She told us that Elisa bore her bereavement with astonishing fortitude and when the old lady expressed her satisfaction at seeing her so compose she replied that it was the grace of God alone that enabled her to do so. It was that that sustained her. Mattie told us that when James was brought home she brought a bowl of water and washed his face, took everything out of his pockets and took of(f) his watch and when others offered to do it she said no it was the last she could do for him and she would do it, that she felt as though she did not want any one to do anything for him that she could do. She tried to comfort her Mother in law and also the man that killed him. She had just mad(e) a fire in their front room and drawn his chair to do it and placed his slippers ready for him when he should return from his hunt and did not know of his death untill a few moments before they brought him in a corpes. I do not know whether she blaimes herself for not letting him to the army or not but I think I should if [I] was in her place. [?] is still with her, and Mattie think she will make her home in Decator.[60] . . .

Another distressing occurrance is the burning of our College.[61] Some speake of it as a mysterious dispensation of Providence. But I rather think it was a plain dispensation of Carelessness. I am graitful however that the whole building did not go. I am inclined to think if Providence had anything at all to do with it, it was that part of it, for it does seem a wonder that it was saved. Another disagreeable feature in the matter is that there was only two thousand dollars insurance on it. Which Mr Stacy was responsible for. The other men having neglected to pay up, because of the hard times. After the fire was oute the walles still stood and seemed but little injured. A meeting of the trustees was held last Monday night and they determined to repair it. But the wind blew quit[e] hard Tuesday and part of the wall fell. Some fear that the Trustees will be broken up. Mr. Lurton is in for several thousand. He is wonderfully oute with the Methodists in town and declairs that they will not get any more money from him. That they made him a trustee in the first place without his knowlege and then would not let him off. That when they want money it is Brother Lurton, Bro. Lurton. But when he wants to get an office to support his family not a Methodist will vote for him. You must know he run for the office of Assessor this month and was beaton in town, but the other places in the county elected him. It must have been rather trying to his vanity to be beaton at home. I will entrust you with that secret. Mother may know it if she will keep it. It is not very marvelous.

From: Hephzibah
To: Jemima

Sunny Dell   Dec 23rd 1861

My Dear Sister

. . . I have five letters that I wish to write before the year is oute. This is the first and it should keep me buisy to get them all done besides the many other things I wish to accomplish. The reporte aboute those College girls getting so badly hurt was circulated in town, also I think one thing that gave rise to the report was this. As soon as the news of the fire reached Mrs. Lawsons she like a good sowl ran down to Mr Lurtons to try and help them. And as Joe [a

Lurton daughter] was sick in bed with an attack of pleurisy she had her taken up to her house, as it was feared Mr. Lurton's house could not be saved. Joe gave rather a laughable account of her trip, she says. They took me out of bed and as I had nothing on but an old calico nightgown they rolled me in a comforter and off we started with night cap on. When we got to the gate Ma sent me her shawl and my hood. I put it on and the string was sticking out but I did not care. The streets was ful of people and the way they did look at me and some asked if I was hurt. It was thought I was one of the College girls. When I got to Aunt Evelines ever so many came in to ask where I was burnt and how I was hurt. One fellow declared he saw a girl jump out of a window and break her leg. Of course he only imagined it as none of the girls was hurt at all. I went to the Phi Nu exhibition lately and in one of the papers a girl enumerated seven wonders of the day one of which was "the girl that jumped from the sixth story of this building without receiving any injury!" As the t[w]o societies have lost all their property by the fire, the Phi Nus asked a contribution of the friends in attendance for the purpose of replenishing their library. I don't know how much was given. Some promised books, I among the number. As I had nothing else to give I sent them my Elliot on Slavery two vol. that Ma gave me years ago,[62] which I have never read though I very much wished to do so. It was rather more than I bargained for, but I thought it might do them some good and it did not seem likely to do me any as I saw no prospect of reading it. There are so many works I want to read. I did right didn't I?

. . . I received a letter from Iowa last Saturday they were well except colds and John complained of haveing hurt his hip in Oct. and of having chills at the time he wrote. He spoke of being exceedingly busy, said he had made 1 1/2 bbls of molasses for themselves and 27 gal for a neighbor. That he had 100 bush of wheat thrashed and as much more in the stack, 30 hogs fattening with a rather poor prospect of getting a very good price for them when they were fat. The girls were going to school and Maggie seemed in earness about it for which I am glad. Lizzie is buisy too as a matter of course. She had just got 18 yds of linsey and 2 blankets home from the weavers and was getting more ready.

. . . I suppose you know that Mr. Leaton[63] takes James' [Barger's] place and Dr. Akers takes the station.[64] The Dr was here the same day that Mr. B. was, also Mr. Crain and James. We wished very much to hear the Dr tell about the events now transpiring in the country as we all think him one of the wisest men of the age, but he staid such a short time and there was so many here beside that we had no chance. I believe some say that he thinks all the old world will be engaged in the war before it is done and then the Millimum will begin. What does Ma think of Englands takeing sides against us. I was loude in my condemnation of her course in case she should go to waring with us because of the capture of Mason and Slidell. And I dont know but I went so far as to [say] if it did i would disown her. Dont you think it would be a great shock to her national dignity if I should do that? I fear it would be more than she could bear. To tell the truth I did not believe the reporte. I have believed all along and still believe that the masses of the English people are with us. I have expected England to behave magnanimously in this contest and am not prepared to be disappointed.

I am reading a book at present entitled Armageddon or the United States in Prophesy. I'll tell you about it in my next if you wish me. I assure you there is some strange things therein: I have sent you this letter for the Publishers. Pleas send it as soon as possible that they may get it before the year is oute. . . . I must close much against my will. Write soon. My love to all [?] in particular.

Eppie

[*upside down*] I have tried at 4 places to get this bill changed to no purpose so Ill send it to you and you must get it changed and send the .75 back to me in the form of stamps.

From: Jemima
Envelope address: Mr. Daniel L. Cheney, Camp McClennand, Cairo, Illinois[65]

Carlinville, Illinois
Jan 11th 1862

Friend Dan

You see that you were mistaken when you thought I should not answer your last letter, which I confess should have been done some weeks ago, but really I have not had time to do it. Perhaps I had better give you some idea of what we have to do and then you can judge how our time is taken up. Every day in the week a school of from 50 to 90 scholars engnasses [engages?] all the time from half after eight in the morning to five in the afternoon at night. The remainder of the time is devoted to sewing, knitting, visiting the sick an attending meetings which are held on Tuesday night and Wednesday night, and every other Thursday the Soldiers Aid Society meets in the afternoon and at night. They ladies have sent away three or four boxes to the hospitals. I wish you and Ben could get those warm gloves which I have knit for the soldier and some of the most needy had the warm socks but I hope they may be sent where they are most needed. We have not heard much about the health of the troops recently.

We have more sickness here at presen[t] than during the fall, and it is quite fatal or at least there have been a number of deaths. Mr. J. T. Daw[e]s the President of the Agricultural Society of Carlinville died on the 27th of Dec. As he was my class leader and our Sabbath School Superintendant. We have sustained a great loss, yet I rejoice to say that our loss is his infinite gain. His toils and cares are over, his quiet immovable breast will be heaved by affliction no more. He is associated with Moses, Daniel, Job, Abraham, Paul, Steven and a host which no man can number and the best of all is Jesus our redeemer is there.

His happy spirit is forever free from sin with God eternally shut in. Say you not in the language of one of yore "let me live, the life of the righteous and let my last days be like his?" In the world we have tribulation but in Christ we may have that peace to which the world is a stranger, which it cannot give, neither can it take away. As we look out over this world by means of the News-papers, we regret to say that we see little else but confusion blood-shed tyranny—and death. In anguish of heart we are ready to exclaim surely the powers of darkness are let loose and the king of sin reigns supreme in all lands.

Perhaps you get the news concerning the war as soon or befor us, however I have seen nothing worth naming recently. The most encouraging news is that your fleet is so near ready for a move down the river, near 70 vessels I think. I suppose you begin to think that the war will be lengthy as so little progress is made toward suppressing the rebellion, and those that should aid, are looking on carelessly or encouraging our enemies but surely the Lord is on our side;[66] and if so, what power or combination of powers, shall be able to crush us, or destroy us. . . . It is very easy to speak of others faults but we can not see our own the truth is we try to think we have none, and with beams in our own eyes we are trying to take the moats out of our brother's eye. I do not mean to say, however, that our sins are more numerous than those of the South. Not by any means. But I do mean to say we have faults and we should repent and bring forth works meet for repentence that the wrath of God might be turned away from us.[67]

We as a nation have sinned extremely. Of our national sins perhaps first in enormity Slavery in all its forms; and [bearing?] next is covetousness with its attendant evils; pride falshood and sacrilege each of which would bring a curse upon us, but we have and are guilty of all. As far as my information extends nearly all the nations of earth have been guilty of the sin of slavery not only enslaving blac[k] but their own children for it was in 1015 a law was passed forbiding the selling of their children in England,[68] but as civilization and christianity have progressed slavery and tyranny have disappeared in the same racio [ratio] "Do unto others as ye would that men should do unto" would forever forbid the enslaving of men women and children whether black or white but some presume to say that the scriptures teach the doctrine—yea that it is a command, and of course should elicit our attention, but there is a very striking difference between slavery of ancient and modern times, *then* the Jews might [buy?] of the heathen and all of the Gentile world were by the Jews denominated heathen. consequently in former times we were sold into slavery. Yet we could not convince an American or a European that it was just to enslave him never. O no but you may the black. What strange inconsistency. Were some to hear me to speak on this wise of slavery they would say, do you wish to live with the blacks and make them our equals? I would simply say <u>never</u>—they are a distinct people and God never designed it should be otherwise.[69] Yet while we could by no means make them our companions we should carefully avoid oppressing them and although many are opposed to the emancipation of the slave I firmly believe peace never will be restored unto us untill we as a nation repent of our profanity covetousness [?] and place our feet upon the neck of the monster slavery.

Sometimes [I] think I should be glad to visit the camps, and see many of my friends in the army but thus far it has not been practical and perhaps I never shall see them again in time . . .

Let me urge you and Benny Stead to be as faithful to the Captain of our Salvation as to the Stars and Stripes, for what profit would it be if you should gain the whole world and lose your precious immortal Souls . . . Ma joins me in my love to you and Ben and says she thinks of and prays for you every day. Write soon and I will try to be more prompt next time.

Jemima Dumville

I wish you a happy New Year, J. D.

From: Benjamin G. Stead, Cairo Illinois
Envelope address: Miss Gemima Domville, Carlingville Macoupin Co Ills

Jan the 29, 1862[70]

Dear friend,

It is snowing so i thought i would right you a few lines to keep out of mischief for you know thear is mischief of all kinds goen on of all kinds. Hear it is a hard place for a christian to live but i doe try to doe as near right as i can and i know my friends at home air praying for me and it does me good to know that they have not forgot me although[h] i am a good way from them. . . . I suppose you have heard of our march through kentucky before this time more than i can tel you. it was a bad time and it maid agreat maney of the boys sick. . . . Thear was 2 of our boys died last week . . .

Benjamin G. Stead
to Miss Gimma Dumville
give my best respects to all enquireing friends.

From: Daniel Cheney
To: Hephzibah

Direct your Letters to Co O 32 Reg Ills or whare ever you heare of us last.

Forte Henry Tenn   Feb 14th/62
Miss Domville

Dear Hep

I recevd your kind & interesting letter yesterday evening and you have no idea how glad I was to heare from you and the friends at home. It was a rich treat for it was the firs[t] line I have received from Carlinville since I have been down in the land of Secesh [Secessionists] or as we sometimes say down in Dixie. We ware Stationed at Birds Point MO for a week then ordered heare. We got here last Monday night. We are just beginning to learn some of the hardships of War in the way of being up all night bored & hungry tho we doant complain. I suppose you have heard long before this of the batle heare and perhaps more than I can tell you but I will Try and tell you Something. This place was very Strongly fortified for miles round. The Rebels have bin at work heare for long months but we took it in one hour 10 minutes with 19 large Canon & a lage amount of ammunition. You can see plenty of blood heart & brains laying around the canon, yet we found [?] men buried in one hole insid the fort.

We have all bin wild with excitement to day. They are fighting over at Forte Dolesson [Donelson] about 12 miles off to day. We could hear the canon roar very plain and messengers coming in every few hours. It is very hard fight tho I supose we have got them completely hemmed in their Forte. We must have some 60 thousand troops thare. The firings has seased this evening. We are in expectation every hour of hearing of our victory. I feel truly that God is on our Side tho we may loose many preshious lives. We are all anxious for a fight & come very near being in this.

. . . . If I never should I expect to meet you all in Heaven with our dear loved ones who have gone before oh what a happy thought when we all shall meet in heaven Dear Sister will you Grand Ma and my old Class still pray for me yes I know you will thanks be to God for what I [?] is mine & I am his and Heaven is my home while I writing and thinking of these things the silent tear is stealing down my cheake I would So wish to spend a week or two at home. . . .

There is some sickness in our company. It is the Mumps. Three or four of our boys is left behind sick at Mound City above Cairo. Will Perviance was one of [?] them. It could not be helped. Tell George to study & learn fast. I am Dear sister very Respectfully yours in Christ, A. D. Keller[71]

Feb 15

I have concluded this morning to write a fiew more lines. We are having a very cold bad spell of wether heare now. It is very Sevear on the men on the batle field. Night before last it Rained, hailed, then froze hard and last night it Snowed 2 or 3 inches deep. Before this it was so warm our boys was all in their shirt sleaves and the buds had begon to swell but perhaps you are getting tiard [tired] of reading. Give Grandma my respects and tell her I have not forgotten her. . . . What a strange world this is. Some Praying, Some fighting, Some Swearing & Cursing the God that made them. The Batle over at Fort Donelson has been Renewed this morning. Thare is a constant roar of Cannon. This is agoing to be one of the hard fought batles. This is the third day. Our side has not suffered much yet is the [?].

I was very Sory to heare of the death of Sue Rogers but Rejoice to learn she died hapy. Good Bye write soon and often. Direct your letters To [?] Henry [?] 32 Reg Ills Vol . . .

Dan

Dan Messick[72] sends his Respects to you and you are not forgotten by him.

From: Hephzibah
To: Jemima

Sunny Dell March 17th 1862

Dear Sister

I am spending this beautiful afternoon alone grandpa and grandma having gone to town. . . . You asked me if I thought the war would not end soon. I think if as good a months work is accomplished this as was last we will have a prospect of peace very soon. Though I am disapointed aboute the Nashvilleites. I hoped the Union sentiment would be strong if it only had a chance of showing its self without fear but the contrary seems the fact. It is passing strange to me how people can be so deluded.

I am glad Mr Lincoln would not change the sentance of Gordon the slave Capt. from hanging to lifelong imprisonment.[73] Though for forty years slave catching has been pronounced piracy, and the punishment death, yet in all that time not one has received the punishment. The honor of the execution belongs to old Abe. Our other Presidents have not had courage to do their duty in this matter. But I believe the days of Slavery are nearly numbered, and I expect to see the end of them.

I could not realize when reading the account of the death of Suesan Rodgers that it was Sue H. that used to be. I was expecting it was some one els that I did not know. It seemed inpossible that one so young so beautiful and promising for a long life should be called. But if she was prepared as she no doubt was she has escaped a world of sorrow. No one at Conference last year seemed more like living long than James Barger and Sue Rodgers.

I have not heard from Iowa since I wrote. Do you intend answering Johns letter or does Mother intend getting some one els to write. That is an unpleasant state of affairs and ought not to be so. I fear both you and John are a little too stif in the neck. I suppose Ma would say you will have to have some more bones broken. I think though in this case Sis that you are most to blaim.

Grandma was very much pleased with her letter and grandpa pronounced it the best one he had seen for some time which led him to think Ma had gotten one of the preachers to compose and write, she furnishing the principal ideas. But I assured him that Ma was the compositor and Mr. Robbison the writer. I expect Ma will get an answer but I don't know how soon.

So Ben has been in battle. I hope he bore it bravely. How little we thought such would be the case when we playd [as] children together. I should like to see him remember me when you write. I hope he may not come home crippled for life. I think I'd rather die.

Was Col Logan in the battle of Donelson? I hear so much about Logan being wounded I should like to know. I heard to day that Palmers regiment had all been taken prisoners in Alabama but I dont believe it I cant think what they would be so far South for just now. It must be Arkansas if any where. I hope it is not true.

There has been three fires in town since I wrote to you. Mr. Capps[74] dwelling was partly burned. The Factory was not injured, the house was insured. A store and Catlins book store was burned also some other houses in another part of town but I cant tell where. The last two fires started from drinking saloons, but you may be sure they lost nothing by it. No such goodluck. I must tell you of an occurence which took place the 22nd of last month. Mr. Mathews a noted drunkard went to town, started home in the evening drunk, several persons asked to drive for him. No, he wouldnt let them. On his way he got on the rail road west of the Blind Asylum and came on to the first cattle guard leading to our pasture then turned and went back to town on the railroad. Turned around again and came on to the rock bridge, which was being repaired at the time. There was nothing to walk on but the ties. But the poor abused horse went on and while there the Express coming East came on full speed. Seeing something dark on the bridge blew the horn and stopped but not untill the carriage had been knocked from the bridge and the poor horse torn to atoms. Mr. Mathews had gotten out of the carriage before the train came up and when he saw it coming on he stepped [to] one side and fell through the bridge. He was taken on to the cars and left at Franklin and the next Monday he was in town again. I have not heard whether he has been drunk since or not. It seems little less than a miracle that he was not killed, and the cars thrown off the bridge. There was two passenger cars full, and the cars rocked very much in passing over the poor beast. The horse was one that had been given his daughter by her brother on his death bed. . . .

Fred has returned and will remain with us this summer. There is talk of Bob Kerr joining the army. I had no reason for asking about Nettie only I wished to know if you was friendly. I hope you will not let me wait long for an answer.
Eppie

[In the margin:]
Inclosed I send some Japonica seed. Plant them carefully and try to get them to grow as they are very choice flowers. It is a shrub. You may have seen it when here though I think you never saw the bloom, which is a deep red. I fear the seed will not come up, but try. It will not bloom for several years yet if it does come up. The rose slips are growing. Write soon.

I have seen no mention of the money we sent to Cin[cinnati] [where the *Advocate* was published] having been received. I think I will write about it to Mr. Poe and Hitchcock unless you will do it and save me the trouble.

From: Hephzibah
To: Jemima

Sunny Dell   April 15th, 1862

Wether your letters are magnificent or other wise I take not upon myself to say. But I assure you they are allways joyfully received by Eppie. I enjoyed your account of the closing of your school very much. Should like to have been there. I expect you felt as proude of your boys when making their speaches as you do that time they got that old stove for a drum and went marching round the square. Don't you feel it sometimes: a "Delightful task to rear the tender thought and teach young ideas how to shoot."[75] I hope it is not too much to wish that the ideas of your boys may always shoot in the right direction.

Apr 16th

You have no doubt heard of the late dreadful battle [Shiloh]. I went to Mrs. Bargers a few days since to learn if she had heard from her boys. She told me that Mr B. had gone the night before to see after them and feared he would not [be] allowed to go as none but nurses were permited to go. She said that she felt very uneasy about them but relied very much on Mothers prayers for their preservation. I heard afterwards that news had come that they were both wounded and that William had passed the boat on which his father was going to Cairo on his way up to St. Louis. So today I was in town and went over to hear the truth. She told me that they telegraphed to St. Louis to hear if the Barger there was her son and today learned he was not. Last night she got a letter from her son William at Pittsburg landing Ten, written the two days of the battle in which he told them that though he and John was in the heat of the battle neither were hurt thanks [to] the prayers of pious parents and friends. Mrs. B. said when she heard her boys were safe she felt as though she could "Run through a troop and leap over a wall." She had a letter from Mr. B at the same time written from Cairo. He had not heard of the boys and has gone on. Mrs. Eliza Barger is expecting to go to Carlinville as soon as Mr. B. comes home as she expects to go in carriage. She looks quite delicate, and rather sad. I asked her if she would take a few rose slips to you that I put to root last fall and she thought she could. In this letter I will send you some verbena seed which you had better plant in a crock or box as soon as possible. I sent a letter to Iowa yesterday in which I sent some also to Lizzie. I received a letter from John at the same time of your last. They were all well except Lizzie who had the head ache. He spoke of the times being very hard and that he could not collect that which was owing him and those whom he owed had no mercy on him but seemed to think he had no reason to complain as he was better off than many. They seemed to have a little hope that perhaps we would visit them this season, he said the Davenport and Iowa City rail-road came to 27 miles of them and if I would let them know when we were coming he would write and let me know what I had best do when we got to the stopping place. I told him there was not much hope of our coming as I had left it to Ma and she was talking of going to housekeeping.[76]

I hardly expect Ma will go into her own house as the Gen. [probably a reference to Major Burke] desires her to keep the children. It does seem as though some one ought to take care of them. I should like very much to come home but have little hope of so doing and for that reason have said nothing about it. Don't be uneasy about my health. I am very seldom troubled lately with sick spells and then not badly. I know that I lack a great deal of having all I desire, but I sometimes feel as though if I had a good education I could be content. But I am in dispair of ever getting it now, and will have to try and do the best I can with what I have and try to feel thankful for what of good I do possess which is more than I merit. . . .

I think it very likely that John Delzell was in the last battle. I don't know whether he is wounded or not. He has been in a number of engagements, and has been wounded twice. He was at Manchester and was struck by a ball in the cheek. When he wrote the 25 of March he was preparing five days rations and thought they were to go to Richmond, but I guess it was to Pittsburg landing. I am glad to hear that [Island] No. 10 is ours for though the loss there was comparitively nothing the position is of immense importance.[77] I am expecting to hear of hard fighting now any day at Corinth also on the Miss. river and in Virginia. I almost dread the next appearance of the Merrimack. I am afraid the Rebels have made her so strong and placed such guns on her that she will be more than a match for the Monitor, but we must trust in "Providence and keep our powder dry," surely then we will succeed.[78] I am sure the Lord is on our side we have been so favored, and I hope the war will soon be over. . . . You and Ma have been very spry indeed. I expect you will get that nice little crooked lot so adorned with trees before I see it again that I shant recognize it. Does Ma have the corners of it as well as ever? I cant think she would love it as well if it was straight, for as it is she will have a chance to exert her ingenuity in beautifying it and it will admit of improvements to such fine purpose. Dont think I am making fun, but it does seem so laughabile that Ma should eulogize the [?] so.

Grandpas health is no better I dont know but he is rather more feble than hitherto. I should have told you to plant those seed immediately in any place you think best as the shrub is hardy, though I fear the seed will not come up. . . . Fred sends his respects. Give my love to all. Write again as soon as possible and if you will send as long a letter as the last it will suit me very well.

Your devoted Eppie

I wrote to Poe & Hitchcock but have as yet received no answer

From: Benjamin Stead
Envelope address: Miss Jemmima Domeville, Carlinville Macoupin Co Illinois

May the 6th [1862]⁷⁹
Pitsburg landing tenese

Dear Friend
    ... We are about 12 miles from Pitsburg Landing. That is about half way from between Pitsburg Landing and Corrinth. We still keep moving on slowly but thear has bin so much rain it is most impossible to get along but we have troops [with] in about 11 miles of Corrinth we air kept back on the redy [reserve(?)]. We expect every day when the fight will commence. I was not near at the fite at Pitsburg landing but since i have bin hear I have bin over agood deal of the battlefield and from the marks on the treas and the graves everything goes to show that it was a dreadful battle. I am rather of the opinion if you know about the Seches [Secessionists] they mean to hold on as long as they can but if we whip them out hear they cant last long and I [-] aney ways uneasy but whill whip them but it is going to cost many a good man's life. Ah if it could stop right hear I would give all that i am worth or ever will be but nevertheless we have to bair it the best way we can. God knows all things and it appears it [h]as bin our lot to half to meat our fellow man face to face with our guns and weapons to mow them down as men would go into a slauter pen to butcher oxen. It does look hard but i hope thear is better day acoming. Sometimes i am most ready to dispair and give up but still God bairs [bears?] me on. I must write a little on another sheet.
    I think you was verry kind as to send a stamp after paying for the one I sent before. Dear friends I will ever remember you for your kindness to me and the advice you give and may you [be?]long and keep on in the way you air and if we air not permitted to meat on hearth I hope and trust to meet you all in heaven at last it is my prayer for Christ Sake amen. Oh Dan is well and in good spirits and was glad to hear from you and told me to tel you howdy for him. Well I have rote already more than will interest you probably so I will come to a close hoping to se you all soon Give my love to all specially gran ma fair well dear friends. Right soon from your friend Benjamin Stead to Miss domville

From: Hephzibah
Envelope address: Miss Jemima Dumville, Carlinville Ill

Sunny Dell   July 18th 1862

Dear Sister,
    I received yours the day after the Fourth. I hope you spent that day as pleasantly as I did. Fan Becraft had been at our hous a bout a week and on that day Grandpa and Grandma and myself went home with her.
    There was a number of others came after we arrived, and upon the whole, I think it was the pleasantest Fourth I ever spent. I enjoyed [Lou's?] visit here so

much she is a splendid girl. It would do you good to hear her talk on the times, slavery, or indeed on any subject she is so sensible. Although all her family and relatives are Southern in feeling she is as strong an Abolitionist as we. She told us that when news came of victory to our arms and the canon was sending forth the sound of triumph though every report sent a thrill of joy to her heart, she sat and *quietly* enjoyed it. For then all the rest were sad and sometimes almost sick about it. Said she: "It is enough for me to know that we are succeeding. So I say nothing for it gives me no pleasure to see those I love sad. But when they get news of the South being beaten they rejoice aloud and seem to forget all about me."[80] While she was here news came of the taking of Richmond. The people in town almost lost their wits about it. They were so wild with joy. Of all the blowing of horns ringing of bells, firing of cannon, hurrahing and yelling that took the lead. It was a sad taking down of our hopes to hear the true statement. Still I hope, and expect the others do to. But I am longing for the good news to hurry along.

I hope you will not think that I felt it a task to root those flowers. I assure you the part that fell to my share was no trouble but rather a pleasure. but I did not like the idea of trying so often to send such things and never succeeding.

. . .

. . . For my own part I feel very much inclined to come home indeed. I want to come, and I am not at all sure that its my duty to stay here [at the Striblings]. I don't want to do wrong but it can't be expected that I'll stay here always and I think they can spare me now as well as they will ever be likely to. I hardly expect them ever to be willing to give me up though they may. . . . Grandma wants to know if Ma feels any assurance that their prayers will be answered soon and their prospects be less gloomy. She still intends writing when she can make up her mind what she can say.

I am in town today the first time in two weeks. Sarah is here and looks rather thin. She wished to be remembered to you all. Willie spoke of English intervention and Sarah whispered "Peace is made between England and America. For my part I do not fear intervention much. Though some make a very big bugaboo of it. England had better not for if she does Mrs Walter intends sending her boys to fight in that case. I very much [?] John Bull will be badly whipped. I hope he will take warning in time to prevent such a serious occurrence.

. . .

I have to go up soon so must close. I hope your roses are doing well. Your devoted Beulah.

From: John Williams

Aug 11 1862

Dear Sister H. B. [Hephzibah Beulah] I again take the time to send you a fiew hasty lines to let you know that we are all well & have enjoyed moderate good health thus fare through the season. Youre young friend [Fred Bechly] called on us Saturday [e]vening. We was very glad to see him. He talks of leaving us today. The secesh [secessionists] has not yet sent me under nor will they do it without some trouble. I have rented my farme for two years I expect to come to See you this fall & also want to get a small place that I can make a living during that time among our friends. We want to start about the 20th of Oct. We can tell you more than I can rite. We expect drafting to comence here soon & there is no telling whoo will have to go. If it is my lot to go I do not see how I shall arange my buoisness . . .

Youre favor come in a special time of need. The young man[81] offered me $35,00 I declined taking 4 of it. Inclosed I send you a note for thirty one.

I have one of the interesting Sabath School class that I have taught. We have the best School in the neighborhood. The quakers think, I know it all. I have 40 acre of corne 10 of wheat. I have worked very harde this summer to make my crop but one nigger[82] wont do on a farme of 90 acres. I rented out 37 acres. They did not halfe tend the corne. . . . If some unforeseen ocurence Shoulde prevent us of seeing each other here let us so live that we shall see each other in a land wheare wars & rumors of war is unknown.

John W. Williams

From: Margaret Emily Williams (John and Elizabeth Williams' daughter)

Aug 11 1862

Aunt Eppy I want to see yo very bad We hav no chool if we come out to see you we will go to school all the time. Mary Ellen is a very purty baby. Gorge is so bad that I canot doe any thin With him. Martha dont try Lurn her leson but she is not so bad as Gorge [?]

Margret Emily Williams

From: Hephzibah
To: Jemima

Sunny Dell   August 15th 1862

Dear Sister

. . . I only received your letter yesterday but as I have some news I will write without further delay. Freid [Friedrich Bechly] has been talking all Summer of going to Iowa to see the country and did not know but he might go as far as brother's [John Williams]. He left us last Wednesday week and started in his [?] expecting to be gone a month but lo and behold he was back again this morning having gone only a little more than a week. However he was at Johns and spent two or three days with him. He happened there very opportunely as John was about to be sued by some of his Secession neighbors. I told Fried before going if

John was very much in need of money when he got there to let him have what he could spare and I would repay him on his return. So it happened in the very nick of time. Fried let him have thirty one dollars and John sent his note to me for it. [See letter of August 11, 1862.] I have twenty dollars which I received sometime since for interest and I hope I shall get the other twenty soon and if I don't Grandpa owes me more than enough to pay Fried. I think John felt very grateful to me for in the letter he sent by Fried he called me "dear" a thing he is not in the habit of doing.[83] You will be surprised to hear that John has rented out his farm for two years and intends coming to Illinois and rent a farm here so as to send the children to school. They are surrounded by secessionists and if John is drafted Sister will come at once. If you intend building this fall it would be well if you could [?] they come as you will be so crowded. I [?] this as I dont expect you to build now.

I will send those thing to you or try as soon as you want them. I am in favor of sending them in wagon I think it would be less trouble as then they would be delivered to you at your door and no trouble to you. I think it would not be worth while to try to sell anything I should get next to nothing for them and we should spend as little money as possible [in] these times. I dont expect to go with the things if I send them in wagon. I don't care about riding all day with some strange man and I dont know yet who Ill send them by. I shall come with John when he comes if not before . . .

Grandma is a[s] unwilling as ever.[84] I hope she will become reonsiled in time. . . . I bought "Parson Brownlow Among the Rebels[85] not long since and I have several other books which with those we have will [?] at present. The best way will be for us to get one book at a time when we see one that we like. We had better not burden ourselves with such things though if Grandpa will let me have MacCaulays History of England and Rowllins Ancient History I will be glad to get them. . . . I will send you aboute the arrest that lately took place. It looks as though the danger comes nearer and nearer. [See discussion above regarding the internment of Southern sympathizers.] I am in to[o] great a hurry to write at present. Write soon, your devoted Beulah

From: Hephzibah
To: Jemima

Sunny Dell   Sept 18th 1862

Dear Sister

I expect you are wondering what can have happened to prevent my writing before now. The long and the short of it is I have been planning about getting your things to you. First I thought I would not send them on the cars because it would be some trouble for you to attend to haveing them taken from the depot, so I spoke to Mr. Kegy a neighbor of ours to take them down in wagon. He promised to do so and this morning was the time to get ready and he intended to start at noon, because he said it would take him two days and a half to go and return, as it took him that long last fall to move Mr. R—. He asked at the rate of two and a half a day and find himself which I thought little enough, but when I thought the matter over I concluded I had better not send any of my wearing clothes untill I was sure of going myself. My bed you would not need to be present, and the bed-stead that Ma has here I thought Lizzie would have again if she should need it and they should stay near J—[Jacksonville] if not they perhaps could take it with their things. My bed-stead and yours and Mas boxes would not be a load so all things considered I thought best to send the three last named items by the cars, which I'll do as soon as I can get them taken to the depot. I don't know how soon it will be as Fried [Bechly] is going to cut corn next week and I shall have to wait till some day when he can't cut corn and then he'll fix my things up and take them in for me. The price per hundred weight is 18 cents from here to S—I could not learn what it was beyond. About the same I suppose. It has rained so hard today that if I had not changed my mind Mr. K would not have started.

I am glad the news I sent you had such good effect. I see happy people so seldom it is a treat to hear of such especially when they are so near to me. Should like to have heard your maiden speach. take care of it that I may see it when I come.

Grandma does not seem any more reconsiled to my leaving her. She expects me to do so, I think, still she feels badly about it. What makes the matter worse just now is, that Grandpa has become so hard of hearing lately that he can scarcely hear a word of common conversation.

What does Ma say about my coming home. I should like to know. I have told you how I feel about the matter. If I dont come home now I hardly expect I ever shall. I wish I knew what to do. It does annoy me to see Grandma so sad and yet I cant help feeling like coming home. I think I shall not lock the boxes and then I can send the keys. Will fasten them otherwise.

. . . There is a regiment at the Fairground, they have preaching every Sabbath afternoon. Went last Sunday for the first time. There are very few that I know. Josiah Belt is second Lieutenant of Capt Mays Company. Saw him outbound but not speak. He looks thin. Felt sad when I saw the soldiers carrying their babes around and their wives walking beside them looking sadly enough. I thought the soldiers all looked gloomy. Perhaps the bad news is the cause. But I hope that the tide has turned in our favor at last. I must close now as I wish to send this by Fried who is just about to start and can't wait. Write soon again and send me a long letter. I have written to Iowa but dont much expect an answer but Love to all. Grandma sends her love. Your affectionate sister, Eppie

P.S. Of course, you knew that Mr. Barger and all his boys had gone. We heard two weeks since that Mr. Jaquess was dead, which is not true we suppose.[86] Write soon and just tell me what to do.

From: Hephzibah
To: Jemima

Jan 27th 1863

. . . I always feel more anxious to hear from you soon after coming away from you than after I have been away a long time. I can fully sympathize with your feeling of my visit being a dream. I can scarcely realize it myself. As you have gone into a detail of what you did after my leaving I will tell you something of my own employment.

Week before last I was buisy and working a three week washing, besides which I worked a little on my furs and made a carpet for the kitchen out of an old one of Mrs. Lurton's. Last week I worked almost all week on my furs and Saturday they were done at least so I thought except the tails, but last night Fred went out hunting and caught another opossum so now he wants me to take one of the [tabs?] of what is peaced several times and put this one on when he gets it tan[n]ed so I seem to be as the Irish man would say "advansing backward in refferance to getting done my furs. Nevertheless I wore them in town to day and they all pronounce them beauties and so they are. The prettiest I ever saw of the kind.

You will perceive that our employment is very different. I have only been to town once since since my return except today as you will preceive that I am writing it in town and if you only knew the commotion that is going on among the children you would surely look over all blunders if they are as numerous as grasshoppers in prairie grass. I received a letter from Mary Mc[Elfresh] and answered it last Monday week but have heard nothing from John yet. I have finished the sto[c]king I was knitting with you and began the other. My coller too is one third done. How are you getting along with yours. Has Mr[s]. Plain finished hers yet? And how is Mr[s]. Brown getting along with her [belting?]? . . .

Fred wishes one to give you his thank for sending his friend Napelion to him. He likes him and has finished it. I am not well into the merits of it yet, as I was behind with the Advocate two weeks when I came home and with reading that and other papers which we sometimes get. I don't have time to read much els. The church bell is ringing which makes me remember that I have not been to church since I came home, but I read sermons at home and upon the whole dont pass the time altogether unprofitably.

The [roads?] have been and still are so bad that there is no such thing as getting about with the carriage. . . . I saw Mr. [P?] the last time I was in town and told him what Ma had said. He remarked that he wished she was here to say "Amen for him that it used to do him great good. . . .

Have you seen Gen Butler's speech in Lowell Mass.[87] I intended sending it to you but forgot it. I'll do it yet if you have not seen it. You think my book is such a poor thing: read the father's legacy to his daughter and tell me what you think of it. My love to all, Eppie

From: Hephzibah [with postscript from Jemima]
Envelope address: Miss Jemima Dumville, Carlinville Illiniois

Jacksonville Illilnois   June 2nd 1863

My dear Sister [Mary][88]
 A thousand thanks to you for sending us that beautiful family picture. I should think you would feel a motherly pride in seeing your self surrounded by such an interesting group of children. I am sure from the expression of Jane's countenance that she is an amiable and dutiful daughter. Emily does look a little serious, but she and Mary Hannah both are very sweet looking little girls. Charls and Mr. [H?] look very much alike I think, and John resembles you more than any of the others. I suppose he is the student. I see he has a book and he looks as grave as a Judge on the bench. Mother says Charls looks like his father but I have not the least recolection of how his father looked. I do rember hearing him and brother John[89] speak to father after we had started to America and I asked if Mary had come. I felt as though I could leave everything in England better than you sister. But you have changed since then as well as myself for when I look at you I have not the least remembrance of ever having seen you before. You said I should not find you looking as well as I did in my likeness. I don't expect to look as well when your age.[90]
 But I must say something about the state of the country and leave sister to tell of family matters because I read the papers more than she has time to do. Thus far no battle has been fought in the soil of the free states. Most of the fighting has been done in the border Slave States yet nothing would please the Rebels more than to get into the Free States especially Illinois because she is the fourth in amount of population of any State in the Union and the first in agricultural production. Grain is what the rebels sorely need beside Illinois has sent at least a hundred and sixty thousand volenteers to the war and no troops fight braver than the Illinois boys. If the rebels get here we need expect no mercy for we shall receive none. I believe they'll burn and destroy and lay waste like very demons and I am not with out my fears that they will get here yet for we have so many traitors in our midst. Many of them have run from the States where the war is raging to save their property and still their sympathys are all with the South and they rejoice to hear of the rebel cause gaining and make no secret of it either. But such things have been born[e] longer than it was safe for loyal people and now an order has been isued by the commander of his department to arrest all openly disloyal persons and send them beyond our lines or treat them as spies.[91] I hope the order may be carried out to the letter. In the early part of last year our Army gained the victory in almost every

engagement, but for a year now the tide seems to be against us. We don't lose ground but we dont gain very fast either. A battle has been raging at Vicksburg at intervals for over a month. I dont know how it will end.

I am very sorry indeed that you could not get the picture, but you shall have one yet if there is any other in town to be had. I think likely I shall be able to get another though I tried to get one this evening but could not find w[h]ere they are kept. The one who sold them has moved. Sister Jemima sent your portraits to me the day after they reached her and I received them on Saturday. I would have had a copy of it taken to send to Sister Lizzie today but it was too cloudy. I know Sister Lizzie will be as happy to see you all as any of us. I shall have this one framed and keep it until I visit Mother and likely I shall have a copy taken for myself if I can get a good one. If not I should like to have you send one for me. I'll tell when I write again. I promise to Mary H. another [?] of hair. The center is father's the other is mine. I hope your helth is better now as you did speak of being troubled with asthmah in your letter. I feel as though this is a poor short letter but I want Sister to send it in her letter so I am in a hurry. My love to all your children and all other friends.

[*In margin*]

If I can get that picture I'll send it soon and when you get it please let me know soon after. I hope to hear from you soon. Your devoted Eppie

-----

[*In margin, different handwriting*]

Yesterday when I sealed my letter I could not find Sister's letter but as I found it I concluded to open it and send it and the piece of hair for Mary H. This was written before all the [said?] victories were gained but as I have no other to send you from Sister I will send this. August 7th 63. Jemima Dumville

From: N. H. Coop[92]   **Corinth, Mississippi**
Envelope address: Miss Jemima Dumville Carlinville, P. O. Macoupin County, Ills

Corinth Miss   June 2nd 1863

Miss Jemima

. . .

Since I was with you last I have seen a great many ups and downs, as the saying goes. While we remained at Trenton Tenn we had general good times.[93] But since we left, there we have had some very hard times. I shall not at this time attempt to describe them. I have had my health tolerable well much of the time. Our f Company has been quite healthy Considering the suden change of Climate and water. One has died. Two have been killed, 2nd liuet. and one Private. One deserted, [?] John Odle, And eleven taken prisoners. And two of them are discharged. All taken together reduces our numbers to only 40 strong. There are great movements going on now the result of which I hope will prove to be with much success to the National Army, Especialy so in the western portion of it. I will now conclude by Asking an Interest in your Prayers. May God Protect you with his mercy. And may you be instrumental in doing much good in the world that is now. And in the world to come may you be crowned with everlasting life.

. . . Good bye. Your devoted friend, N. H. Coop

From: Margaret Emily Williams [John and Elizabeth's daughter, age 12]
To: Jemima

July the 20 [1863][94]

Dear Aunt Gemima

We was glad to hear from you but we could not ixpect you to rite eany sooner then you did. We are all well at present. We are going to school now to Angia [G?]ause. We hant [haven't] went to school mutch this summer We would went more then we did but we had to mutch other work to doe. We have got about t[w]o hunderd and fifty chickens. Paw has got A reeper and he has not got time to rite. We went to the forth of July. The Copperheads marched round town three time. We have got forty geas[e]. Paw is going off to reap in the morning and he will be gon all the weak** [asterisks in original]. Joseph Lauson was killed last weak he went out earlia in the morning a fore breakfast and told his wife that he would be in dreackely [directly] but he never come and she never told eany body till a bout five oclock in the after noon Eliza Jane went up thare on a visit and she sent Eliza Jane right back to tell the neighbors and thare was several came to hunt him. When they found him he was dead and he had got killed by A load of rails sone way. He was mashed up A gainst a tree. When tha [they] found him the dogs had got to him. His Wife had been to or three times righ at him nearlia but the brush was so high that that she could not see him. He was right black. Maw and Miss Lancaster Was the second one that got to him. Tha [they] help take the rails off uf him. He didant have aeny horses to the wagon. Maw said she did not out see how he did get killed. His wife Was not Well and she had a right yong baby and other boy was t[w]o years old. We went to the barring [burying].

I study reading and spelling and arithamatic. I have not said but one lesson in my arithmatic yet. The teacher out [ought] lisson [listen] to [us] resite. Martha studies spelling and reading. Gorge studies spelling. He has got so he can spell right well. Thare is t[w]o more weeks of our school Mary Ellen is as pretty as eve[r]. She has cut her ha[i]r off like a little boy. I sent my picter to Aunt Eppie but i se you have seen it. A fore now I was skard [scared] when I had it taken but it looks natcherl.

We have A Sunday school. Paw teaches the bible class. Angia [G?]ause teaches the testment class. Maria frazer teaches the little spelling Class as you did. Rite me A see scrett [secret?]. I will tell you I was at play with the rest of the children. Maw red the letter A fore I did. Mister pike fetched the letter out of the offis and she red it A fore I did and now she tries to pleg [plague] me A bout it. We have got twenty peaches.

We have got fiv Apple trees and there [three?] churry trees that bars [borders?] our garden. Didant do eany good this year it is burnt up with the sun & our pinks all died but one root. Maw wants you to send her some more pinks seeds.

Cousin [?] Williams talks of cumming to Jacksonvill to see Mary Jane. She is at the insain ospittle [Hospital]. I don't [k]now hardly w[h]at she is A doing. She is A going to stay six months. She gits fifteen Dollars A month.[95] As I told you A bout Joseph Lawson I will tell you some more. He went to run his wagon down A hill and out of the brush. The Wagon catched him between the wagon and the tree. Maw said she never see sutch A site in her life. The rails was run thrue his head.

Well Aunt Gemima the Copperheads is Going by to there peas meeting in wagons and buggies and every other way. Tha [They] are gitting very strong and well armed. Tha [They] have shut up the school house against all republican preaching. We have meeting at our house now. Thare is meeting at our house in the morning. Maw sais she don't believe it will be long till the Copperheads and republican has a fuss.[96]

Maw is making me a new dress. I will send you A peas of it. Mary ellen sais she loves Gran maw A half a bushel. George sais he wants Gran maw to fetch him some canday when she coms. Maw sais Gorge stutters as bad as logan[97] Mary Ellen stuters some but not like George. Maw sais Martha puts her in mind of aunt Eppie When she was little. Martha is just as mean and lazy as she can be. George sais he wants paw to go Whare gran maw is. He sais that thae hant [ain't] no Copperheads thare. He cride last night for paw to come out thare where you was. Maw sais she don't want you and Granmaw to be uneasy about us. Thare is A Compney of home Gards in Montzuma and thar [they] are gitting up a Compney of home gards at blue point and paw has joined them. Tha [They] are gitting up A Compney of home Gards at Lynnville. We[e]k A fore last thare was betwen sixty and seventy Copperheads A gathered up to take for storm but tha [they] did back out Cause tha [they] was A fraid to undertake it. Paw has sett out orcherd A twice and the winters kills them. We have A bout twenty trees now that is living. Thare is some kind of A worm that works in the root of the tree. We have got A plenty of corn bushes. Granmaw you ne[e]dant to be uneasy A bout us. We have enough flannel and linsy to do us next winter that is not made up. Maw has made A new feather bed this summer of her ges [geese]. Maw sais she would like to Come and see granmaw I will bring my letter to A Close. I have made severl mistake but I cant help it now. Rite soon Aunt Gemima so no more.

We sold our sheep to John Mathes but paw is A going to buy some more.

Gran maw[,] maw Wants you to send her age. We all have our ages put down in the bible but maw.

Margaret Emily Williams

From: William Stribling
Envelope address: Mrs. Ann Dumville Carlinville Ill

Morgan County Ill   Dec. 12th '63

Esteemed and beloved sister,

The subject of death is the first in place. I attended at the house of Br. Carr on yesterday, and heard Bro Reed preach the funeral of Miss Annie E. [?] She had been teaching in Franklin highly esteemed by all. She suffered about a week, and died in great triumph. . . . Would you not rejoice in God for your daughters to depart, even *now* (were it the will of God) could they only depart in holy triumph; unless they were doing something in the way of benevolence, and religion?

Ah me! I sorrowed almost to despair when my youngest daughter[98] departed! O! if our firstborn had gone home in holy triumpth, what darts of agony had miss'd my heart! But now first see and behold!!!

My beloved sister I might say, "Now thou art risen a mother in Israel" I therefore speak the words of our matters to you suposing that perhaps she may yet feel some of the regard to you, that the youngest daughter should have, to the religious and prudent & loving mother. Perhaps you made some venture in intrusting to our care, your younger, and loving daughter. We have felt for her. And when her labour appeared [pressing?] we have felt for her, in no common degree. We hoped devoutly that when she should leave us, she woulld leave us in a manner to rise in holy enjoyment, and aid you and yours benevolently and religiously. But Alass! Alass!

Sister, words & ideas are of great importance Words leading to immediate action, upon which much depends should be spoken in time. If our daughter H had only told us in time that she wished us not to employ F [Fred Bechly], in consequence of his efforts made against her previously, I would not have employed him even if he had been able to do the work of a dozen men at the price of one, we could not have been prevailed upon to employ him even at half price; & we would not have been willing for him to be about our house; but alass! not a word is spoken to us about the affair; also when the cow, bed, & bedstead are presumed to be [?], if they had been calld for, they were at hand: & I had sold I think 2 or 3 cows about that time at $10^{00} each, and how easily could I have furnished them if I had known there was a call for them on the part of H—But not a word. I had always supposed that these things were to be given when called for; Particularly when leaving us. They were at hand and we would much rather have furnished them than the money, then or now, but in a [?] to accomodate, particularly a <u>loving daughter</u> of a <u>loving</u> and <u>esteemed</u> mother in our Israel. But [?] But that which perhaps would appear to many <u>more terrific</u> than all the rest, is leaving us making upon us the impression that she was going to visit the mother & sister & soon return; but Alass! Alass! Alass! arrangements it seems, had been made, for F—to fall in quickly & for them to marry and push off to the house of Bro & Sister Williams.[99] If I mistake not, these are things of peculiar characteristics.

To make a full settlement of matters that have been [?] on as long as our matters have been on [?] with H. requires some attention. We always held ourselves disposed to settle up with her so as to give satisfaction to all concerned, but when the <u>affair</u> was conducted in the stile [style] in which it was, who was prepared to meet all emergencies? Matters that had been in rather a loose condition for a while, required some close thought. <u>Thought</u> that is conducted in the way of familiar converse with one another.

In this way matters may be <u>explained</u> and adjusted but how can all these little things be brought to a satisfactory close, when friends are trying to conduct it unless they are <u>together</u>, to make proper <u>explanations</u>. To write to each other and wait for the mails, the difficulty is quite considerable. Had everything been arranged and put in for <u>eternal</u> separation, <u>we</u> would have made the arrangement; but alass! alass!

We supposed that everything had been arranged satisfactorily, for all future time. We had <u>try'd</u> to make everything satisfactory. It was indicated by sister Jemima that she would be satisfied with $500.00 dollars. We supposed this was about the proper amount. We were willing to give it. The calculations made by H—was a fraction over 400.00. I thought that not enough. I requested that it should be made up <u>at least</u> to 500.00. I do not say <u>that a 100 was added</u>, to the amount, but so near it that for round numbers a 100 has occasionally been mentioned.

About bed, 'sted, cow, &, & we always would have been willing to hand them over, & would greatly have preferd it to giving the money. . . .

After we had handed over the amount to H, named above, we desired that she should in her writings learn whether the amount given was satisfactory; the reply was <u>that</u> that it was <u>satisfactory</u>. Thus our minds were set at rest about the matter. We feel fairly assured that we paid fully all the expenses for the tuition &. Thus it appears passing strange that anything was said on that account. We hoped when you departed everything was made satisfactory for we had tryd to go fully up all reasonable claims. . . .

Mrs. S and <u>yourself</u> conversed openly about her matters in relation to H., & Mrs. S. never desired to make any improper impression upon your mind and hoped that every thing was satisfactory & clear but when the letter was received from H—, every thing appeared in quite a different view. I hope you will write immediately and tell us your mind without any reserve. We cannot think that there can be an item of disagreement between us, if the facts in the case are fully known.

I very much desire these matters may be brought to a close so as for full satisfaction to be given to all concerned. Please therefore write a line or two address'd to Revd L. Pitner stating the sum that will be satisfactory, and inclosing a receipt covering the whole ground of our matters: instructing him to hand it over to us if we pay the sum; if otherwise, instruct him to retain it.

. . .

[–] yours (perhaps) till we meet in the world of spirits. W. G & M. Stribling

———

[*In margin*] . . . It appears that sanctification in the highest degree is required, that Willie may be delivered from his [?] particularly in the way of music to companies set against the Christian spirit. We desire that you should pray that he may be sanctified and throughout & perserved from all improper influences in his music and all other [?] that we urge these matters with warm desire upon you. &

7. The Letters End

There are no later letters in the archive.[1] By using information from public records, however, we can extend the story. In the next few years, the lives of Hephzibah and Jemima ran parallel. Both married within a few months of the end of the letters,[2] when Jemima was thirty-three and Hephzibah was thirty, well past the age at which most nineteenth-century women married.[3] Jemima married James Holme, a widower from a town near Carlinville. Her first child was born the following year, after Jemima and Holme had moved to rural Missouri, near St. Joseph, where they eventually established a substantial farm.[4] They had four children, two boys and two girls,[5] and the couple also cared for two children born to Holme's first marriage. At least three of the children entered the professions. As we saw in chapter 6, Hephzibah left Jacksonville in 1863 with Fred Bechly, with whom she had worked at the Stribling farm. They went to Iowa, to the farm owned by Elizabeth and John Williams,[6] and in due course had a son and a daughter. Their son became an osteopathic physician.[7]

    The story of the Dumvilles is a picture of life in the antebellum, rural Midwest as it was lived by women of modest means. No doubt that picture is representative in some ways but not in others. We have only four women, all from the same family, not a large or diverse sample, and it would be absurd to argue either that they were typical of women at that time and place or that they were truly extraordinary and transcended their circumstances. Neither is true. Instead, they are examples, four distinct examples, of how some people lived then and there. A review of the situations and experiences of each of the Dumville women may permit us to see how their lives were shaped as the Midwest was transformed by settlement, technological innovation, commercial development, and cultural change.

Ann Dumville was a widow. With the rigors of daily existence, the ravages of cholera and typhoid, and, later, the toll of the war, there were a great many widows. Like more than a few of them, Ann often resided in other people's homes, the homes where she worked. Jemima and Hephzibah also lived with other families; Hephzibah was with the Striblings for sixteen years. The separation meant that letters were the primary way the family shared experiences and emotions. In this respect, at least, the Dumvilles were like many families; a large share of all households had unrelated lodgers or help.

Ann did not write and she may or may not have been able to read, but she was certainly familiar with the Bible—knowledge that had been gained through one medium or another. Reading aloud to others was then common practice, and it is likely that Jemima read to her. Ann may have concentrated on familiar texts, reading (or listening) "intensively," as many people did in the late eighteenth and early nineteenth centuries.[8] It appears that neither Ann nor Jemima read newspapers, and they therefore relied on Hephzibah to summarize news in her letters. This meant that they were somewhat remote from the broader world, certainly less cosmopolitan than Hephzibah.

In the 1870 Census, Ann Dumville was listed at the residence of Don Burke, the son of Major B. T. Burke, but the records of her estate indicate that, at the time of her death three years later, she still owned a house in Carlinville. There are varying accounts of where she lived in her last years.[9] It seems likely that, despite her ownership of a home, she returned to the Burkes when Jemima married and moved to Missouri.[10] The subject of the following story reported by Leaton is surely Major Burke:

> One of those for whom she kept house was a man of great wealth, whose heart was wholly absorbed in the things of this world. One evening after spending some time in examining his accounts, noticing Mother Dumville gazing at him, he asked her of what she was thinking. "I was thinking," she replied, "of Bunyan's man with the muck rake."[11] He understood the reproof and received it. Though so worldly himself and at times profane, he resolved that he could not doubt the reality of religion from seeing the consistent walk of Mother Dumville who was never ruffled under any of his irritations, and who was never afraid to reprove him.[12]

The Dumvilles' fondness for John Bunyan's *The Pilgrim's Progress* is easy to understand. It is a story of a quest for salvation.

In March 1873 Ann became ill, and she was then taken to Missouri to be with Jemima and her family. She died a short time later at age seventy-eight.[13]

Her body was returned to Sulphur Springs, where it was buried next to that of her husband, Thomas.[14]

The second of the four women, Elizabeth, lived on relatively isolated farms, first in Illinois and then in Iowa. She does not appear to have attended concerts or paper readings, such as those given by the Phi Nu society and Belles Lettres, which Hephzibah and Jemima enjoyed in Jacksonville. Elizabeth's husband, John, went out into the markets to buy supplies and to sell grain and hogs, but she had little need to deal with commerce while John was alive. According to a history of Poweshiek County, he enlisted in the Iowa volunteers in 1862 and fought at Shiloh, Corinth, and Vicksburg. There is no mention of this, however, in the 1862 or 1863 letters—indeed, those letters include evidence that he was still farming in Iowa at that time.[15] He did, however, serve in the army later, and he died on Sherman's march through Georgia, late in 1864, four miles from Savannah. A Bible found in his pocket was inscribed, "My name is John W. Williams and my wife's name is Elizabeth, Lynnville, Iowa."[16] John's death left Elizabeth with four young children (two other children had died earlier), and Elizabeth moved into town (Grinnell) in 1866 so that the children could attend school there. In the 1870 Census she was listed as "keeping house" and having real property of $7,000. This suggests that she still owned the farm and that the Bechlys were then tilling that land or that Elizabeth had tenants. She did not remarry but lived forty more years.[17] Her life was difficult, certainly.

For most of the years covered by the letters, Jemima lived in Carlinville, in proximity to her mother. Only a few of Jemima's letters survive, and both the style and the content of those letters conform to the conventions of Methodist discourse. But she was not content to remain a serving woman, and this ambition may have contributed to her conflict with William Stribling. Her ambition was of a conventional sort—her work as a teacher was a nurturing role that conformed to the ideology of domesticity, "true womanhood," and she pursued that career only until she married. Jemima was commended for her work at the elementary school and was active in the church, teaching Sunday school and collecting money for missionary work. Indeed, she apparently considered becoming a missionary to Texas or Africa, but she did not. The breadth of her interests is not really clear. Hephzibah's letters say that Jemima was too busy to read newspapers. She appears to have been more attracted to religious literature, and she probably read intensively rather than extensively, in the older mode, as did Ann. In the 1870 Census, Jemima was recorded near St. Joseph, Missouri, and listed as "keeping house." Her husband, then age fifty, was a farmer with real property valued at $9,500 and personal property of $2,500, well above the average. Jemima died in St.

Joseph in 1919 at age eighty-eight of "apoplectic stroke due to old age." The death certificate was signed by her son, Dr. Edward Holme.

Hephzibah's case is more complex, perhaps because we know more about her. She wrote the majority of the letters in the archive, and those letters make it clear that she was creative. She was the youngest of the Dumvilles, and the family's meager resources could not provide for her. Although Jemima was more successful in conventional terms, Hephzibah appears to have had more wit or spark. Certainly, she was willing to challenge authority. Other family members found her outspoken, perhaps contentious. She was acutely aware that she was not as accomplished as she might have been, given her intelligence, and this generated frustration and some anger. We cannot be certain that she actually had less schooling than Jemima, but she does not appear to have sought any sort of credential, certification, or career. Nonetheless, she read broadly.

Hephzibah often sought guidance in the tenets of the Methodist Church, but some of that guidance was, at best, unclear. On the one hand, Methodists embraced the ideology of true womanhood. On the other, the Church supported the education of women, especially training for jobs as teachers. The endorsement of domesticity provided doctrinal support for the separation of men's and women's roles—women would make the home a well-ordered refuge, a place for support of the efforts of their husbands and for the nurture and moral instruction of the next generation.[18] But the education of women held the "seeds of destruction"[19] of the woman's exclusive devotion to domesticity. Education gave women a broader view, stimulated their interest in public issues, and provided tools they needed in order to advance their objectives.

In a letter written in May 1861 Hephzibah balanced the competing norms concerning the proper role of women. She observed that "a girl that had to work for herself away from home was not as much respected as others," but she also said that her mother and Mrs. Stribling thought that "so long as a girl behaved herself well and kept a regular home she could not see why she was not as much respected as any one els." Hephzibah clearly valued education, but it is less clear why she valued it. It may be that she sought learning less for its practical utility than for its inherent intellectual appeal and its contribution to self-esteem. Moreover, self-improvement was seen as a religious duty—one should make full use of the talents and potential provided by God.

Hephzibah's social standing was ambiguous. She certainly aspired to be middle class, and she had some of the attributes: she had attended a college; she was acquainted with prominent, influential clergymen such as Peter

Cartwright, William Milburn, James Jaquess, and Levi Pitner; and she had wit and read extensively. But she did not have skills that were valued in the market, and she did not have independent means. One's social class, in any functional sense, is determined by labels applied by others—an essential characteristic of prestige is that the deference is granted voluntarily.[20] Hephzibah was, at the end of her life, the wife of a small farmer and was, in that respect, more akin to Elizabeth than to Jemima or even Ann. Ann owned a home, and Jemima's husband owned a large, successful farm. In contrast, when the Bechlys moved to Iowa they almost certainly tended the Williams farm, not land of their own. Married women were ordinarily assigned the social class of their husbands—had Hephzibah married a shopkeeper, a skilled craftsman, or a resident preacher, her level of education would have been sufficient to qualify her for middle-class status. Without such a husband, it was not. Hephzibah's letters say relatively little about marriage prospects, but she met young, unmarried clergymen who would have been regarded as suitable mates. In January of 1859 or 1860 [the date is unclear], Hephzibah was corresponding regularly with a young man from Virginia, a small Illinois town not far north of Jacksonville, but she reported that Mrs. Stribling was "sure that I should be stooping very much to take him as a partner for life." Mr. Stribling told Hephzibah that she would "throw [herself] away entirely" if she married him. The Striblings, it appears, wanted to retain the benefit of Hephzibah's services, and this may have influenced the advice they gave her regarding potential suitors.

Although she wanted to be compensated fairly, Hephzibah did not appear to be much concerned about money. She was, however, conscious of the problem created by her lack of an agreement "about what I was to get for staying with them" [the Striblings].[21] It is probably significant that she used the phrase "staying with," instead of, for example, "working for." She did not think of herself as an employee. Two years earlier, she had used the phrase "making my home with." Hephzibah was sensitive to social class distinctions—as we have noted, she referred to one of the Methodist congregations in Jacksonville as being located in "the aristocratic part of town," and she commented with some asperity that she was not invited to particular weddings or parties.[22]

Hephzibah Dumville Bechly died on April 6, 1869, at age thirty-five, less than six years after leaving the Stribling farm and only eleven months after the birth of her second child.[23] Her letters often began with the dateline "Sunny Dell," the name of the Stribling farm, which was no doubt meant to suggest a place of comfort and enlightenment. The search for such a place is one of the recurring themes in the lives of the Dumvilles. They left England and came to America in the hope of finding opportunity, a better place. Hephzibah and Jemima experienced religious conversions that were seen as a quest for moral improvement, a higher plane. They eagerly sought education, perhaps hoping for social advancement, a superior position. For most of her short life, Hephzibah searched for a place where she belonged. Her life apparently had more sorrows and frustrations than joys and notable accomplishments, but she participated actively in the community around her, she took an interest in the religious, political, and intellectual issues of the day, she had a marriage and children, and she left an extraordinary set of letters.

The Dumvilles made the transition from hardscrabble lives in a sparsely populated region to settled lives in thriving communities with schools, churches, railroads, and mills, and their concerns and accomplishments reflect the early development of the American middle class. The letters demonstrate their interest in consumer goods—Jemima bought a piano; Hephzibah bought dresses for Elizabeth's daughters; Ann sent Hephzibah earrings—and they played their small part in the growth of mercantile enterprise. They met the new world with considerable success, despite the very real challenges and even tragedies in their lives. Life was arduous and disease and death were common. Hephzibah and Jemima struggled to obtain schooling, never managed to advance in their studies as far as they would have liked, and confronted the severe economic, social, and political instability created by the battles over slavery and, eventually, the Civil War. Nonetheless, they persevered, and prevailed. Their social mobility was, no doubt, aided by the fact that they were white, English, and Protestant—not black, Irish, or Catholic—but they overcame being unskilled newcomers, female, and impoverished. They transformed themselves from immigrants to Americans, and they progressed from rural poverty to ownership of homes and farms. Their letters, noting both their success and the limitations on that success, provide a rare view of the transformative changes then taking place in the American West.

Notes

Preface

1. The Emily Dickinson Museum at Amherst, Massachusetts, notes: "Dickinson most often punctuated her poems with dashes, rather than the more expected array of periods, commas, and other punctuation marks. She also capitalized interior words, not just words at the beginning of a line. Her reasons are not entirely clear . . . the dash was liberally used by many writers, as correspondence from the mid-nineteenth-century demonstrates." See http://www.emilydickinsonmuseum.org/poetry_characteristics (accessed November 5, 2013).

2. The "long s," which strongly resembles an f, is used in some of the letters; see Sacks, 296–97.

3. See http://about.usps.com/publications/pub100/pub100_022.htm (accessed December 10, 2013).

4. "In 1856 only 3.5 letters per capita were sent from northern rural districts, compared with 30 and 40.8 from New York and Boston respectively. Even the northern countryside fared better than similar areas in the South, which sent only 1.6 letters per capita that year." Zboray, 72.

5. See Watters.

6. John Heinz is a great-great-grandson of B. T. Burke. He did not, however, bring family knowledge or information to this project. He was not aware of the existence of the letters until the late 1990s, and he read the letters only after they had been donated to the Abraham Lincoln Presidential Library.

Chapter 1. The Dumvilles and Their Times

1. Watters, 148. Her words were not recorded, and most versions of what she said were written long after the fact. We have found seven accounts, but the substance is essentially the same. One, written by her grandson, Dr. Thomas L. Holme, suggests

that she was eager to keep the college out of the hands of "Roman Catholics." Everett Turnbull's version includes more details; see Turnbull, 284–85.

2. McElfresh, 10.

3. The name Hephzibah Beulah was surely taken from Isaiah 62:1–4: "You shall be called My Delight is in Her" [*Hephzibah* in Hebrew] and "your land Married" [*Beulah* in Hebrew].

4. William is a mystery. The manifest listed his occupation as "weaver." He is not mentioned in the letters. He was born in 1821, and Ann and Thomas were not married until 1828; but Thomas was a widower, and there were children born to his previous marriage. William may have been one of them.

5. Leaton, 18–19. See also Bestor. The MacMurray College archives include a draft of an unpublished speech about Ann Dumville written by Mrs. C. J. Lumpkin, *c.* 1946. The draft includes this sentence: "Her husband, Thomas Dumville, was a foreman in a cloth weaving factory in England and they came to St. Louis where a communistic society had established a store and which, like all other similar societies, failed." In the draft, "communistic" is crossed out and "cooperative" is written in.

6. Leaton, 19.

7. *Seventh Census* and *Ninth Census*.

8. Established in 1846, the college changed its name three times, becoming MacMurray College in 1930.

9. They are listed as "Irregular Students" in the College catalogue (*Illinois Conference Female College*, 1852).

10. Doyle, 113–14. Before 1880 the U.S. Census does not make it possible to identify relatives with differing surnames.

11. We examined thirteen manuscript pages of the Carlinville portion of the 1860 U.S. Census. The 103 households recorded on those pages included 523 individuals. Only eight of the 103 households were headed by females.

12. The preacher was Peter Cartwright (Cremin, 432).

13. Jemima appears in the 1850 U.S. Census at both the Tiller household in Carlinville and her older sister's home in Scott County, Illinois.

14. See letters of May 6, 1861, and March 17, 1862. The 1870 U.S. Census noted that Ann could read but not write, which was a standard entry at that time. Her will is signed with an X, but the will was executed only a few days before her death and she was ill; her will is on file at the Macoupin County courthouse. We obtained the record of the marriage of Ann and Thomas Dumville from the Church of Manchester, England. The husband and wife were required to sign their names—Thomas did, but Ann signed with an X (Ancestry.com). *Lancashire, England, Marriages and Banns, 1754–1936* [database online]. Original data: *Lancashire Anglican Parish Registers*, p. 212. Preston, England: Lancashire Archives.

15. There is a brief postscript to one letter that is signed "Elizabeth Williams" (September 29, 1861).

16. Lambert, quoted in Watters, 147.

17. The account of her dress is based on Turnbull, 44, and on Lambert, quoted in Watters, 147.

18. Leaton, 19.

19. *History of Macoupin County*, 76.

20. Watters, 146.

21. Leaton, 25.

22. Leaton, 25.

23. McElfresh, quoted in Watters, 148.

24. Hempton, 65–67.

25. Just over half of the letters (51 percent) deal with religion or with church affairs, and more than one-third (35 percent) deal with both death/illness and religion.

26. Melton, 109–10.

27. Katharine Dvorak observes, "For some men, circuit riding and celibacy went together; married preachers were likely to 'locate'" (pp. 113, 124).

28. "Discipline and Institutions, Conditions of Membership," Fox and Hoyt, 187.

29. Fox and Hoyt, 188.

30. Reid, 87.

31. American Colonization Society, 92–93; 114–17. After the Civil War, Seys became the U.S. consul general in Liberia. See also Spooner.

32. Hatch, 202–6.

33. Peter Cartwright was a prominent figure in the Methodist Church and in Illinois politics. He became a Methodist minister in 1802 and ten years later was made a presiding elder of the Church (a supervisory office), a position he then held for fifty years. He is reputed to have baptized twelve thousand converts. In 1846 he ran for Congress but was defeated by the Whig candidate, Abraham Lincoln; see Bray, 139–40. Cartwright's autobiography makes no mention of Abraham Lincoln. Cartwright lived near Jacksonville, in Pleasant Plains, and Hephzibah referred to him as "Uncle Peter."

34. "The pew system must necessarily be extremely offensive to the Lord's poor, and we should all remember the words of Jesus Christ, that it were better that a millstone were hanged about our necks, and we drowned in the depth of the sea, than that we should offend one of those little ones that believe on him" (Cartwright, 217).

35. Illinois Conference Female College, 21.

36. In 1835 Beecher published *An Essay on the Education of Female Teachers*.

37. Cremin, 146–47; see also Sklar, 124–27, and P. Palmer.

38. Cherry, 120, includes an excerpt from Lyman Beecher, "A Plea for the West."

39. Beecher, 167.

40. Methodists had proselytized through print since the early 1800s, building on and encouraging literacy with publications distributed by the circuit riders. At the same time, they were setting a reading agenda (Zboray, 90–91; Hatch, 126, 142–44). See Lehuu, 148, for the view of the novel as "reprehensible entertainment"; see also Hart, 53.

41. Watters, 51.

42. Kirkland, quoted in Miyakawa, 135. Ralph L. Rusk (p. 76) observed: "The typical frontiersman felt a stolid pride in his disdain for intellectual attainment. The few who possessed unusual culture were generally forced, if they wished to gain the confidence of their neighbors, to adapt themselves as rapidly as possible to the more primitive environment." Welter (p. 165) notes: "The female was dangerously addicted to novels, according to the literature of the period. She should avoid them, since they interfered with 'serious piety.'" A study of the demand for books at a subscription library in New York City found that the circulation of novels increased from 21 percent of the books charged out in 1847–49 to 45 percent in 1854–56 (Zboray, 164).

43. Cremin, 63–64. See also Stratton, 160; Monaghan, 134–35.

44. Although bound books remained too expensive for most people to afford in the antebellum period, the spread of railroads and the increasing circulation of newspapers provided literature to a growing portion of the country (Zboray, 11–13; 31).

45. Lehuu, 16–19, 132, citing Zboray, 96–109; Cremin, 490–91. "Basic literacy" differs from "advanced literacy." The 90 percent rate surely refers to the former standard. Although manuscript census records indicate that Elizabeth could read and write, the evidence in the letters suggests that at most she had a very minimal level of proficiency in writing, and there are no references to her reading.

46. Lehuu, 16.

47. The November 4, 1852, issue of the *Illinois Daily Journal* (Springfield) includes two stories that illustrate the importance of these technological advances. One, originally published in the *New York Tribune*, describes a trade mission to Japan that transported train track, wire for a telegraph, and daguerreotype equipment to show to the emperor of Japan. The other story includes presidential election results that, the newspaper notes, came by telegraph. See also, Dudden; R. Brown, 13–15.

48. Zboray, 127 passim; see, for example, *Illinois Daily News*, November 4, 1852.

49. See Blumin, 330.

50. Dudden, 43.

51. "Largest stock of new goods," *Jacksonville Constitutionist*, November 6, 1852, 4 (advertisement).

52. See Dudden, 104–7.

53. For analysis of the *Ladies' Home Journal*, which (somewhat later) promoted the consumer culture through the publication of extensive advertising, see Scanlon.

54. Fackler and Lippy, 241.

55. Rose, 83.

56. Matthaei, 123; Dudden, 130.

57. For an example of the role of women in the creation of markets in frontier Illinois, see Faragher, 104–5, 208. For the role of markets for household and decorative goods, which developed in the context of the "cult of True Womanhood," see, for example, Rose; Matthaei; Welter. For the importance of advertising and mass media in the development of consumerism and external displays of wealth, see Fackler and

Lippy; Scanlon; Garvey. The literature on the implications of the development of the "leisure class" is large. For a review of some of the historical trends, see Horowitz discussing Simon Patten.

58. Dressmaking was, of course, both functional and creative. Hephzibah's sewing was probably done by hand. The first practical sewing machine was patented in 1846, but the machines were initially quite expensive. Until the early 1870s, sewing machines were manufactured in relatively small numbers, but by 1873 annual production, made by several companies, had reached half a million. See Cooper, 19, 40, 47. Prior to the introduction of sized dress designs by Ebenezer Butterick in 1863, seamstresses tore apart existing dresses and adjusted design and size for their new projects. See Walsh, 299–313; Wass and Fandrich, 275.

59. Blumin, drawing on the work of John Gilkeson, has also noted the "direct connection between the emergence of reform organizations (in particular temperance and antislavery societies) and the crystallization of middle-class consciences in the antebellum era" (Blumin, 334).

60. Letter of January 26, 1857.

61. Letter of November 13, 1856.

62. Sheumaker, 53.

63. They had also saved some of her father's hair; see the letter of April 22, 1860.

64. See Becker, 17.

65. Cole, 320.

66. Ferrie, 35.

67. Cole, 315.

68. Ferrie, 187.

69. See Baltzell.

70. Watters, 19.

71. Later, the town had an important role in the founding of the new Republican Party, which was strongly abolitionist (Eames, 135).

72. Foner, 12, 47, 130.

73. Leaton, 19.

74. For a detailed and nuanced description of the influence of regional differences on the organization of abolitionist activities, see Robertson.

75. Ferrie, 59.

76. Stampp, 37.

77. Sutton, 341. Sutton comments: "Know-Nothing voters in Illinois, as in other states, were absorbed by the Republicans. Even Danenhower [leader of the Know-Nothings in Illinois] turned up a Republican during the Civil War and was recommended by Lincoln for a patronage job in Washington. After 1856 Lincoln himself solicited the support of the Know-Nothings, stressing in the process the similar views of the two parties on foreigners and Catholics."

78. As one might expect, there were soldiers from Carlinville and Jacksonville who were killed in the war, but there is no mention of those deaths in the women's letters.

79. The concept of homemaking as a vocation developed in the nineteenth century (Faragher, 118). See also, for example, Ellet, 18; Lerner, 130–33; Matthaei, 155–61.

80. In the 1850 Census a column was provided for "Profession, Occupation, or Trade of each Male Person over 15 years of age." In 1860 this became "Profession, Occupation, or Trade of each person, male and female, over 15 years of age," and in 1870 "Profession, Occupation, or Trade of each person, male or female." Despite the changes, however, occupations were seldom listed for females in either 1860 or 1870. Some were listed as "At Home" or "Keeping House," and others as a teacher or seamstress. In 1870 children were commonly listed as "At School."

81. Heilbrun, 16–31.

82. Rose, 80.

83. See, for example, Hempton, 138–39.

84. See Motz; George; Hampsten.

85. But see Dudden.

86. The Dumville letters differ in this respect from the sample of women's letters analyzed by Marilyn Motz, where the emphasis was on personal, immediate, and local matters. In those letters, even discussions of the Civil War focused on personal losses, not political, military, or religious matters (Motz, 72).

Chapter 2. Family Matters

1. The author of the centennial history of MacMurray College comments, however: "When one recalls the picture often given of the ignorance and lack of intellectual interest of the women of that day, it is remarkable to discover the scope and character of the reading of this schoolgirl [Hephzibah] who spent a great part of her days in physical labor" (Watters, 90).

2. Brush, 36. See also Faragher, 124.

3. See letters of September 7, 1857, and July 20, [1863].

4. Brush, 36. Fifty years later, in rural Iowa, Bess Corey wrote letters about her experiences teaching in one-room schools. See Gerber and Wright. See also Stratton.

5. He was an early supporter of Lincoln, one of the founders of the Republican Party, served as military governor of Kentucky, and was elected governor of Illinois as a Republican, but he then left the Republicans and was elected U.S. senator as a Democrat. In 1896, after the nomination of William Jennings Bryan, Palmer became the presidential candidate of the National (Gold) Democrats at age seventy-nine. The *New York Times* supported his presidential candidacy (see "The Choice" and "Where the Democratic Vote Belongs"). See also John Palmer; and Palmer and Lewis.

6. Cremin, 471.

7. Cremin, 435.

8. Illinois created a public school system in 1825 "open to every class of white citizens between the ages of five and twenty one" and provided for taxation within the county as well as State appropriations. Two years later, however, the tax was made optional. In 1845 the state legislature authorized the creation of a state superintendent of common schools as well as county superintendents, among whose duties was the

examination and licensing of teachers. It was not until 1855 that taxes were mandated to support common schools (Walker, 237–38). See also *History of Morgan County*, 332–33.

9. Watters, 50–52; Pruitt, 160, notes that the preparatory department offered reading, writing, spelling, geography, arithmetic, natural science, and needlework. The collegiate department provided a four-year classical course that included Latin and Greek.

10. See letter of November 28, 1859.

11. See letter of February 20, 1858. On September 12, [1859], Hephzibah wrote to Jemima, "While I write this they are singing 'The Old Cabin Home,' but to take the piano alone I would rather here my sister play than any one els" [emphasis in original].

12. See Miyakawa, 111–15.

13. Hempton, 68–74.

14. Here is the first verse of "Innocent Sounds," a "spiritual song" written in 1805 by Jeremiah Ingalls: "Enlisted in the cause of sin,/ Why should a good be evil?/ Music, alas, too long has been/ Press'd to obey the devil./ Drunken or lewd or light the lay,/ Flows to their souls' undoing./ Widen'd and strewn with flow'rs the way,/ Down to eternal ruin" (quoted in Hatch, 146–47). "The Wesleyan set of prescriptions for the life of scriptural holiness left no room for levity or carelessness." Hempton, 59.

15. Sweet, 82–83. The last letter in the archive (see chapter 6), written by William Stribling, includes an incomplete marginal note that refers to "improper influences" in music and to music "set against the Christian spirit."

16. Augst, 72.

17. Note that the letter is written using capital letters at the beginning of each line, as in poems of the period. This may suggest that she was using a book, perhaps a book of poetry, as a model.

18. This is a reference to her older sister Elizabeth's three children. At this time, Elizabeth and John Williams farmed in Scott County, Illinois, about two hours' ride by horseback from Jacksonville. Jemima appears to have moved frequently among Jacksonville, where she went to school and worked for the Striblings, Carlinville, where her mother lived, and Scott County, where she helped her sister.

19. Although the envelope was addressed to Jemima, the salutation was to their mother.

20. Her use of the French closing, "adieu," may have been regarded as humorous, or perhaps not. In either case, it suggests some sophistication.

21. Jemima had probably visited Elizabeth and John Williams.

22. The Striblings lived in Kentucky before moving to Illinois.

23. Jaquess was president of the Illinois Conference Female College and an elder in the Jacksonville Methodist Conference; Watters, 42–44; Burnette, 27–31.

24. The School for the Deaf and Dumb was opened in 1843 (Doyle, 69–73).

25. Thomas Dumville, her father, had been a member of the Odd Fellows in England.

26. Thomas Huckstep was a successful farmer in Lynnville, located about five miles southwest of Jacksonville.

27. "Pluck the beam…": Matt 7:3–5; Luke 6:42.

28. According to the *New York Times* ("Consistency, Thou Art a Jewel"), this popular phrase has no known source in literature, although it is frequently used.

29. William Hindall was an elder in the Clinton district, west of Jacksonville. He is mentioned as active in circulating *Uncle Tom's Cabin* and encouraging anti-slavery sentiment; see *Historic Morgan County*, 138.

30. The Saundersons lived near the Striblings. Mr. Saunderson was a local politician. Their daughters attended the women's college with the Dumvilles.

31. The style of this letter includes echoes of the language of the pulpit. This may have been Ann's own choice of words, reflecting her devotion to the church, or it may be that a preacher served as the scribe and he embellished her thoughts.

32. We do not know whether the writer may have altered Ann's words. She assumed that Jemima and Hephzibah shared her letters.

33. The proposed trip to Texas was probably for missionary work.

34. Ann was working as a housekeeper for the three McClure brothers, who farmed near Carlinville. James may have suggested taking her money for deposit in a bank.

35. Harris Point was a small settlement near Sulphur Springs.

36. The Chicago and Alton Railroad, connecting Alton and Springfield via Carlinville, was completed in 1852 (*History of MacoupinCounty*, 308).

37. Farm work was often shared by the employee and the employer but was divided by gender.

38. We do not know how Hephzibah's schooling was financed. Perhaps the Striblings were willing to pay the tuition, but attendance at school was permitted only when household duties had been completed.

Chapter 3. Cholera

1. See Custer.

2. John Snow published a theoretical paper on the causes of cholera in 1849; his definitive work on cholera was published in 1855, based on careful study of the water supply in Soho, London, documenting the manner in which cholera is spread. See Snow.

3. Jacksonville completed a water system and sewers in the 1870s; see Eames, 173, 179, 193. See also C. Smith, 165.

4. By 1856 there were 2,135 miles of railroad lines in Illinois (Doyle, 79).

5. The trip from Jacksonville to Carlinville now takes about an hour by automobile, by a more direct route.

6. The Dumvilles were enthusiastic customers of the local photographers. In the 1870 Census, two men in Carlinville listed their occupation as "photographer."

7. Hudgins, 561; Daval, 54. When photographs made as negatives became available and multiple copies of a picture could then be produced, prints were often glued onto small pieces of cardstock and used as calling cards. The cards, popularized in France

and known as *cartes de visite*, came into vogue in the United States by the 1860s. The photograph of Ann Dumville reproduced in chapter 1 is from a *carte de visite*.

8. Miyakawa, 187.
9. Fox and Hoyt, 204.
10. See Miyakawa, 90.
11. Cartwright, 189–90.
12. Atherton, 25.
13. Miyakawa comments (p. 164): "It was the successful preachers at camp meetings, Cartwright and Finley among them, even more than the opponents of revivalism, who most vividly described the hysteria, turbulence, confusion, and noise at these meetings with hundreds or thousands shouting, bellowing, and screaming, others in convulsions, and at times many in free-for-all fights. Cartwright, like others, dealt summarily with trouble makers, often cracking their skulls together. The whisky dealers who set up stands nearby were blamed for some of the wild fights."
14. Hatch, 195.
15. Hatch, 204.
16. Cartwright, 100; 217–19. After describing some of the excesses in behavior at a large revival, Rusk commented: "A few of the less emotional leaders were alarmed at such extraordinary proceedings; but the majority, especially the Methodists, had long been accustomed to regard extreme religious enthusiasm as indispensable" (47).
17. See Dvorak, 113; see also Miyakawa, 90–96.
18. Cartwright, 181, quoted in Miyakawa, 94. Cartwright also said that "illiterate Methodist preachers actually set the world on fire."
19. Miyakawa, 95.
20. Miyakawa, 96.
21. Miyakawa, 50–51.
22. Hempton, 124; Miyakawa, 110–11.
23. Dvorak, 124.
24. Hempton, 138–39.
25. Hempton, 140.
26. Motz, 7.
27. Illinois College was established by Presbyterians from the Yale College missionary program; see Eames, 57–58; Doyle, 21–23 passim; Burnette, 21.
28. Although Jemima was teaching, some of the spelling in this letter departs from standard usage, even for the time and place.
29. Jemima had moved to Carlinville to teach.
30. Given Jemima's several changes of residence, it is not clear what "home" refers to. Martha was one of the Williams children, born in 1854.
31. The Walter family had probably gone to Texas as missionaries.
32. Hephzibah assumes that Jemima had already heard of the death of Logan, Elizabeth and John's second child. He was five years old.
33. Sitting up was part of the ritual of a death vigil.
34. Sarah was the Williams's oldest child, born in 1848.

35. Margaret was the Williams's third child, born about 1852.

36. Since Jemima was teaching, her friend's compensation would no doubt be of interest.

37. Enoch March was an early settler in Jacksonville, a miller and merchant (*Morgan History*, 63). Mary March attended school with the Dumvilles.

38. Calling three physicians suggests the seriousness of the case and perhaps the prominence of the patient. Steven Stowe, discussing nineteenth-century physicians, notes that "their aim was to take charge of the patient's body and to roll back disease. But to do so, they had to organize and direct the often fractious and social bedside" (141). Stowe also observes that "bedside drama has lived on in sentimentalized accounts of 'frontier' doctors, a mixed image in which physicians are portrayed—with reference to twentieth-century medicine—as both heroic and ignorant" (132).

39. Only after describing the stages of his illness does she finally give the diagnosis, "cholera."

40. Richard Yates was at this time a congressman. He was later governor of Illinois (1861–65) and then a U. S. senator (1865–71). He had attended Illinois College in Jacksonville and practiced law there.

41. Hephzibah's friends, the Walter family, had returned from their missionary trip, finding that the conditions were too challenging.

42. Hephzibah is probably referring to employees at the Stribling farm. The Richardsons farmed nearby.

43. The Poseys were close neighbors; the daughters attended the College with the Dumvilles. They were early settlers in the area and founders of the Presbyterian church there (Eames, 56).

44. There were two Pitners, Levi and Wilson, both of whom were Methodist ministers. The one discussed here is Wilson, not Levi. We know this because Levi's wife was a daughter of Peter Cartwright, and Cartwright did not own slaves or reside in Tennessee. Wilson later moved to California.

45. The account given in the letter is not entirely clear, but our interpretation is this: Pitner's wife was one of the heirs of her father, who had recently died. The father had lived in Tennessee, and Pitner went to Tennessee to claim her inheritance, but the estate included slaves. Although Pitner was willing to free the slaves, to do so would have required the consent of all the heirs, and at least one of them was not present. Therefore, in order to divide the assets of the estate, the slaves were sold, and Pitner was then "turned out [of the church] . . . for selling men and women into perpetual bondage."

46. Note her concern for his loss of the labor of the children.

47. Jacob Plain was Major Burke's financial agent. He may have been called "Jake." The fact that Plain's mother was French may explain the rendering of his name as "Jacque." Plain was later Mayor of Carlinville. He also owned a land title abstract office in Carlinville (*History of Macoupin County*, 121).

48. This Mary is probably Hephzibah's half-sister, the daughter of Thomas and his first wife. Mary remained in England, married, and was then widowed.

Notes to Chapter 3

49. "Liney" may be a reference to linen, or possibly to linsey-woolsey, a fabric with a linen (or, sometimes, cotton) warp and a woolen weft. It was considered a less-valued fabric, associated with slave labor and the poor.

50. This appears to be a reference to barege, "a lightweight dress fabric made with yarns that have been highly twisted, usually silk . . . and worsted wool. . . . When the count was very low, the resulting fabric would be almost gauze-like and could be worn for veiling. When a higher count, the fabric remained lightweight but would be used for dresses" (Stamper and Condra, 203–4).

51. Bishop sleeves were gathered or pleated at both top and bottom. Often they were "shorter at the inside of the arm, so that the resulting shape is curved with fullness over the elbow" (Stamper and Condra, 96). They were especially popular in the 1850s and 1860s. See Wass and Fandrich, 302.

52. The editors do not recommend this treatment. The laudanum (that is, opium) mixed with brandy, taken "every five minutes," might well make the patient feel better, however, until the point at which he or she stopped breathing.

53. Possibly after taking the laudanum treatment?

54. Goldsmith, "Humorous Poems: II. Miscellaneous Elegy on Madam Blaize," lines 9–12.

55. Belle is another name that Hephzibah used during this period.

56. According to the *Oxford English Dictionary*, the term "blues," used in the sense of low spirits or melancholy, is of mid-eighteenth-century origin.

57. Biographical information concerning William Stribling notes that he "lived near Salem Church 3 mi East of Jacksonville. It was one of the earliest religious societies formed in the county" (Whitaker Genealogy).

58. In 1693 Cotton Mather published a book titled *Wonders of the Invisible World*, in which he defended his role in the prosecution of witches.

59. See Finley.

60. In Jacksonville in 1860 the highest paid male teacher received eighty dollars per month; the highest paid female received forty dollars per month (Eames, 157). We do not know whether the students were male or female. Elementary school students would not have been called "Mister"; her bill was probably sent to their fathers.

61. The Iowa state census of 1856 lists in the Williams household a nine-year-old named Ezra [Pisro?] who had been born in Illinois. Microfilm of Iowa State Censuses, 1856, Sugar Creek, Poweshiek County.

62. For a similar account of the rigors of homesteading on an unsettled frontier, although at an earlier period in Illinois, see Burlend.

63. "Bedstead" refers to the frame or structure of a bed, including the headboard, footboard, and rails, but not including the mattress. As we will see in chapter 6, the possession of the bedstead became an issue when Hephzibah prepared to leave the Stribling farm.

64. See note 70, below, regarding Helen Burke Denby.

65. "Orphan's father" likely refers to Major Burke; "widow's" probably refers to Ann Dumville.

66. Joseph Benson (c. 1748–1821) was a preacher, teacher, and scholar. During his early years he preached in Manchester, where Ann lived at the time of her marriage. Adam Clarke (c. 1760–1832) was a popular preacher sent out by John Wesley; he was also an influential scholar. See Wesleyan Heritage Collection. The memoir of James Laver (p. 20), a British author, art critic, and museum curator, includes an interesting comment on Clarke:

> Pride of place, in the great glass-fronted mahogany bookcase, was taken by the ten fat volumes of Dr Adam Clarke's *Commentary*. This, apart from the Bible itself, was my great-aunt's only reading, and very good reading it was, as I discovered at an early age. Adam Clarke was Methodism's most learned man, and his work, for the early nineteenth century anyway, was a monument of scholarship. It is true that many of his co-religionists regarded his views as dangerously sceptical, even tinged with heresy.... But he sprinkled his pages with Greek and Hebrew, showed diagrams of such mysteries as the Dial of Ahaz, and when he found a parallel to some Biblical story in one of the Hindu epics, printed the page in full.

67. See Cartwright, 205.

68. The Pitner mentioned here is Levi. He subsequently moved to Evanston, Illinois, and became an influential real estate developer and Prohibition Party politician (Sheppard and Hurd, 511–13).

69. William Milburn served several terms as chaplain of the U.S. House of Representatives and later was chaplain of the U.S. Senate from 1893 until his death in 1903. Milburn was blind and lectured widely; see Milburn.

70. A letter in the archives at MacMurray, written April 11, 1945, by Major Burke's granddaughter, Helen Burke Denby, includes this addendum: "A family story—Major Burke built a lovely new home & had it furnished & decorated quite lavishly for that day—carpets! even upon the stairs! His sister & a brood of children descended upon the household in his absence. Grandma D[umville] couldn't refuse to let them stay, though she did not want them—but she made them take off their shoes when they stepped on the carpet—so they soon got disgusted & left. Grandma was a diplomat."

Chapter 4. Political Awareness

1. As vice president, Fillmore became president in 1850 upon the death of Zachary Taylor. He served the remainder of Taylor's term, leaving office in 1853.

2. See Sutton, 326–41.

3. Dubin, 164.

4. Steckel, 583–603.

5. Steckel, 597–99.

6. Methodist preachers in Illinois generally favored abolition, and Democrats and Southern sympathizers thus advocated the separation of the ministry from politics. At Carthage, Illinois, an effort was made to establish an offshoot of the Church that

prohibited "politics in the pulpit," which was denounced as the "degeneracy of the church" (Cole, 423–24).

7. Using the University of Michigan database, we searched *The Ladies' Repository* and found no references to " Know-Nothing," "Know Nothing," "Fillmore," or "American Party," although there were hundreds of references to abolition and slavery.

8. Regarding Lurton, see Eames, 332.

9. Doyle's study of Jacksonville describes Republican efforts to build support through public meetings, partisan clubs, and parades. By the 1856 election, the Democrats were adopting similar approaches. (Doyle, 173–75).

10. In 1855 the Reverend Henry Ward Beecher, one of the brothers of Harriet Beecher Stowe and Catharine Beecher, raised money in Connecticut to buy rifles for abolitionist troops in "bloody Kansas." A company of volunteers, "the Beecher Bible and Rifle Colony," marched through New Haven armed with Sharps rifles provided by his fundraising (Applegate, 281–82; see also Goodwin, 183–84, and Byers, 19–20).

11. See Gayler, 154–69.

12. Even at an assembly of women's rights advocates—the convention at Seneca Falls in 1848—the resolution advocating women's suffrage was barely adopted. It passed by a narrow margin only after Frederick Douglass had made a persuasive speech supporting it. See Banner, 42; Ginzberg, 59–61.

13. According to Welter, "True Womanhood . . . could be divided into four cardinal virtues—piety, purity, submissiveness and domesticity" (152). "The true woman's place was unquestionably by her own fireside—as daughter, sister, but most of all as wife and mother. Therefore domesticity was among the virtues more prized by the women's magazines" (162).

14. Ellen Carol DuBois argues that "the development of feminism before the war was restrained by the organizational connection of its leaders with the antislavery movement, which kept them from concentrating on the mobilization of women around a primary commitment to their own rights" (19). It is also the case that the outcome of the Civil War and the long-sought abolition of slavery through adoption of the Thirteenth Amendment emboldened social reformers. Elizabeth Cady Stanton said: "Out of this struggle we must come with higher ideas of liberty, the masses quickened with thought, and a rotten aristocracy crushed forever" (quoted in Banner, 53).

We searched *The Ladies' Repository* for mentions of either "woman's vote" or "women's vote" from 1830 to 1863, when the letters stopped. We found only five mentions, and only between 1852 and 1863. Neither "woman's suffrage" nor "women's suffrage" was mentioned during that period. In contrast, the magazine mentioned "slavery" more than three hundred times and "emancipation" more than ninety times by 1863. The *Repository* supported abolition but was unenthusiastic about any "radical" changes in the core principles of "true womanhood." The text of the *Ladies' Repository* is accessible at http://quod.lib.umich.edu.

15. Motz, 72.

16. Baker, 631.

17. Goodwin, 98.
18. Goodwin, 99.
19. Goodwin, 97.
20. Galenson and Pope, 651.
21. Bogue, 51.
22. Galenson and Pope, 655.
23. See Pruitt, 154.
24. In some of the letters, Hephzibah gives people satirical pseudonyms, perhaps reflecting her familiarity with the work of John Bunyan and Jonathan Swift. Presumably Jemima understood the code and the names were intended to be both humorous and communicative.
25. This Mary was one of the Striblings' grandchildren.
26. Aunt Chloe and Black Sam are characters in *Uncle Tom's Cabin*, which was published in 1852 and which Hephzibah was then reading (see end of this letter).
27. Probably a reference to the Striblings' daughter, who lived close by.
28. Venetian blinds had by then been in use for several decades. St. Peter's Church in Philadelphia reportedly had them in 1761.
29. The "safe sugar desk" refers to a piece of furniture used for the storage of sugar, which was costly. Sugar chests, boxes, or desks were often decorated with inlay or figured veneers, as an indication of sugar's value. These were often seen in Kentucky and Tennessee. Since the Striblings had come from Kentucky, it is possible that they brought the sugar desk with them. See Speed Art Museum, exhibition "For Safekeeping: The Kentucky Sugar Chest, 1790–1850."
30. The Belles Lettres Society was the older of two literary societies at the college, founded in 1851; see Watters, 104 passim. Hephzibah often attended the literary events.
31. Phi Nu was the second literary society at the college, founded in 1853; see Watters, 104 passim.
32. The Dellzells were farmers who lived near the Striblings.
33. Internal evidence suggests that this letter dates from sometime in mid- or late June, since she wrote it after June 9 (when she wrote previously) and before graduation, which was in mid-July.
34. Slang term for Irish immigrants.
35. This is apparently a reference to a book she was reading.
36. This is the subtitle of *Uncle Tom's Cabin*.
37. See Ward.
38. Probably refers to Mr. Kerr, whose daughters attended the college with the Dumvilles. The death of Isabelle, one of Hephzibah's close friends, is mentioned below.
39. It is possible that this is a reference to Wilson Pitner.
40. Hephzibah probably means that she did the same thing.
41. Asa S. McCoy was the third president of the school, serving 1856 to 1858; Watters, at 119–23.

Notes to Chapter 4

42. On women's suffrage, see *The Declaration of Sentiments* signed at the Women's Rights Convention at Seneca Falls, New York, in 1848. It included demands for economic, educational, and voting rights for women. The major push for women's suffrage, however, came immediately after the Civil War (Susan B. Anthony Center).

43. Note that the class included only "young Ladies," and that the school is referred to as "Miss Dumville's School." It is not clear whether the school was public or private.

44. The votes from Illinois, Florida, and California were not reported until later, but by November 6 Buchanan had already secured the Electoral College majority. See "Result of the Elections"; "The Election in California"; "The Meeting of Congress."

45. White wedding dresses have been a tradition since Queen Victoria, who wore "creamy white Spitalfields satin" when she married Prince Albert in 1840 (Goldthorpe, 61–62).

46. This may be a reference to her half-sister, who remained in England.

47. Alexander Pope, 1688–1744. This appears to be a reference to Pope's poem, "An Essay on Man: Epistle I, X": "All nature is but art, unknown to thee/ alliances chance, direction, which thou canst not see/ All discord, harmony not understood/ All partial evil, universal good/ And spite of pride/ in erring reason's spite/ One truth is clear/ Whatever is, is right." We do not, however, believe that Pope considered this to be for the best.

48. Members of the McElfresh family were prominent in the Illinois conference. They were founders and staunch supporters of the Illinois Conference Female College.

49. William Milburn's lectures and stories first appeared in newspapers and were published as a collection as early as 1857.

50. Perhaps Julia Palmer, John McAuley Palmer's sister. She attended the college in the 1850s and taught there in the 1870s (Watters, 271).

51. Jemima had worked as domestic help at the Tillers' farm.

52. Milburn, 137–209.

53. Milburn, 162.

54. This appears inconsistent with her efforts to obtain further education. Perhaps she was intimidated by Milburn.

55. In the United States, first Massachusetts and then other states required smallpox vaccination. By 1897 smallpox had largely been eliminated in the United States. See Hopkins.

56. For the history, sociology, and art of picnics, see Barter, 96–99.

57. Thomas M. Eddy, D.D., (1823–1874), editor from 1856 to 1868. *Advocate* was published in Chicago.

58. 1 Thes 2:4: "But just as we have been approved by God to be entrusted with the message of the gospel, even so we speak, not to please mortals, but to please God who tests our heart."

59. Captain Vicars was a young British officer who died in the Crimean War. Earlier, while stationed in Canada, he was inspired by a chance reading in the Bible and became an ardent religious spokesman (Vicars, 32, 288–91).

60. Dr. Peter Akers was a presiding elder and one of the founders of the Illinois Conference Female College (Watters, 29–33).

61. See Sanders.

62. See Ray.

63. See Mitchell.

64. Josiah Williams was perhaps a relative who lived in Scott County.

65. See Hallwas, 10.

66. Elias was John's cousin and was one of the first settlers of Poweshiek County, having bought a farm in 1846.

67. Mr. Sinnock was a Methodist minister in Jacksonville.

68. The Poor Farm was located about a mile west of the Striblings, close to the Jacksonville city limits (Eames, 49–50).

69. We have been unable to find a source for this expression.

70. Utah militia challenged federal troops during "the Utah War" or "Utah Expedition," 1857–1858. The settlers feared invasion by Federal forces (Fleek, 81–96).

71. We know that Ann bought a house in Carlinville at about this time. In the 1860 Census, she and Jemima were listed as living in their own home.

72. On the Financial Panic of 1857, see Stampp, 213–38.

73. Beginning in May 1857, soldiers of the Bengal army attacked British officers. A year later the East India Company disbanded (Adas, 1–19; see also Herbert).

74. Gaslights for public streets were first used in London in 1807; they arrived in Jacksonville in 1857 and in Carlinville in 1869 (Walker, 425).

75. Although President Lincoln did not declare Thanksgiving a national holiday until 1863, it had been celebrated since the beginning of the nineteenth century by many states. The growth in popularity of the holiday may have reflected the increased attention to domestic arts and science, as well as its social function. See Wass and Fanduck, 266; Salmon, 217; Matthaei, 140–41, 173 passim.

76. Barter, 41–55.

77. Note that the farm laborer would go to school, but Hephzibah could not be spared.

78. Her "theology" is a reference to her letter a month before, on October 29, 1857, in which she set forth her ideas about the existence of hell.

79. Cartwright, first published a year earlier.

80. Cartwright, 80.

81. Cartwright, 99–101.

Chapter 5. The Lincoln-Douglas Elections

1. Another matter of national consequence noted in these letters is the attack by John Brown and twenty-one other abolitionists on the U.S. armory at Harpers Ferry, Virginia (now West Virginia), in October 1859. They occupied the armory but were then surrounded by Federal troops commanded by Robert E. Lee. Brown was wounded, captured, convicted of treason, and sentenced to death. There was considerable popular support for Brown in the North. See, for example, Henry David Thoreau,

"A Plea for Captain John Brown." Nonetheless, Brown was hanged on December 2, 1859.

2. Burnette, 31–34.

3. The curriculum of the Illinois Conference Female College included a course for sophomores listed as "Domestic Economy—Miss Beecher's," a reference to the textbook. See Watters, 51.

4. Baker, 634.

5. Hewitt, 157.

6. Starting in the 1830s Jacksonville called itself "the Athens of the West." This claim was based in part on the educational institutions in the community (Doyle, 32–33).

7. Perhaps this means the "functional equivalent of" bed cords and a table.

8. Cartwright lived until age eighty-seven. He died in 1872.

9. Methodists and other Christian groups had attempted to proselitize in India, starting in 1856. Ten years later the Methodists had twenty-five European missionaries there (Missionary Society, 73–74).

10. The neighborhood effort probably intended the construction of a small elementary school, financed by subscriptions.

11. George was born in 1857, after Sarah, Logan, and Margaret Emily.

12. Doyle, 75n29, describes the split among Methodists in Jacksonville that led to the creation of an "East Charge" and a "West Charge": "The establishment of the academy [that is, the women's college] also opened a serious rift between Methodists on the east and west sides, each of whom wanted the school at their end of town. The 'East-Enders' won, but Jacksonville's Methodist church later split into 'East Charge' and 'West Charge' congregations" (see Watters, and also Pratt, 271–78).

13. The creek ran close to the Lurton and Stribling properties, on the way to the Illinois River; see figure 5.

14. Mary Spaulding's father was an abolitionist on the faculty of the college (Watters, 109).

15. Probably Virginia, Illinois, about forty miles north of Jacksonville.

16. Lurton's store was located in downtown Jacksonville.

17. The mention of the "splendid orator, Mr. Colfax," refers to Schuyler Colfax, a congressman from Indiana, who later became speaker of the U.S. House of Representatives and then Grant's vice president. He was only thirty-six years old when Hephzibah heard him speak. He may have come to the attention of the organizers of the Jacksonville celebration through his prominence in the Independent Order of Odd Fellows, which is given considerable attention in Hephzibah's letter. She was especially interested in the Order because her father was a member; see letter of June 8, 1854.

18. "The worst" to which Ann Dumville refers never came to light in other letters or contexts. We do not know what this refers to.

19. This letter appears to be addressed to an English cousin.

20. Based on Psalm 65:5: "A father to the fatherless, a defender of widows, is God in his holy dwelling."

21. Perhaps this letter is a copy that Hephzibah made prior to mailing Jemima's letter and her own to England.

22. "Bottom land" refers to land adjacent to a stream or creek, at a lower elevation than the surrounding land.

23. Grinnell was the largest town in Poweshiek County.

24. Gardening is often mentioned in the letters. It was both an entertainment and a necessity. In 1854 a business directory listed only one grocer in Morgan County (Jacksonville) and none in Macoupin County (Carlinville); see Montague. But flowers were also cultivated, and the letters mention tulips, daffodils, verbena, roses, and japonica [Japanese quince]. Seeds were available by mail order from catalogs (for example, Thorburn); the library of the Smithsonian Institution has a collection of ten thousand seed and nursery catalogs dating from 1830. Exchanging seeds, however, was obviously more economical than buying them, and the exchange appears to have had a social element as well. Seeds were enclosed in some of the letters.

25. This letter is on the other side of the same sheet as Hephzibah's letter of October 10, 1859, the next letter in the archive. They conserved stationery.

26. The reference to Jacob and Joseph comes from the Old Testament (Genesis 37: 1–35), but the meaning of this reference in the Williams's letter is unclear.

27. Hephzibah then passed this sad news to her mother and Jemima. At that time, newspapers did not carry obituaries unless the decedent was a prominent citizen, and letters were therefore the primary way that such information reached people living elsewhere. It took two weeks for this devastating news to be passed on. Although the telegraph was available in Jacksonville by the mid-1850s, telegrams were expensive, brief, and impersonal, and in rural areas telegraph offices were often several miles away.

28. For homesteading farmers, children played an important role in the economic unit; see Faragher.

29. White missionaries working in Liberia suffered from tropical diseases, and many died (Hempton, 157). Four of the Seys children died while there in the 1840s (American Colonization Society, 114–15).

30. Methodist traveling preachers and deacons were responsible for identifying and recruiting potential members and for ministering to established congregations within a district that could cover four hundred to five hundred square miles. Local preachers were licensed annually and appear to have been relocated often (Fox and Hoyt, 181–85).

31. At this time, Jaquess was president of Quincy College. There were financial problems at the college, which resulted in controversy (Burnette, 44–45).

32. Perhaps she is referring to erysipelas, a bacterial skin infection.

33. Although she was twenty-six years old, Hephzibah appears to have followed Mrs. Stribling's social cues.

34. No year is stated in the letter, but the references to her social acquaintances suggest that it was written in 1860.

35. Mrs. Posey was forty-seven years old at the time of her death. A widow, she farmed nearby and had seven children. Her daughters were good friends of Hephzibah's. Shortly after Mrs. Posey's death, the 1860 Census listed John (then age twenty-one) as a farmer with real property valued at $12,000 and personal property of $1,200. John was listed as the head of household even though his sisters were older, but the property may not have been solely his.

36. Hephzibah's attempts to name the disease that afflicted Mrs. Posey are consistent with Steven Stowe's observations concerning nineteenth-century medical practice in the South: "People eagerly attached names to what they suffered, drawing upon a vocabulary of diseases heard about, seen before, and diagnosed by doctors, family, or friends. Names were a gesture toward control, implying that a malady was a known thing with a predictable 'course'" (Stowe, 135; at page 133 he suggests that calomel, a laxative or purgative, was overused).

37. A tornado damaged property and injured people in Carlinville on April 16, 1860 (*St. Louis Republican*, April 17, 1860, and *Chicago Press and Tribune*, April 23, 1860).

38. Benjamin Stead was a young Methodist friend of the Dumvilles from Nilwood, near Sulphur Springs. He joined the army in 1861 and corresponded with Jemima during the war.

39. "As Methodist and Baptist churches grew wealthier, they built substantial sanctuaries, installed organs" (Hatch, 195).

40. This refers to the tornado in Carlinville on April 16, noted above. The bad weather in Jacksonville that Hephzibah discusses in this letter was not a tornado—it was apparently localized and caused no major damage. There was, however, a tornado in Jacksonville the year before, in May 1859 (Eames, 217).

41. This is probably a reference to the work of William G. Sewell, who was on the editorial staff of the *New York Times* and wrote extensively about the effects of emancipation in the West Indies. See Sewell.

42. It may be that Hephzibah was referring to George Thompson, a well-known English abolitionist who lectured frequently in the United States.

43. Based on internal evidence.

44. By 1860 Don Burke, Major Burke's son, was a student at McKendree College in Lebanon, Illinois. Don later graduated from St. Louis University. Don's sister, Ellen (or Ella), was ten years old at that time.

45. This may be a reference to the next annual conference, which was held in Carlinville, September 11–14, 1861 (*Minutes of the Conference*, 1861, cover page). Or, perhaps, Hephzibah may have been planning to leave the Striblings the following year.

46. The Van Winkle daughters attended the college with the Dumvilles; Mr. Van Winkle was a Methodist.

47. Brothers George and William Rutledge were elders. William served as a chaplain in the Civil War and was subsequently a founder of the Grand Army of the Republic (*History of Morgan County*, 462, 933).

48. Gift books were usually "small books of duodecimo size ... published annually for holiday rituals of gift giving ... primarily a gift and a sign of taste and social status" (Lehuu, 76–77).

49. "Constitutional slavocrat" is probably a reference to Stephen Douglas.

Chapter 6. The War

1. During the fighting, U.S. Senator Edward Baker of Oregon, a close friend of Lincoln, was killed. Baker was serving as a colonel in the Union army.

2. Matthews, 1590.

3. Klement, 3–4.

4. See postscript to letter of December 23, 1861. Matthews, 1670, quotes the *Chicago Tribune* of May 1861 as using the term "stumptail currency." It is defined as follows: "At the outbreak of the Civil War, those bank notes secured by Southern state bonds and depreciated Northern issues were called 'stumptail' and were, as the name denotes, circulated at a discount."

5. Klement, 3–4.

6. Klement, 6–9.

7. He was a cousin of the more famous Major General John A. "Blackjack" Logan of Murphysboro, Illinois. See Emery.

8. The army commissioned its first female chaplain in 1979. See www.armyhistory.org.

9. The losses on both sides were extraordinarily heavy. "Americans ... suffered more casualties in the daylong fight at Shiloh than all of the casualties during the American Revolution, the War of 1812, and the Mexican War *combined*" (Groom, 16).

10. The Statue of Freedom (a fortified woman) was installed at its top on December 2, 1863.

11. For example, Jemima's letter of January 11, 1862, to Daniel Cheney, and Hephzibah's letter of March 17, 1862, which was addressed to her mother and sister.

12. McPherson, 117.

13. See "Gleanings from the Mail."

14. Milburn, 96–97.

15. Doyle, 264, table 7.

16. Stribling's letter assumes that they were already married at that time, but he was probably mistaken. Macoupin County records report that "Hephzibah B. Dunville" [sic] married "Frederick A. Beckley" [sic] on August 16, 1864.

17. See Dudden, 88.

18. After 1856 there was a German Methodist church in Jacksonville. It is possible that Fred Bechly found his way to the Stribling farm through that network (Doyle, 131).

19. Stowe suggests, "People's accounts of sickness and care-giving often become small devotional tales, enlivened for many by the broad language of Christianity that

allowed the idiosyncrasies of personal suffering to flow into lessons of courage and moral character" (Stowe, 136).

20. Hephzibah, who writes straightforwardly, simply, and with wit, was impressed by Mary's baroque, pretentious style.

21. Mrs. Jaquess taught practical life courses at the college in the 1850s (Watters, 67; Burnette, 30).

22. Clarinda Olin taught science and math at the college in the 1850s (Watters, 67; 68–69).

23. The juxtaposition of the decoration of the chapel and the hog killing is striking. It illustrates the variety of daily experience and the relative lack of social hierarchy in the rural Midwest of the 1860s.

24. See note in chapter 2 regarding Clarke and Benson.

25. At this time the Lurtons had five children living at home; Benjamin was born in 1860.

26. This is probably a reference to Mary Dumville Cooke, Hephzibah's half-sister, who remained in Huddersfield, York, England.

27. This is a reference to the Garden of Eden story in which the serpent tempts Eve and she is then cast out of paradise. Also see *Paradise Lost*.

28. Such rhetoric continued through the war years: for example, an article in the *New York Times*, July 19, 1863, states, "There are parallels of depravity in a class of men who endeavor to embarrass the Government we love, in its struggle with traitors. I mean Copperheads of to-day—worthy compeers of Tories of the Revolution." (See "The Fourth of July at Port Hudson.")

29. This letter was written four days after Lincoln's inauguration.

30. Her friend and neighbor.

31. Hephzibah's reading broadened her vocabulary.

32. By the 1870 Census, John Posey had moved to Wisconsin, where he farmed a small piece of property. He and his wife had five children under age nine, all of whom were born in Wisconsin. It is likely, then, that John left shortly after this incident.

33. Margaret was their older sister.

34. South Carolina seceded first, on December 20, 1860; Mississippi, Florida, Alabama, Louisiana, and Texas had seceded by February 1861.

35. Virginia seceded on April 17, 1861, five days after the battle of Fort Sumter and about five weeks after this letter.

36. In commending Lincoln's silence, she endorsed the view of those who were concerned with maintaining presidential authority during the transition.

37. William H. Seward became secretary of state a few days before this letter was written, but Hephzibah is probably referring to a speech that Seward made on January 12, 1861, while he was still a U.S. senator. That speech was an effort to save the Union by making concessions to the South, and it was widely reported. The *New York Times* article "Mr. Seward's Speech" (January 14, 1861) said that "a few Republicans declare that the Senator has cowed before his enemies." In the speech, Seward argued that an

escaped slave should "be delivered up, on claim, to the party to whom his service is due" and that "domestic slavery, existing in any State, is wisely left by the Constitution of the United States exclusively to the care, management, and disposition of the State; and if it were in my power, I would not alter the Constitution in that respect." But he also said, "I certainly shall never, directly or indirectly, give my vote to establish or sanction slavery in [the U.S.] Territories, or anywhere else in the world." In a piece from "News of the Day") in the same issue of the *Times*, there was a vivid account of the event: "The largest crowd that ever collected inside the Senate-house assembled on Saturday to hear the speech of Hon. WM. H. SEWARD on the National Crisis. The full Diplomatic Corps were in attendance, the galleries were crammed almost to suffocation, and numbers went away unable to obtain admission."

38. Jemima had considered becoming a missionary in Liberia. Hephzibah is replying to this.

39. Hephzibah does not mention that four Seys children died in Liberia in the 1830s and early 1840s.

40. Livingstone was a medical missionary, funded in part by the London Missionary Society, an association he found agreeable because of "its perfectly unsectarian character.... [It] sends neither Episcopacy, nor Presbyterianism, nor Independency, but the Gospel of Christ to the heathen. This exactly agreed with my ideas of what a missionary society ought to do" (Livingstone, introduction).

41. This may be a reference to "From Greenland's icy mountains, From India's coral strand, Where Africa's sunny fountains Roll down their golden sand." Hymn written in 1819 by Reginald Heber, a distinguished Anglican priest and the bishop of India.

42. Based on internal evidence—the letter indicates that she had worked at the Stribling farm for fourteen years.

43. Kansas entered the Union as a free state on January 29, 1861, but violence between pro-slavery and anti-slavery forces continued to erupt there throughout the Civil War. The Methodists maintained a missionary program in the state.

44. Arrangements for domestic service rarely included a contract. The position was often short term, with only an informal understanding about the terms (Dudden, 88–89).

45. This flurry of correspondence may have been stimulated by Hephzibah's letter of March 11, 1861, concerning her employment status with the Striblings.

46. Payment for services sometimes included reimbursement for expenses.

47. Dudden reports evidence that the usual compensation for housework in the 1850s was about one dollar per week (102). At that rate of pay, sixteen years of work at the Stribling farm would amount to $832. When Louisa May Alcott was young, she worked as "help," and her mother asked Louisa's employer about Louisa's wages. The employer replied: "My dear madam, in a case like this let us not use such words as those. Anything you may think proper we shall gladly give" (quoted in Dudden, 87). Mrs. Alcott did not pursue the matter, and Louisa's wages, in the end, proved to be grossly unsatisfactory. This reported conversation has striking similarities to the Reverend Stribling's letter to Ann Dumville.

48. Framing Mrs. Stribling's perspective as spiritual support rather than as a financial matter was consistent with the usual terms of discourse among religious women. But Hephzibah uses instrumental language, similar to John's (March 11, 1861)—for example, "what she should get." It is, of course, possible that Mrs. Stribling did not agree with Mr. Stribling.

49. Home Guards were local militia organized to support the Union forces; see www.iowahistory.org/battleflags/iowa_in_the_war.htm.

50. The conference was in Carlinville, September 11–14, 1861 (see Leaton). This serves to date the letter.

51. At this time General Winfield Scott was in command of the Union Army. He resigned his command in November 1861.

52. The term "democracy" refers to members of the Democratic Party. Matthews says that "stumptail" designates "a person or thing that is damaged or inferior" (1670).

53. Southern sympathizers were active in Iowa. The rhetoric on both sides was heated, with intimidation and threats. See Klement; see also Byers.

54. Oskaloosa is about thirty miles south of Powesheik County and was a trading and shipping point.

55. In 1861 the draft was used only in states that did not provide sufficient volunteers. When a draft was imposed, it was administered by the state, not by the federal government, and a quota was allocated to each county. One could therefore avoid the draft by moving to another state (Klement, 25–26). Iowa filled its troop requirements with volunteers, at least until late 1863 (Byers, 334). Illinois did not have a draft until late in 1864. According to the Illinois State Archives, of 259,000 soldiers from Illinois, only 3,538 were draftees.

56. The stationery features a military seal and an inspirational poem.

57. The Harris family was prominent in Nilwood Township, the Sulphur Springs neighborhood. Cheney was also from that area.

58. Mechanical apple peelers had been available since the early 1800s. Given Hephzibah's previous references to the time-consuming task of drying fruit, it is possible that after the tornado in the spring of 1860 (May 8, 1860 letter), the Striblings invested in a newer and more efficient dry house and peeler (Thornton, 58–61).

59. James Barger was a Methodist elder and the son of an elder. He was killed in a hunting accident.

60. Decatur is seventy-four miles east of Jacksonville.

61. For discussion of the fire, see Watters, 148–52.

62. See Elliott.

63. James Leaton was a prominent younger member of the Illinois Conference. He later became its historian.

64. Dr. Akers was a leader in Methodist higher education as well as an elder in the conference.

65. This letter from Jemima to Daniel Cheney was found among the Dumville family correspondence. That raises an interesting question: How did it get there? Did Cheney return the letter to Jemima? Did the letter fail to reach Cairo before

Cheney had left for action in Tennessee, so that the letter was returned to Jemima by the army? Military records indicate that Cheney did not die in the war. This is not a draft or a copy of a letter—the archive includes the stamped, postmarked envelope in which it was mailed.

66. Lincoln strongly rejected claims by both North and South that God was a partisan. In his second inaugural address, he said: "Both read the same Bible and pray to the same God, and each invokes His aid against the other. . . . The prayers of both could not be answered. That of neither has been answered fully. The Almighty has His own purposes." But the "Battle Hymn of the Republic" does not hesitate to invoke Divine Providence: "Mine eyes have seen the glory of the coming of the Lord. . . . I have read a fiery gospel writ in burnished rows of steel:/ As ye deal with my contemners, so with you my grace shall deal;/ Let the Hero, born of woman, crush the serpent with his heel./ His truth is marching on" (see Howe).

67. Jemima's religious perspective is quite different from the patriotism and hope for survival expressed by Cheney (for example, October 18, 1861) and Stead (January 29, 1862).

68. This is probably a reference to the ordinance of 1015, in the reign of King Ethelred, which provided that "Christian men and uncondemned be not sold out of the country, especially into a heathen nation." See Smith; see also Stubbs.

69. It should be noted that Jemima's distaste for living "with the blacks" was typical of even some abolitionist opinion at the time. It is consistent, indeed, with statements made by Lincoln. See Foner, 224; Johannsen, 664.

70. In the original, this letter was written without any punctuation—no periods, no commas, and no capital letters except for people's names. The stationery includes military symbols.

71. Abram D. Keller, from Carlinville, was a forty-one-year-old lieutenant in the 30th Ill. Infantry. Daniel Cheney, from Nilwood, close by, was in the 32nd Ill. Infantry. The signature appears to be in the same handwriting as the rest of the letter, which was signed by Dan Cheney. Perhaps Keller was a mutual friend.

72. Daniel Messick, from Carlinville, was in the same unit. He was killed in battle on March 1, 1862, two weeks after this letter was written.

73. Nathaniel Gordon was the captain of a ship that brought slaves from the Congo. In 1860 his ship was seized with 897 captives on board, most of whom were children. He was convicted and sentenced to death. Lincoln initially stayed Gordon's execution, but only for two weeks. Gordon was hanged less than a month before Hephzibah's letter. As she notes, no other slave trader had been executed.

74. Capps owned a mill that produced cloth and, later, clothing; see Heinl.

75. These lines come from James Thomson (1700–1748), "Spring. A Poem," first published in 1728. In another passage, not included here, Hephzibah attributes them to "Cowper." The *New York Times* of February 16, 1879 (" The Trials of School-Teaching"), also attributed the image to Cowper: "When Cowper wrote about the 'delightful task, to teach the young idea how to shoot'. . . ." Hephzibah and the *Times* may have traveled in the same literary circles.

76. At about this point, Ann went back to work for Major Burke as his housekeeper.

77. After the surrender of Forts Henry and Donelson, Confederate forces under the command of P. G. T. Beauregard sought to control traffic on the Mississippi River by reinforcing a garrison at Island Number 10, near New Madrid, Missouri. The island was then attacked by Union gunboats and the Union army, and the siege continued from early March until the Confederate forces surrendered the island on April 7, only a few days before Hephzibah's letter. Palmer's troops took part in this battle.

78. The *Monitor* and the *Merrimack* were both ironclad ships, the former a Union vessel and the latter a Confederate ship (built on the shell of the *USS Merrimack* and then renamed the "Virginia," but northerners continued to refer to it as the *Merrimack*). The two ships met in an inconclusive battle on March 8 and 9, 1862, at Hampton Roads, Virginia, near where the James River enters Chesapeake Bay. Confederate forces were trying to break the Union blockade of Norfolk and Richmond. Hephzibah's letter reflects concern that the Confederate ship would be further strengthened, but the two vessels never met again.

79. Although no year is provided, the battle of Pittsburg Landing was fought in 1862.

80. Many residents of central Illinois had come from the South. This letter is an interesting comment on how the resulting conflicts were handled in "polite society."

81. This is a reference to Fred Bechly.

82. The term "nigger," of course, was in common usage in both North and South at this time; see Mathews, 1117–21. It seems that he was referring to himself, meaning one who did hard labor.

83. Contrary to Hephzibah's assumption, John's letters customarily used "Dear" in the salutation. This is the only letter in the archive that John mailed to Hephzibah. We believe that Jemima was the person who saved most of the surviving letters, but Hephzibah may have saved this one or she may have forwarded it to Jemima.

84. This appears to refer to Hephzibah's departure from the Striblings.

85. William G. Brownlow, known as "Parson Brownlow," was a Methodist minister who became editor and publisher of the *Knoxville Whig*. Although a Southerner, he opposed secession. An article in the July 1862 issue of *The Ladies' Repository*, published shortly before Hephzibah wrote this letter, said: "Mr. Brownlow is never neutral on any subject, is not over-fastidious in the use of language, and loves to pile up epithets denunciatory and objurgatory upon his opponents.... [I]n his personal habits he is singularly pure; he never tastes liquor, never has used tobacco, never has seen a play at a theater, and never has dealt a pack of cards—a remarkable record for a Southerner."

86. Jaquess, who resigned as president of the women's college in 1855, continued to work in education until he entered the Union army (Watters, 115–16). His later life was considerably more colorful; see Burnette, 95–152.

87. General Benjamin Franklin Butler lived in Lowell, Massachusetts. He gave a speech at Huntington Hall there on January 12, 1863, and the next day he spoke at Faneuil Hall in Boston. In his remarks at Lowell, Butler said: "I have found that

this rebellion is a rebellion against the working classes, without distinction of color; ... The rebellion was begun, and is carried on for the purpose of creating a landed aristocracy" (see "General Butler at Home"). The *New York Times* reported that, at the Boston speech, "Faneuil Hall was overflowing. ... When the General entered the hall the effect was very grand, the handkerchiefs of nearly two thousand ladies waving him a brilliant welcome home" (see "General Butler in Boston").

88. Although the envelope is addressed to Jemima, it is likely that Hephzibah was writing to Mary, her half-sister in England, and expected Jemima to forward the letter to England.

89. There was no John Dumville listed on the ship's manifest, and John Williams, Elizabeth's husband, was born in Indiana. "Brother" was a term used to refer to fellow Methodists, so this may be a reference to a friend who came to America with the Dumvilles.

90. Mary was fifteen years older than Hephzibah.

91. Lincoln had suspended the writ of habeas corpus to permit suspicious persons to be held without trial, and a man named Milligan, who was suspected of being a Confederate spy, was arrested in Indiana and imprisoned by the military authorities. After the war ended, the U.S. Supreme Court held that Lincoln's order exceeded the constitutional powers of the president because civilian courts had been open and functioning in Indiana and were capable of adjudicating the case. *Ex parte Milligan*, 71 U.S. 2 (1866).

92. Nathan Coop was a twenty-six-year-old farmer. The Coops were among the earliest settlers of Macoupin County. "Coop's Mound" is near Sulphur Springs.

93. Trenton, Tennessee, is in a rural area, located in the western part of the state, about one hundred miles north of Memphis and thirty miles east of the Mississippi River.

94. Internal evidence indicates that this letter was probably written in July 1863. The handwriting and grammar are more mature than that seen in her August 11, 1862, letter; moreover, Copperhead activity was an increasing problem in Iowa in 1863.

95. The reference to compensation may suggest that Mary Jane was employed at the hospital or that she was a patient who had some duties there.

96. Eleven days later, "Tally's War" took place about forty miles away. A Copperhead rally in a neighboring (and Republican-leaning) county became violent. The Copperhead leader, George Cyphert Tally, was killed, and one or two others were injured (Byers, 474); See also "Troubles in Iowa: Outrageous Conduct of the Copperheads," from the *Davenport (Iowa) Gazette*, August 6, 1863, republished in the *New York Times*, August 12, 1863.

97. Logan probably refers to the Williamses' son, Hardin Logan Williams, who died in 1854 at age five (see letter of May 4, 1854).

98. The Striblings had a daughter who died at age sixteen.

99. As indicated above (see note 16), Hephzibah and Fred did not marry until August 1864.

Chapter 7. The Letters End

1. Hephzibah and Jemima surely continued to write to their mother and to each other, but no subsequent letters have been found.

2. Records of the State of Illinois show (with misspellings) that "Jemima Dunville" married "James H. Holmes" on June 9, 1864, and that "Hephzibah B. Dunville" married "Frederick A. Beckley" on August 16, 1864. Both marriages took place in Macoupin County (Carlinville). The 1860 Census listed Holme, age forty, as married and as a miller in Gillespie, Illinois, near Carlinville. His wife died a short time later.

3. See Jones, 201–19, 208 (table 5). The average age during the period from 1851 to 1900 was 22.3. The Dumvilles' marriage prospects were, no doubt, limited by their lack of dowries.

4. At common law, under a doctrine known as "coverture," the husband and wife were "one person in law," which effectively meant that married women could not own property nor enter into contracts. As the nineteenth century progressed, married women's property rights were gradually modified, but husbands nonetheless continued to have managerial control. See Chused, 1359n26.

5. Born between 1865 and 1872.

6. Fred Bechly later owned a small farm in Iowa. The 1870 Census reported that he owned real property valued at $1,000. It is unclear when he acquired this property.

7. In addition to the son born in August 1865, the Bechlys had a daughter born in May 1868.

8. Lehuu, 16, 132.

9. Leaton reports that "for the last eighteen years of her life, indeed until near her death, she kept house for Major Burke near Carlinville" (20). This is not necessarily inconsistent with the Census report that she lived at Don Burke's residence in 1870—she could have lived at the son's house but cared for the father's. But her obituary in the *Macoupin County Enquirer*, April 3, 1873, said that she "for many years resided with Major Burke."

10. An unpublished speech held by the archives of MacMurray College says that "she did not remain in that home [the Burkes' home] through the years but returned to the side of her old employer when his second wife died and he again had small motherless children" (Lumpkin, 3). Major Burke survived three wives. His second wife died in 1852. Eleven years later he married the third wife, who died in 1866, apparently as a consequence of childbirth. Two children born to the second marriage survived, as did two born to the third marriage (*History of Macoupin County*, 95). Hephzibah's letter of April 15, 1862, suggests that the children needed someone to care for them. The children of Burke's second marriage were then twelve and seventeen, and he did not marry his third wife until the following year.

11. This is a reference to a character in John Bunyan's *The Pilgrim's Progress* (1678).

12. Leaton, 22–23.

13. Leaton reports that "she lingered for a few days and then passed away" (26).

14. Thomas's gravestone is now broken in half, but Ann's remains intact although barely legible.

15. A letter written by Hephzibah to Jemima on August 15, 1862, suggests that Williams was in Iowa at that time, four months after the battle of Shiloh. She says that Fred Bechly had just visited Iowa and had "spent two or three days" with John Williams. The Williams family considered moving back to Illinois at that time. We think it probable that some 1862 and 1863 letters are missing.

16. *History of Poweshiek County*, 697.

17. John's place of burial is unknown, but there is a memorial to him in the Forest Home Cemetery in Poweshiek County, near Elizabeth's grave (Iowa Cemetery records).

18. "Who can estimate the value of the amount of Educated Female minds, every year accumulating, and spreading over the country as sisters, wives, and mothers of those who are soon to direct the destinies of this nation" (*Illinois Conference Female College*, 20).

19. See Welter, 174.

20. Shils, 104.

21. Letter of March 11, 1861.

22. Dudden (pp. 28, 120–21) observes that nineteenth-century serving women sometimes saved their money to buy a special dress. This did not alter their inherent status.

23. She is buried in the Forest Home cemetery in Poweshiek County, Iowa, in the Williams family plot with Elizabeth, Elizabeth's daughter, Sarah, and the memorial to John. Fred Bechly remarried three years after Hephzibah's death. He died January 21, 1916, and is buried in the Odd Fellows cemetery in Searsboro, Iowa, beside his second wife.

References

Adas, Michael. "Twentieth Century Approaches to the Indian Mutiny of 1857–58." *Journal of Asian History* 5, no. 1 (1971): 1–19.
American Colonization Society. *The African Repository*. Vol. 47. Washington City, 1872.
Applegate, Debby. *The Most Famous Man in America: The Biography of Henry Ward Beecher*. New York: Doubleday, 2006.
Army Historical Foundation. Available at http://www.armyhistory.org.
Atherton, Lewis. *Main Street on the Middle Border*. Bloomington: Indiana University Press, 1954.
Augst, Thomas. *The Clerk's Tale*. Chicago: University of Chicago Press, 2003.
Baker, Paula. "The Domestication of Politics: Women and American Political Society, 1780–1920." *American Historical Review* 89, no. 3 (June 1984): 620–47.
Baltzell, E. Digby. *Puritan Boston and Quaker Philadelphia*. New York: Free Press, 1979.
Banner, Lois W. *Elizabeth Cady Stanton: A Radical for Woman's Rights*. New York: Little, Brown, 1980.
Barter, Judith A. *Art and Appetite: American Painting, Culture, and Cuisine*. Chicago: Art Institute of Chicago, 2013.
Becker, Howard S. *Outsiders: Studies in the Sociology of Deviance*. New York: Free Press, 1963.
Beecher, Lyman. *Autobiography of Lyman Beecher*. Vol. 2. Edited by Barbara Cross. Cambridge, Mass.: Harvard University Press, 1961.
Bestor, Arthur Eugene, Jr. *Backwoods Utopias: The Sectarian and Owenite Phases of Communitarian Socialism in America, 1663–1829*. Philadelphia: University of Pennsylvania Press, 1950.
Blumin, Stuart M. "The Hypothesis of Middle-Class Formation in Nineteenth-Century America: A Critique and Some Proposals." *American Historical Review* 90, no. 2 (April 1985): 299–338.

Bogue, Allan G. *From Prairie to Corn Belt: Farming on the Illinois and Iowa Prairies in the Nineteenth Century*. Chicago: University of Chicago Press, 1963.

Bray, Peter. *Peter Cartwright, Legendary Frontier Preacher*. Urbana: University of Illinois Press, 2005.

Brown, Candy Gunther. *The Word in the World: Evangelical Writing, Publishing, and Reading in America, 1789–1880*. Chapel Hill: University of North Carolina Press, 2004.

Brown, Richard D. *Knowledge Is Power: The Diffusion of Information in Early America, 1700–1865*. New York: Oxford University Press, 1989.

Brush, Daniel Harmon. *Growing Up with Southern Illinois, 1820 to 1861*. Edited by M. M. Quaife. Chicago: Lakeside, 1944.

Burlend, Rebecca. *A True Picture of Emigration; or, Fourteen Years in the Interior of North America*. Nabu Public Domain Reprints, originally published 1848.

Burnette, Patricia B. *James F. Jaquess: Scholar, Soldier and Private Agent for President Lincoln*. Jefferson, N.C.: McFarland, 2013.

Byers, Samuel Hawkins Marshall. *Iowa in War Times*. Des Moines, Iowa: Condit, 1888.

Cartwright, Peter. *Autobiography of Peter Cartwright, the Backwoods Preacher*. Edited by W. P. Strickland. London: Hall, Virtue, 1862.

Cherry, Conrad, ed. *God's New Israel: Religious Interpretations of American Destiny*. Englewood Cliffs, N.J.: Prentice Hall, 1971.

"The Choice." *New York Times*, September 30, 1896.

Chused, Richard. "Married Women's Property Law, 1800–1850." *Georgetown Law Journal* 71 (June 1983): 1359.

Civil War Preservation Trust. Available at http://www.civilwar.org/education/pdfs/civil-was-curriculum-medicine.pdf.

Cole, Arthur C. *The Centennial History of Illinois: The Era of the Civil War, 1848–1870*. Vol. 3. Springfield: Illinois Centennial Commission, 1919.

Cole, Arthur. "The Passing of the Frontier." In *The Prairie State: Colonial Years to 1860*, edited by Robert P. Sutton, 314–26. Grand Rapids, Mich.: Eerdmans, 1976.

"Consistency, Thou Art a Jewel." *New York Times*, February 26, 1888.

Cooper, Grace Rogers. *The Sewing Machine: Its Invention and Development*. 2nd edition. Washington, D.C.: Smithsonian Institution Press, 1976.

Cremin, Lawrence A. *American Education: The National Experience, 1783–1876*. New York: Harper and Row, 1980.

Custer, Milo. "Asiatic Cholera in Central Illinois." *Journal of the Illinois State Historical Society* 23, no. 1 (1930).

Daval, Jean Luc. *Photography: History of an Art*. New York: Rizzoli, 1982.

Doyle, Don H. *The Social Order of a Frontier Community*. Urbana: University of Illinois Press, 1983.

Dubin, Michael J. *United States Presidential Elections, 1788–1860: The Official Results by County and State*. Jefferson, N.C.: McFarland, 2002.

DuBois, Ellen Carol. *Feminism and Suffrage: The Emergence of an Independent Women's Movement in America 1848–1869*. Ithaca, N.Y.: Cornell University Press, 1999 [1978].

Dudden, Faye E. *Serving Women: Household Service in Nineteenth-Century America*. Middletown, Conn.: Wesleyan University Press, 1983.

Dvorak, Katharine. "Peter Cartwright and Charisma." *Methodist History* 26 (1988): 113–26.

Eames, Charles. *Historic Morgan and Classic Jacksonville*. Jacksonville, Ill.: Daily and Weekly Journal, 1885.

"The Election in California." *New York Times*, November 26, 1856.

Ellet, Mrs. *The Practical Housekeeper: A Cyclopeadia of Domestic Economy*. New York: Stringent and Townsend, 1857.

Elliot, Charles. *Sinfulness of American Slavery: Proved from Its Evil Sources; Its Injustice; Its Wrongs; Its Contrariety to Many Scriptural Commands, Prohibitions, and Principles, and to the Christian Spirit; and from Its Evil Effects; Together with Observations on Emancipation, and the Duties of American Citizens in Regard to Slavery*. Vol. 1. N.p.: Sormstedt and Power, 1850.

Emery, Tom. *The Other John Logan: Col. John Logan and the 32nd Illinois*. N.p.: History in Print, 1998.

Emily Dickinson Museum. Available at http://www.emilydickinsonmuseum.org/poetry_characteristics (accessed November 5, 2013).

Ex parte Milligan, 71 U.S. 2 (1866).

Fackler, Mark, and Charles Lippy, ed. *Popular Religious Magazines of the United States*. Westport, Conn.: Greenwood, 1995.

Faragher, John Mack. *Sugar Creek: Life on the Illinois Prairie* New Haven, Conn.: Yale University Press, 1988.

Ferrie, Joseph P. *Yankees Now: Immigrants in the Antebellum United States, 1840–1860*. New York: Oxford University Press, 1999.

Finley, James Bradley. *Pioneer Life in the West: The Autobiography of James Bradley Finley*. Edited by W. P. Strickland. Cincinnati: Cranston and Curts, 1853.

Fleek, Sherman L. "The Church and the Utah War, 1857–58." In *Nineteenth-Century Saints at War*, edited by Robert C. Freeman, 81–106. Provo, Utah: Religious Studies Center, Brigham Young University, 2006.

Foner, Eric. *The Fiery Trial: Abraham Lincoln and American Slavery*. New York: Norton, 2010.

"The Fourth of July at Port Hudson." *New York Times*, July 19, 1863.

Fox, Henry J., and William B. Hoyt. *Quadrennial Register of the Methodist Episcopal Church, and Universal Church Gazetteer, 1852–56*. Hartford, Conn.: Case, Tiffany, and Hamersley, 1852.

Galenson, David W., and Clayne L. Pope, "Economic and Geographic Mobility on the Farming Frontier: Evidence from Appanoose Country, Iowa, 1850–1870." *Journal of Economic History* 49 (1989): 651.

Garvey, Ellen Gruber. *The Adman in the Parlor: Magazines and the Gendering of Consumer Culture, 1880s to 1910s*. New York: Oxford University Press, 1996.

Gayler, George R. "The Mormons and Politics in Illinois: 1839–1844." In *An Illlinois Reader*, edited by Clyde C. Walton. DeKalb: Northern Illinois University Press, 1970.

"Gen. Butler at Home: Grand Reception by His Neighbors." *Chicago Tribune*, January 19, 1863.

"General Butler in Boston: A Grand and Enthusiastic Reception." *New York Times*, January 14, 1863.

Genesis 37: 1–35. *Holy Bible*, RSV.

George, Susanne K. *The Adventures of the Woman Homesteader: The Life and Letters of Elinore Pruitt Stewart*. Lincoln: University of Nebraska Press, 1992.

Gerber, Philip L., and Charlotte M. Wright. *An Iowa Schoolma'am: Letters of Elizabeth "Bess" Corey, 1904–1908*. Iowa City: University of Iowa Press, 2011.

Ginzberg, Lori D. *Elizabeth Cady Stanton: An American Life*. New York: Hill and Wang, 2009.

"Gleanings from the Mail: An Illinois Town; Some of the Celebrities of Jacksonville: Eccentric Ministers, the Blind Preacher, and the War Senator Flowers in the Scale of Justice." *New York Times*, May 5, 1877.

Goldsmith, Oliver. "Humorous Poems: II. Miscellaneous Elegy on Madam Blaize," lines 9–12. Bliss Carman, et al., eds. The World's Best Poetry. Volume 9 (Tragedy: Humor). 1904. Available at http://www.bartleby.com (accessed May 24, 2015).

Goldthorpe, Caroline. *From Queen to Empress: Victorian Dress 1837–1877*. New York: Metropolitan Museum of Art, 1988.

Goodwin, Cardinal. "The American Occupation of Iowa, 1833 to 1860." *Iowa Journal of History and Politics* (1919): 98.

Groom, Winston. *Shiloh 1862*. Washington, D.C.: National Geographic, 2012.

Hacker, J. David. "A Census-Based Count of the Civil War Dead." *Civil War History* 57, no. 4 (December 2011): 307–48.

Hallwas, John E. *Keokuk and the Great Dam*. Chicago: Arcadia, 2001.

Hampsten, Elizabeth. *Mother's Letters*. Tucson: University of Arizona Press, 1993.

Hart, James D. *The Popular Book: A History of America's Literary Taste*. New York: Oxford University Press, 1950.

Hatch, Nathan O. *The Democratization of American Christianity*. Yale University Press, 1989.

Heilbrun, Carolyn G. *Writing a Woman's Life*. New York: Norton, 1988.

Heinl, Frank J., "Centennial: J. Capps and Sons, Ltd." Jacksonville, Ill.: Jacksonville Journal-Courier Company, 1939.

Hempton, David. *Methodism: Empire of the Spirit*. New Haven, Conn.: Yale University Press, 2005.

Herbert, Christopher. *The Indian Mutiny and Victorian Trauma*. Princeton, N.J.: Princeton University Press, 2007.

Hewitt, Nancy A. "Taking the True Woman Hostage." *Journal of Women's History* 14, no. 1 (Spring 2002): 156–62.

Historical Encyclopedia of Illinois and History of Morgan County: Biographical Sketches. Chicago: Munsell, 1906.

History of Macoupin County, Illinois. Philadelphia: Brink, McDonough, 1879.

History of Morgan County, Illinois: Its Past and Present. Chicago: Donnelly, Lloyd, 1878.

History of Poweshiek County, Iowa, 1880. Available at http://www.beforetime.net/iowagenealogy/poweshiek/HistoryOfPoweshiekCounty1880.

Hobbs, Catherine, ed. *Nineteenth-Century Women Learn to Write*. Charlottesville: University of Virginia Press, 1995.

Hopkins, D. R. *The Greatest Killer: Smallpox in History*. Chicago: University of Chicago Press, 2002.

Horowitz, David. "Consumption and Its Discontents: Simon N. Patten, Thorstein Veblen, and George Gunton." *Journal of American History* 67, no. 2 (September 1980): 301–17.

Howe, Julia Ward. "Battle Hymn of the Republic." Lyrics. 1861; first published in *The Atlantic Monthly* in February 1862.

Hudgins, Nicole. "A Historical Approach to Family Photography: Class and Individuality in Manchester and Lille, 1850–1914." *Journal of Social History* 43 (Spring 2010): 559–86.

Illinois Conference Female College. *Fourth Annual Catalogue of the Officers and Students of the Illinois Conference Female College, Jacksonville, Illinois*, 1852.

Iowa Census, 1856. 1885 Poweshiek County.

Jacksonville Constitutionist, November 6, 1852 (advertisement).

Johannsen, Robert W. "Lincoln-Douglas Debates." In *The Reader's Companion to American History*, edited by Eric Foner and John A. Garraty. Boston: Houghton Mifflin, 1991.

Jones, Carl E. "A Genealogical Study of Populations." *American Statistical Association* 16, no. 124 (December 1918): 201–19, 208 (table 5).

Kay, Betty Carlson, and Gary Jack Barwick. *Jacksonville Illinois: The Traditions Continue*. Mt. Pleasant, S.C.: Arcadia, 1999.

Klement, Frank L. *The Copperheads in the Middle West*. Chicago: University of Chicago Press, 1960.

Lambert, Belle Short. *College Greetings*, November 1921, 32–35.

Laver, James. *Museum Piece; or, The Education of an Iconographer*. Boston: Houghton Mifflin, 1964.

Leaton, James. *Methodism in Illinois. Vol. 2: Minutes, Illinois Conference, 1840–51*. Illinois Conference Society, 1889.

Lebsock, Suzanne. *The Free Women of Petersburg: Status and Culture in a Southern Town, 1784–1860*. New York: Norton, 1984.

Lehuu, Isabelle. *Carnival on the Page: Popular Print Media in Antebellum America*. Chapel Hill: University of North Carolina Press, 2000.

Lerner, Gerda. *The Majority Finds Its Past: Placing Women in History*. New York: Oxford Press, 1979.

Livingstone, David. *Missionary Travels and Researches*. London, 1857.

Lumpin, Mrs. C. J. Unpublished manuscript: Ann Dumville. Jacksonville, Ill.: Archives of MacMurray College (c. 1946).

MacMurray College. Web site at http://www.mac.edu.

Macoupin County Enquirer (Carlinville, Illinois). "Obituary," April 3, 1873.

Marty, Martin E. *Pilgrims in Their Own Land: 500 Years of Religion in America.* New York: Little, Brown, 1984.

Matthaei, Julia A. *An Economic History of Women in America.* New York: Schocken, 1982.

Matthews, Mitford M. *A Dictionary of Americanisms.* Chicago: University of Chicago Press, 1951.

McElfresh, G. R. S. *College Greetings*, June 1902, 10.

McPherson, James M. *For Cause and Comrades: Why Men Fought in the Civil War.* New York: Oxford University Press, 1997.

"The Meeting of Congress." *New York Times*, December 1, 1856.

Melton, J. Gordon. *Log Cabins to Steeples: The United Methodist Way in Illinois, 1824–1974.* Nashville: Parthenon, 1974.

"Methodist Heritage in Lincoln, Illinois." Available at http://www.gbgm.umc.org (accessed July 30, 2012).

Milburn, William Henry. *The Pioneer Preacher; or, Rifle, Axe, and Saddle-bags, and Other Lectures.* New York: Derby and Jackson, 1857.

———. *Ten Years of Preacher-Life: Chapters from an Autobiography.* New York: Derby and Jackson, 1859.

Minutes of the Thirty-Eighth Session of the Illinois Annual Conference of the Methodist Episcopal Church, 1861.

Missionary Society. *Seventy-First Annual Report of the Missionary Society of the Methodist Episcopal Church for the Year 1889.* New York: Missionary Society, January 1890.

Mitchell, Samuel Augustus. *Mitchell's Primary Geography: An Easy Introduction to the Study of Geography; Designed for the Instruction of Children in Schools and Families.* Philadelphia: Thomas, Cowperthwait, 1845.

Miyakawa, T. Scott. *Protestants and Pioneers: Individualism and Conformity on the American Frontier.* Chicago: University of Chicago Press, 1964.

Monaghan, Charles. *The Murrays of Murray Hill.* Brooklyn, N.Y.: Urban History Press, 1998.

Montague's Illinois and Missouri State Directory, 1854–55.

Motz, Marilyn Ferris. *True Sisterhood: Michigan Women and Their Kin, 1820–1920.* Albany: State University of New York Press, 1983.

"Mr. Seward's Speech." *New York Times*, January 14, 1861.

"Our Wesleyan Heritage." United Methodist Church. Available at http://www.umc.org/what-we-believe/our-wesleyan-heritage (accessed May 20, 2015).

Oxford English Dictionary. "Blues" entry. Available at www.oed.com/view/Entry/20615?rskey=Zk6UBm&result=1#eid.

Palmer, G. T., and Lloyd Lewis. *A Conscientious Turncoat.* New Haven, Conn.: Yale University Press, 1941.

Palmer, John M. *Personal Recollections of John M. Palmer: The Story of an Earnest Life.* Mrs. John M. Palmer, 1901.

Palmer, Phoebe. *A Present to My Christian Friend on Entire Devotion to God, 1845*. London: Heylen, 1857.
Pratt, Henry E. "Peter Cartwright and the Cause of Education." *Journal of the Illinois State Historical Society* 28 (1936): 271–78.
"Presidential Election." *New York Times*, November 27, 1856.
Pruitt, Linda Carlisle. "Ann Dumville: A Woman of Conviction." *Methodist History* 25, no. 3 (1987).
Ray, Joseph. *Ray's Arithmetic, Second Book: Intellectual Arithmetic by Inductions and Analysis*. New York: Wilson, Hinkle, 1857.
Reid, J. M. *Missions and Missionary Society of the Methodist Episcopal Church*. Vol. 1. New York: Phillips and Hunt, 1879.
"Result of the Elections." *New York Times*, November 6, 1856.
Robertson, Stacey M. *Hearts Beating for Liberty: Women Abolitionists in the Old Northwest*. Chapel Hill: University of North Carolina Press, 2010.
Rose, Anne C. *Voices of the Marketplace: American Thought and Culture, 1830–1860*. Woodbridge, Conn.: Twayne, 1995.
Rusk, Ralph Leslie. *The Literature of the Middle Western Frontier*. 1925. Westport, Conn.: Greenwood, 1975.
Sacks, David. *Language Visible: Unraveling the Mystery of the Alphabet from A to Z*. New York: Broadway, 2003.
Salmon, Lucy Maynard. *Domestic Service*. New York: MacMillan, 1897.
Sanders, Charles W. *Sanders' Spelling Book Designed to Teach Orthography and Orthoepy of Dr. Webster*. New York: Newman, 1845.
Sanders' Spelling Book: Containing a Minute and Comprehensive System of Introductory Orthography. New York: Ivison, Blakeman, Taylor, c. 1846.
Scanlon, Jennifer. *Inarticulate Longings: The Ladies' Home Journal, Gender and the Promises of Consumer Culture*. New York: Routledge, 1995.
Sewell, William G. *The Ordeal of Free Labor in the British West Indies*. New York: Harper, 1861.
Sheppard, Robert D., and Harvey B. Hurd, eds. *Northwestern University and Evanston*. Chicago: Munsell, 1906.
Sheumaker, Helen. *Love Entwined: The Curious History of Hairwork in America*. Philadelphia: University of Pennsylvania Press, 2007.
Shils, Edward. "Deference." In *Social Stratification*, edited by J. A. Jackson, 104. Cambridge: Cambridge University Press, 1968.
Sklar, Kathryn Kish. *Catharine Beecher: A Study in American Domesticity*. New Haven, Conn.: Yale University Press, 1973.
Smith, Carl. *City Water, City Life: Water and the Infrastructure of Ideas in Urbanizing Philadelphia, Boston, and Chicago*. Chicago: University of Chicago Press, 2013.
Smith, G. Barnett. *History of the English Parliament*. London: Warwick House, 1894.
Smith-Rosenberg, Carroll. *Disorderly Conduct: Visions of Gender in Victorian America*. New York: Knopf, 1985.

Snow, John. "On the Mode of Communication of Cholera." 2nd ed. London: Churchill, 1855.

Speed Art Museum, Kentucky Collection. Available at www.speedmuseum.org/collection/kentuckycollect/1994_1.html.

Spooner, Matthew P. "W. N. Lewis vs. Rev. John Seys: Power, Ideology, and Race in Colonial Liberia." Paper presented at the American Historical Association meeting, Boston, January 8, 2011.

Stamper, Anita, and Jill Condra. *Clothing through American History: The Civil War through the Gilded Age, 1861–1899*. Santa Barbara, Calif.: Greenwood, 2011.

Stampp, Kenneth M. *America in 1857*. New York: Oxford University Press, 1990.

Steckel, Richard H. "Migration and Political Conflict: Precincts in the Midwest on the Eve of the Civil War." *Journal of Interdisciplinary History* 28, no. 4 (Spring 1998): 583–603.

Stowe, Steven M. *Doctoring the South: Southern Physicians and Everyday Medicine in the Mid-Nineteenth Century*, Chapel Hill: University of North Carolina Press, 2004.

Stratton, Joanna. *Pioneer Women: Voices from the Kansas Frontier*. New York: Simon and Schuster, 1981.

Stubbs, William. *Select Charters and Other Illustrations of English Constitutional History*. Oxford: Clarendon Press, 1874.

Susan B. Anthony Center for Women's Leadership. *The Declaration of Sentiments*. Available at www.rochester.edu/sba/suffragetimeline.html (accessed May 20, 2015).

Sutton, Robert P. "Against the 'Drunken Dutch and Low Irish': Nativism and Know-Nothings in Illinois." In *The Prairie State: A Documentary History of Illinois, Colonial Years to 1860*, edited by Robert P. Sutton, 326–41. Grand Rapids, Mich.: Eerdmans, 1976.

Sweet, William Warren. *Circuit Rider Days in Indiana: The Minutes and Journal of the Indiana Conference of the Methodist Episcopal Church, 1832–1844*. Indianapolis: Stewart, 1916.

Thorburn, G. *Catalogue of Kitchen Garden, Herb Flower, Tree, and Grass Seeds, Bulbous Flower Roots, Greenhouse Plants, Gardening, Agricultural and Botanical Books, Gardening Tools, etc*. New York: J. Seymour, 1830.

Thoreau, Henry David. "Plea for Captain John Brown." Read to the citizens of Concord, Massachusetts on October 30, 1859. Published in *The Liberator*, July 27, 1860.

"Timeline of Women in Methodism." Available at http://www.archives.umc.org/interior.asp?ptid=1&mid=2619; www.umc/home/our world/leader resources/Timeline (accessed July 27, 2012).

"The Trials of School-Teaching: Some Recent Experiences in Western New-York—One Teacher Assaulted with an Iron Poker and Another, a Lady, Knocked Down by a Pupil." *New York Times*, February 16, 1879.

"The Troubles in Iowa: Outrageous Conduct of the Copperheads." *New York Times*, August 12, 1863. Originally published in the *Davenport (Iowa) Gazette*, August 6, 1863.

Turnbull, Everett. "A Century of Methodism in Carlinville, Illinois," *Journal of the Illinois State Historical Society* 24 (July 1931).
U.S. Census, *Census of the United States* 1840, 1850, 1860, 1870.
Vicars, Hedley. *Memorials of Captain Hedley Vicars, 97th Regiment*. New York: Carter, 1857, pp. 32, 288–91.
Walker, Charles A. *History of Macoupin County, Illinois*. Vol. 1. Chicago: Clarke, 1911.
Walsh, Margaret. "The Democratization of Fashion: The Emergence of the Women's Dress Pattern Industry." *Journal of American History* 66, no. 2 (September 1979): 299–313.
Walton, Clyde C., ed. *An Illinois Reader*. DeKalb: Northern Illinois University Press, 1970.
Ward, Maria. *Female Life among the Mormons: A Narrative of Many Years' Personal Experience by the Wife of a Mormon Elder, Recently from Utah*. New York: Derby, 1855.
Wass, Ann Buermann, and Michelle Webb Fandrich. *Clothing through American History: The Federal Era through Antebellum America, 1786–1860*. Santa Barbara, Calif: Greenwood, 2010.
Watters, Mary. *The First Hundred Years of MacMurray College*. Jacksonville, Illinois: MacMurray College for Women, 1947.
Welter, Barbara. "The Cult of True Womanhood, 1820–1860." *American Quarterly* 18 (Summer 1966): 151–74.
"Where the Democratic Vote Belongs." *New York Times*, October 20, 1896.
Whitaker Geneaology. Available at http://whitakergeneaology.us/iltrails/ancestors_cass.htm (accessed August 9, 2012).
Zboray, Ronald J. *A Fictive People: Antebellum Economic Development and the American Reading Public*. New York: Oxford University Press, 1993.

Index

abolition, 17–19, 34, 53, 62, 80–81, 118, 150, 173n71, 173n74, 180n6, 181n7, 181n10, 181n14, 184n1, 185n14, 187n42, 192n69; Dumvilles as abolitionists, 19, 34, 41, 54, 111
Abraham Lincoln Presidential Library, xi, xiv, 119, 169n6
accidents, 60; falls, 43, 61; farm, 73, 105, 157–58; fire, 40; railroad, 63, 146
Adas, Michael, 184n73
Advocate (magazine) 70, 81, 111, 129, 138, 147, 154, 183n57
Africa, missionaries to, 10, 98, 129–30, 164
"Africa's sunny fountain," 130, 190n41
agrarian values, 18, 55
Akers, Peter, 71, 140, 184n60, 191n64
American Colonization Society, 171n31, 186n29
American Party. *See* Know-Nothing Party
Andrew, Bishop, 34
Anthony, Susan B., 183n42
anti-Catholic views, 18, 19, 40, 54, 124
antislavery societies, 173n59
apples: drying of, 89, 109, 134, 138; peelers, 191n58
Applegate, Debby, 181n10
Associated Press, 12
"Athens of the West," 185n6
Atherton, Lewis, 177n12
Atlantic Monthly, The, 12
Augst, Thomas, 24, 175n16

Baker, Paula, 81, 181n16, 185n4
Baker, Senator Edward, 188n1

Ball's Bluff, battle of, 115
Baltimore, 49, 62, 96
banknotes, 115–16, 188n4
banks, 1, 93, 132, 176n34; failures of, 115–16, 188n4
Banner, Lois, 181n12, 181n14
Baptist Church, 23, 187n39
barege. *See* fabric
Barger, James: family, 100, 147, 153, 191n59; death of, 138–40, 145, 191n59
Barter, Judith, 183n56, 184n76
"Battle Hymn of the Republic," 192n66
Beauregard, Gen. P. G. T., 193n77
Bechly, Freiderich (Fred): death of, 196n23; immigrant from Germany, 122; place of burial, 196n23; property of, 195n6; travels of 151, 162, 196n15; work as farm laborer, 122, 153
Bechly, Hephzibah and Freiderich (Fred): children of, 162, 195n7; courtship of, 121, 122, 126, 151; marriage of, 121, 195n2
Bechly, Hephzibah Dumville. *See* Bechly, Hephzibah and Freiderich; Dumville, Hephzibah
Becraft, family: Mr., 88; 111; Misses A. and S., 40; Miss F., 149
bedside drama, physician roles in, 178n38
bedstead, 47, 59, 132, 153, 159, 179n63
Beecher, Catharine, 11, 81, 181n10; *An Essay on the Education of Female Teachers,* 171n36, 185n3
Beecher, Rev. Henry Ward, 181n10
Beecher, Rev. Lyman, 11, 171nn38–39

Beecher Bible and Rifle Colony, 181n10
Bell, John, 79
Belles Lettres literary society, 14, 59, 70, 164, 182n30; readings at, 70
Belt, Josiah, 39, 89, 153
Bengal army, 184n73
Benson, Joseph, 51, 125, 180n66, 189n24
Bestor, Arthur, 170n5
Bible owned by John Williams, 164
Bible, references to, 12, 74, 96, 158, 159, 163, 164, 180n66, 183n59, 192n66
Birks, Miss, 48, 52
birth, 90, 100, 125
bishop's sleeves, 42, 179n51
blind asylum (School for the Blind), 5, 146
blindness, 41, 180n69
blues, 43, 104, 130, 179n56
Blumin, Stuart, 172n49, 173n59
Bogue, Allan, 182n21
bonds, Southern, 116, 188n4
border states, as source of settlers of southern and central Illinois, 17, 54, 155
bottom land, 186n22
Breckenridge, John, 79
bridesmaids, 40
Bristow, Mr., 61, 92
Brown, John (Harpers Ferry), 101, 129, 184–85n1
Brown, Miss, 39, 40
Brown, Mr., 26
Brown, Mrs., 154
Brown, Richard, 172n47
Brown, Sarah, 57, 74
Brownlow, Parson William G., 152, 193n85
Brush, Daniel, 22, 174n2, n4
Bryan, William Jennings, 174n5
Buchanan, James, 17, 53, 55, 60, 62, 65,183n44
Bunyan, John, 12, 163, 182n24, 195n11
Burke, Don A., 50, 51, 163, 187n44, 195n9
Burke, Ellen (or Ella), 48, 50–51, 187n44
Burke, Major B. T., xiv, 47, 56, 58, 148, 163, 178n47, 179n65; and Ann Dumville, 48–53, 93, 163, 193n76, 195n9; care of his children, 48–53, 148; and Dumville archive, xiv, 169n6, 180n70; family visit, 49; Hephzibah's view of, 56, 58, 75, 148; letters to, 48–53; travels of, 49, 52; views of abolitionists, 41; wives of, 48–53, 195n10
Burlend, Rebecca, 179n62
Burnette, Patricia, 175n23, 177n27, 185n2, 186n31, 189n21, 193n86
Butler, Gen. Benjamin, 154, 193–94n87
Butterick, Ebenezer, 173n58

Byers, Samuel, 181n10, 191n53, 191n55, 194n96
Cairo, Illinois, 116, 137, 144, 147, 191n65; letters from, 136, 141, 143
calomel, laxative, 105, 187n36
campaigns: political, 17–18, 79; reform, 11; for women's vote, 55
camphor, 73
camp meetings, 35, 61, 92, 177n13
Capps mill, 146, 192n74
Carlinville, Illinois, 3, 4, 175n18, 176n5, 178n47; Ann living in, 3, 163, 184n71, 195n9; businesses in, 176n34, 186n24; demographics of, 4, 170n11; 141; disease in, 43, 141; domestic work in, 4, 170n13; Dumville marriages in, 121, 162, 195n2; education in, 22–23; gaslights in, 184n74; Hephzibah's return to, 120–21; Jemima's teaching in, 11, 164, 177n29; mail in, xv, Methodist church in, 8, 25; Methodist conference in, 187n45, 191n50; newspapers in, 13; opposition to abolition in, 18; photographer in, 176n6; soldiers from, 19, 116–19, 144, 173n78, 192n71, 192n72; teaching in, 11, 177n29; tornado in, 107, 108, 187n37, 187n40; railroad, 33, 49, 176n36; travel to and from, 49, 64, 71, 72, 77, 147, 175n18
cartes de visite, 176–77n7
Carthage, Illinois, 54, 73, 180n6
Cartwright, Peter, 35, 52, 171n33, 177n11, 178n44; autobiography, 34, 77, 83; as congressional candidate, 171n33; conversions by, 171n33, 177n16; financial contribution to college, 126; frontier adventures of, 83; lectures of, 126; political position of, 54; preacher, 74, 170n12, 177n13, 177n18, 180n67
Catholic church, 1
Catholics, opposition to, 11, 40, 54, 124, 167, 169–70n1, 173n77; and Know-Nothing Party, 18–19
Census, Iowa, 179n61
Census, U.S.: Ann's residence, 163, 184n71, 195n9; education data, 23; Elizabeth's occupation, 164; Elizabeth's property, 164; Elizabeth's residence, 164; Fred's property, 195n6; Hephzibah's occupation, 13, 20; Hephzibah's residence, 13; James Holme's property, 164; Holme's residence, 195n2; household data, 4, 170nn10–11, 179n61; immigration data, 17; Iowa farm data,

56; Jemima's occupation, 164; Jemima's residence, 4, 164, 170n13, 184n71; literacy data, 170n14, 172n45; occupation data, 20, 174n80, 176n6; Posey family, 187n35, 189n32; Stribling property, 120; value of church property, 10
chaplains: Rev. Milburn, 180n69; Rev. William Rutledge, 134, 187n47; women as, 117, 188n8
charisma, recruitment through, 11, 35
Charleston, South Carolina, 19, 115
Cheney, Daniel: battle experiences, 144; letters from, 136, 141, 143; letter to, 191–92n65; from Nilwood, 191n57, 192n71; request for prayers, 144; views of war, 192n67
Cherry, Conrad, 171n38
Chesapeake Bay, 193n78
Chicago: immigrants in, 18; population growth, 16; travel to, 70, 95, 109, 114
Chicago and Alton Railroad, 176n36
Chicago Tribune, 187n37, 188n4
childcare, 14, 19–20, 38, 148; by Hephzibah, 13, 27, 70, 96, 146, 154
children's performances, 57, 68
cholera: causes of, 32, 176n2; diagnosis of, 39, 178n39; impact of, 21, 163; outbreak of, 32, 41, 43, 55; treatment of, 43, 176n2
church: camp meetings, 35, 61, 92, 136, 177n13; conversions, 8, 30, 36–37, 52, 84–86, 166–67; dedication of, 10, 49, 52; prayer meeting, 46, 86, 87, 92, 127; preaching, 9–11, 36, 44, 51, 70, 85, 120; preachers, 1, 8–12, 28, 34, 35, 43, 51, 52, 61, 66, 69, 71, 74, 80, 81, 85, 88, 92, 93, 97, 102, 110, 113, 114, 122, 132, 135,145, 159, 170n12, 176n31, 177n13, 177n18, 180n66, 180n6, 186n30; preacher preparation, 35, 97; property, value of, 10; religious education, 95, 100, 110, 112, 141, 158; revival, 8–10, 35, 52, 123, 126, 132, 177n13, 177n16; Salem, 29, 43, 44, 59, 68, 74, 84, 85, 87, 95, 123, 126, 179n57; singing, 24, 92, 190n41; walk to, 7, 36, 46. *See also* circuit riders; Methodist church
Chused, Richard, 195n4
Cincinnati, 147
circuit riders, 9, 171n27, 171n40; attitude toward education, 35; compensation, 35; conflict with resident clergy, 35; preachers, 43, 44
Civil War, xi, 18, 19, 23, 122, 167, 173n77, 174n86, 181n14, 187n47, 188n4; deaths, 119, 188n9; letters from soldiers, 118, 136–37, 143–45, 149, 156
Clarke, Adam, 51, 125, 180n66, 189n24
clothes, 30, 37, 99, 153
Cloude, Rev., 43, 44, 51, 61
Cole, Arthur, 33, 173n65, 173n67, 180–81n6
Colfax, Schuyler, 92, 185n17
college, attendance at, 51, 97. *See also* curriculum
commencement, 27, 60, 70, 86
commercial markets, 14, 16, 20, 81, 116, 172n57
compensation, 20, 35, 49, 178n36, 179n60, 194n95. *See also* serving women, compensation of; teaching, compensation for
Condra, Jill, 179nn50–51
Confederate States of America, 193n78; army, 19, 115–18, 120, 193n76, 193n77; diplomatic recognition; 155, 194n91; war casualties, 188n9
Congo, slaves from, 192n73
Constitutional Union Party, 79
consumer goods, 20, 37, 47, 167, 172n53
consumerism, 172n57
conversion, religious. *See* church, conversions
Cooke, Mary Dumville, 131, 155–56, 178n48, 183n46, 189n26, 194n88, 194n90
Coop, Nathan, 156–57, 194n92
Cooper, Grace, 173n58
Copperheads, 18, 115, 157, 158, 189n28, 191n53, 194n94, 194n96
Corey, Bess, 174n4
Corinth, battle of, 117–18, 148, 156, 164
correspondence, as duty, 21, 24, 36
coverture, 195n4
Cowper, William, 192n75
craft work, 14–15
Cremin, Lawrence, 12, 22, 23, 170n12, 171n37, 172n43, 172n45, 174nn6–7
Crimean War, 12, 183n59
culture, middle class, 172–73n57, 173n59
Curiosity, Brother. *See* pseudonyms
curriculum, 12, 22, 185n3; classical, 124, 175n9; history, 63; religious, 85, 112, 141, 144, 151, 158
Curtis, Major General., 118
Custer, Milo, 176n1

Danenhower, William 173n77
Daval, Jean, 176n7
Dawes, Mr. J. T., 141

death, 8, 32, 37, 49, 104, 105, 116, 142, 173n78; frequency in letters, 9, 171n25; reports of, xiv, 3, 7, 9, 27, 33, 38–39, 40, 41, 44–45, 49, 51, 61, 63, 65, 67, 93, 98–99, 102, 105–6, 117, 122–23, 138–39, 141, 144, 145, 157–58, 159, 163–64, 166, 180n69, 186n1, 186n29, 187n35, 190n39, 196n23; resigned to, 40, 106; vigil, 38, 49, 177nn32–33
debts, 1, 83, 94, 132, 136
Declaration of Independence, 17, 62, 92, 110, 111
Defoe, Daniel, 12
Dellzell, family, 59, 64, 68, 82, 87, 102, 182n32; sons of, fought in Civil War, 134, 148
Democratic Party, 18, 53–55, 79, 116, 174n5, 180n6, 181n9, 191n52
Dempster, Dr. John, 35
Denby, Helen Burke, xiv, 179n64, 180n70
Dickinson, Emily, 169n1
disease, 3, 30, 31, 43, 44–45, 49, 65, 71, 73, 76, 86, 89, 92, 93, 96, 102, 104, 106, 141, 144, 147, 159, 188n19; ague, 94; asthma, 156; bilious fever, 43, 48, 51; boils, 25, 48, 50; brain fever, 41; chills, 31, 48, 73, 86, 94, 96, 140; colds, 29, 37, 44, 51, 69, 83, 104, 114, 140; congestion of the brain, 61; consumption, 102; diarrhea, 96; erysipelas, 99, 186n32; food poisoning, 45; headache, 147; inflammation of bowels, 45; lung fever, 40, 102, 105; measles, 27, 47; mental derangement, 131; milk sickness, 44; mumps, 144; pleurisy, 140; rheumatism, 62, 99; scarlet fever, 76; sore eyes, 41; sore throat, 96, 104; stutter, 158; tooth extraction, 124; whooping cough, 27, 112; winter fever, 104. See also cholera; smallpox; typhoid fever
disputes, neighbor, 135, 151
domestic furnishings, 10, 52, 59, 66, 180n70
domestic management, 20, 48–51
domesticity, 16, 20, 36; and consumer markets, 81, 140; ideology of, 55, 164–65; 172n57, 184n75; in Methodist publications, 165, 181n14; religious emphasis on, 81, 165; training for, 185n3. See also "true womanhood"
Donalson, Andrew, 63
Douglas, Stephen, 17, 18, 60, 90, 113, 188n49; elections of 1858 and 1860, 79–80
Douglass, Frederic, 181n12
Doyle, Don, 4, 120, 170n10, 175n24, 176n4, 177n27, 181n9, 185n6, 185n12, 188n15, 188n118

draft, military, 136, 151, 152, 191n55
dress, 6, 26, 34, 37, 42, 90, 167, 128, 138, 171n17, 183n45, 196n22
dressmaking, 20, 27, 31, 56, 57, 59, 95, 109, 138, 173n58
Dubin, Michael, 180n3
DuBois, Ellen, 181n14
Dudden, Faye, 13, 172n47, 172n50, 172n52, 172n56, 174n85, 188n17, 190n44, 190n47, 196n22
Dumville, Ann: appearance of, xiv, 6; burial of, 196n14; character of, 7; church expansion, 49, 52; Civil War, 117, 135; death of, xiv, 163–64, 195n9; expulsion from church, 18, 34; founding of church in Missouri, 7–8; gifts from, 47, 167; immigration of, 1–3; letters of 1853, 29–30; letters of 1855, 46–52; letters of 1859, 92–93; literacy of, 4, 132, 163, 170n14; marriage of, 170n14; re Catholics, 169–70n1; relations with Striblings, 52, 132; religious zeal, 7–8; residence of, 148, 163; social activities of, 50, 95; speech to Conference, 1; spiritual welfare of others, 29, 30, 49, 50, 51, 52; work as domestic service, 48–51, 56, 193n76; See also visiting
Dumville, Elizabeth (Mrs. John Williams). See Williams, Elizabeth
Dumville, Grandma. See Dumville, Ann
Dumville, Hephzibah (Mrs. Freiderich Bechly): appearance of, 6, 64, 65; character of, 7; children of, 162; compensation of, 130–31, 132, 159, 160; conversion of, 52, 84–86; death of, 166, 196n23; departure from Striblings, 130–31, 132–33, 150, 153; 160; desire for education, 30, 47, 68, 70, 124, 125, 133, 148, 165, 167, 184n77; immigration from England, 1–3, 55, 93; letters of 1851 and 1852, 24–28; letters of 1853, 28, 29, 31; letters of 1854, 37–45; letters of 1855, 47; letters of 1856, 56–62, 63–67; letters of 1857, 67–78; letters of 1858, 82–90; letters of 1859, 90–94, 95–99; letters of 1860, 101–14; letters of 1861, 122–35, 137–41; letters of 1862, 147–52; letters of 1863, 152–55; location of burial, 196n23; marriage of, 162, 166, 188n16, 195n2; marriage prospects, 9, 122, 171n27; missionary opportunities, 30, 37, 176n33; newspapers as source of information, 43, 54, 108; political attitudes, 17, 53, 54, 55, 62, 64, 65, 77, 79, 101, 128–29, 135, 140, 145; reading of, 12, 44, 59, 67, 68, 70, 77, 83, 111, 129, 138, 140, 141, 154, 174n1,

182n26, 182n35, 189n31; references to the war, 133–35, 145–48; relationship with Striblings, 47, 90, 91, 101, 153; romances of, 43, 44, 81, 90–91, 166; self-image of, 44, 77, 85, 90; and slavery, 62, 111, 125, 145; social activities of, 15, 44, 59, 63–64, 68–69, 70, 74, 82, 111, 124; social conflicts, 44, 61, 102; social status of, 133, 166–67; student at college, 170n9; tasks of, 13, 14, 15, 22, 27, 31, 58, 59, 66, 68, 70, 76, 89, 97, 102, 109, 134, 138, 154; views of alcohol, 59–60; views of Catholics, 54, 124, 173n77; views of England, 17, 111, 116, 140, 141, 150; views of Germans, 74; view of Irish, 59, 65, 154, 182n34; views of Lincoln, 129, 145, 189n36; views of Mormons, 54, 75, 77; views of South, 19, 54, 62, 129, 145, 150, 155; work in domestic service, 14, 19, 27, 38, 58, 59, 66, 68, 70, 76, 89, 97–99, 109, 131, 134, 138, 154. *See also* visiting

Dumville, Jemima (Mrs. James Holme): character of, 7; children of, 162, 195n5; compensation of, 45, 100; conversion of, 36–37; death of, 164–65; disagreement with John, 37; as domestic help, 4, 131, 170n13, 183n51; employment as teacher, 28, 29, 45, 77, 89, 98, 100, 105, 107, 141, 147, 164, 177nn28–29; immigration of, 1–3; knitting, 141; letters of 1854, 36–37; letters of 1855, 45; letters of 1859, 99–101; letters of 1862, 141–43; marriage of, 162, 195n2; missionary opportunities, 30, 37, 129–30, 164, 176n33; personality of, 7; property of, 164; relationship with Striblings, 29, 77, 133; residence of, 4, 170n13; sewing of, 98, 100, 141; student at college, 170n9; support for war effort, 141, 143; views of slaves, 142, 192n69; views of war, 101, 141–43. *See also* visiting

Dumville, Thomas, *ix*, 1–3, 175n25; death of, 7, 9, 93

Dumville, William, 1–3, 170n4

Dvorak, Katharine, 35, 171n27, 177n17, 177n23

Eames, Charles, 173n71, 176n3, 177n27, 178n43, 179n60, 181n8, 184n68, 187n40

earthquake, 74

East Charge Methodist church, 5, 185n12

East India Company, 184n73

Easy, Mr. *See* pseudonyms

economic conditions, 54, 75, 77, 104, 115, 167; in frontier, 20, 186n28; in Jacksonville, 4; in South, 19. *See also* financial panic of 1857; recession of 1861–62

Eddy, Thomas, 70, 183n57

education: conflict with domesticity, 132, 165, 176n38; extent of, 23; methods used in, 22, 65, 158; public vs. private, 23, 183n43; and religion, 24, 107, 158; social credential, 66; training of teachers, 11, 20; of women, 66, 165

elections: of 1856, 18, 55, 65, 181n9; of 1858, 19, 79; of 1860, 19, 79, 80, 114

election returns: in 1856, 183n44; in 1860, 79–80

Ellet, Mrs., 174n79

Elliot, Charles, 140, 191n62

emancipation, 11, 118, 143, 181n14, 187n41

Emery, Tom, 188n7

England, in Civil War, 111, 116, 127, 140–41, 150

entertainment. *See* social activities

envelopes, xii–xiv, 175n19, 191–92n65, 194n88

Ethelred, reign of, 192n68

Evanston, Illinois, 35, 180n68

examinations, 27, 37, 40, 174–75n8

fabric: barege, 42, 179n50; calico, 130, 138, 140; flannel, 158; liney, 42, 179n49; linsey, 140, 158, 179n49; merino wool, 42; silk, 102

Fackler, Mark, 172n54, 172–3n57

fair: awards at, 61; county, 9, 80, 88, 92, 112, 123, 134; state, 63

fancywork, 14. *See also* hairwork

Fandrich, Michelle, 173n58, 179n51

Faneuil Hall, Boston, 193–94n87

Faragher, John, 172n57, 174n79, 174n2, 186n28

farms: animals, 46, 48, 49, 104, 112, 136, 159; crops, 21, 45, 112, 136, 151; debt, 94, 104, 135, 136, 151, 152; equipment, 46, 69; land rent, 151; management, 46, 104, 112, 135, 136; prices, 86, 94, 104, 112, 135, 136, 153

fashion, 14, 34, 42, 81, 138; wedding, 64, 183n45

Ferrie, Joseph, 17, 173n66, 173n68, 173n75

Fillmore, Millard, 18, 53–55, 63–64, 180n1, 181n7

financial panic of 1857, 54, 75, 77, 116, 184n72

Finley, Rev. James Bradley, 44, 77, 177n13, 179n59

fire: college, 139–40, 191n61; company, 78, 91; Jacksonville, 99, 146

Fleek, Sherman, 184n70

flowers, 64, 66, 97, 101, 102, 114, 146, 147, 150, 186n24. *See also* garden; seeds

Index

Foner, Eric, 173n72, 192n69
food, 4, 7, 32, 51, 83
Forest Home Cemetery, 196n17
Fort Donelson, battle of, 117, 144, 146, 193n77
Fort Henry, battle of, 116–17, 143–44, 193n77
Fort Sumter, battle of, 19, 189n35
Fourth of July celebration, 17, 110, 129, 134, 149, 189n28
Fox, Henry, 171nn28–29, 177n9, 186n30
free trade, 116
Fremont, John C., 53, 62, 117
French language, 12, 124, 175n20
fruit, 31, 109, 158
fugitive slave laws, 18
funeral. *See* death

Galenson, David, 56, 182n20, 182n22
garden, 58, 106, 109, 158, 186n24. *See also* flowers; seeds
Garden of Eden, 189n27
Garrett Biblical Institute, 35
Garvey, Ellen, 172–3n57
gaslights, 76, 184n74
Gayler, George, 181n11
gender, 19, 36, 121, 176n37; and consumer markets, 14, 16, 36; differences in writing style, 24; and education, 81; effects on social mobility, 133
Genesis, book of, 186n26
George, Susanne, 174n84
Gerber, Philip, 174n4
German immigration. *See* immigration
German Methodist church, Jacksonville, 188n18
Gettysburg, battle of, 120
ghost stories, 44
gift books, 114, 188n48
Gilkeson, John, 173n59
Gillespie, Illinois, 195n2
Ginzberg, Lori D., 181n12
Glass, Robert W., 63
Godey's Lady's Book, 14–16, 36
Goldsmith, Oliver, 43, 179n54
"good death," 8
Goodwin, Cardinal, 181n10, 182nn17–19
Gordon, Nathaniel: execution of, 145, 192n73
graduation. *See* commencement; Illinois College; Illinois Conference Female College
Grand Army of the Republic, 187n47
Grant, Gen. U. S, 116, 117, 185n17
grief, 38–39, 98–99, 120, 122–23, 106–7
Grinnell, Iowa, 94, 164, 186n23

grocers, 46, 186n24
grog shop, 59–60
Groom, Winston, 188n9
gunboats, Union, 193n77

hairwork, 15–16, 102, 107, 156, 173n63
Hallwas, John E., 184n65
Hampsten, Elizabeth, 174n84
Hampton Roads, Virginia, 193n78
Harpers Ferry, Virginia, 50, 101, 184n1
Harper's Magazine, 12
Harris family, 97, 137, 191n57
Harris Point, 30, 110, 176n35
Hart, James D., 171n40
Hatch, Nathan O., 35, 171n32, 171n40, 175n14, 177nn14–15, 187n39
health, public, 32; of troops, 141,156. *See also* cholera; smallpox; typhoid
Heber, Rev. Reginald, 190n41
Heilbrun, Carolyn G., 174n81
Heinl, Frank J., 192n74
help, domestic. *See* compensation, of serving women; domestic service; domestic tasks
Hempton, David, 36, 171n24, 174n83, 175nn13–14, 177n22, 177nn24–25, 186n29
Herbert, Christopher, 184n73
Hewitt, Nancy, 185n5
hierarchy, rural Midwest, 80–81, 189n23
Hindall, William, 28–29, 176n29
Hobart, Mrs. Ella Gibson, 117
holidays, 188n48; Christmas, 25, 76, 78, 82, 98, 99, 100, 123; New Years, 26, 68, 76, 82–83, 125, 143; Thanksgiving, 76, 100, 184n75. *See also* Fourth of July celebration
Holme, family: Dr. Edward, 165; James, *ix*, 162, 195n2; Dr. Thomas L., 169n1
home guards, 135, 158, 191n49
homemaking. *See* domesticity
home manager, 20
homesteading, 179n62, 186n28
Hopkins, D. R., 183n55
Horowitz, David, 172–73n57
Horrell family: Annis, 46, 63, 131; Charles, 38; Charles's letter, 72; L.P., 59, 72, 108; L.P.'s letters, 62–63, 125, 131–32
house construction, 48, 49
Howe, Julia Ward, 192n66
Hoyt, William B. 171nn28–29, 177n9, 186n30
Huckstep, Thomas, 41, 72, 108, 125, 176n26; letter of, 28

Index

Huddersfield, Yorkshire, England, 189n26
Hudgins, Nicole, 176n7
Hughes, George R., 63
Huntington Hall, Lowell, Mass., 193n87
Hurd, Harvey, 180n68
Hurst, Sarah, 40

Illinois College, 5, 23, 36, 177n27, 178n40; commencement at, 60, 86
Illinois Conference Female College (MacMurray College), xiv, 5, 171n35, 175n23, 183n48, 184n60; 185n12, 195n10; attendance at, 182n38, 183n48, 183n50, 187n46; commencement at, 27, 60, 70, 80, 86, 182n33; commencement controversy, 80; curriculum of, 12, 23, 185n3; 189n21; exhibition at, 57, 140; goals of female education, 196n18. *See also* Belles Lettres society; Phi Nu literary society
Illinois Daily Journal, 172n47
Illinois Daily News, 172n48
Illinois population growth, 16, 155
Illinois River, *3, 33*, 123, 185n13
Illinois State Archives, 191n55
Illinois State University, 11
illness. *See* disease
immigration, 17; Dumvilles as immigrants, 16, 116, 167; German, 4, 16–19, 54–55, 122; increase in, 16, 54; Irish, 4, 16–19, 54–55; opposition to, 18, 53, 54
India, 75, 83, 184n73, 185n9, 190n41
Invisible World, 44, 179n58
Iowa, 174n4; economic conditions, 115; land values, 56; migration to, 55, 179n61; prosperity in, 89
Irish. *See* immigration; social class
Island No. 10, battle of, 148

Jacksonian Democrats, 18
Jacksonville: businesses, 102, 178n37, 186n24; division of Methodist congregations, 1, 112–13, 166, 185n12; gaslights, 76, 184n74; partisan differences, 17, 54, 181n9; railroads, 33, 88; sewer system, 176n3; social hierarchy, 80; soldiers from, 19, 116, 118, 133, 134, 173n78; storm, 108, 187n40; wealth, 120
Jacksonville Constitutionist, 172
Jacksonville Sentinel, 13
James River, Virginia, 193n78
Janes, Bishop, 10, 48, 52
Jaquess, James, 26, 27, 29, 97, 124, 153, 166, 175n23, 186n31, 193n86

Jaquess, Mrs. James, 124, 189n21
Jaquess, Willie, 27
Johannsen, Robert W., 192n69
Johnston, Gen. A. S., 117
Jones, Carl E., 195n3

Kansas: Methodist missionaries in, 71, 114, 130, 190n43; political prospects, 77, 190n43; violence in, 54, 62, 83, 181n10, 190n43
Kansas-Nebraska Act, 18, 53
Keller, Abram D., 144, 192n71
Kentucky, 174n5, 182n29; and Civil War, 116, 143; migration to and from 17, 44, 100, 175n22
Kerr, Isabelle, 57; death of, 61
Kerr family, 57, 60–61, 63–64, 68, 82, 102, 146, 182n38
Klement, Frank L., 188n3, 188nn5–6, 191n53, 191n55
knitting, 31, 138
Know-Nothing Party (American Party), 18–19, 53–55, 79, 173n77, 181n7
Knoxville Whig, 193n85

Ladies' Home Journal, 172n53
Ladies' Repository, 14, 36, 60, 106, 193n85; Lord's Prayer in, 103; political positions of, 54, 181n7, 181n14; subscriptions to, 66, 67, 77
Lambert, Belle Short, 170nn16–17
laundry, 38, 56, 59, 76, 97, 99, 154
Leaton, James, 140, 163, 170nn5–6, 171n18, 171nn21–22, 173n73, 191n50, 191n63, 195n9, 195nn12–13
Lebanon, Illinois, 187n44
Lee, Gen. Robert E., 118, 184n1
Leesburg, Virginia, 115, 138
Lehuu, Isabelle, 171n40, 172nn45–46, 188n48, 195n8
leisure, 14, 15, 110, 137, 172–73n57
Lerner, Gerda, 174n79
letter writing, conventions, 24, 25, 76
letters: frequency of, xiv; provenance of, xiv–xv, 193n83; sharing of, 32, 33, 36, 50, 96, 123, 126, 131, 137, 156, 176n32; style of, 24, 25, 32–33, 43, 76
Lewis, Lloyd, 174n5
Liberia, 10, 41, 124, 171n31, 186n29, 190n39; Jemima's interest in, 129–30, 190n38
likenesses. *See* photography
Lincoln-Douglas debates, 79

Lincoln, Abraham: administration of, 116, 173n77, 184n75; congressional election of 1846, 171n33; election of 1858, 19, 79; election of 1860, 17, 19, 79–80, 114, 125, 174n5, 189n29; Hephzibah's enthusiasm for, 129, 145, 189n36; second inaugural address, 192n66; and slavery, 192n69, 192n73; and war, 129, 145, 188n1, 194n91
liquor, 9, 46, 59–60, 146, 193n85
Lippy, Charles, 172n54, 172–73n57
literacy, 171n40, 172n45; rates of, 12
Livingstone, Dr. David, 130, 190n40
Logan, Col. John, 117, 146, 188n7
Logan, Maj. Gen. John, 188n7
Logie. *See* Williams, Hardin Logan
Lowell, Massachusetts, 154, 193n87
Lumpkin, Mrs. C. J., 170n5, 195n10
Lurton family, 5, 52, 54, 93, 181n8, 189n25; James, 14, 26–27, 75, 88, 91, 92, 98, 101, 102, 109–11, 113, 139–40; Joanna, 125, 134, 139–40; Mary Stribling, 37, 42, 70, 93, 125, 154; William, 27, 67, 76, 93, 98, 108, 126, 128, 134, 161
Lurton store, 14, 26–27, 185n16
Lynnville, Illinois, 3, 11, 62, 176n26
Lynnville, Iowa, 158, 164

Macaulay's History of England, 12, 152
MacMurray College, xiv, 170n5, 170n8, 174n1, 180n70, 195n10. *See also* Illinois Conference Female College
Macoupin County, 3, 4, 7, 10, 23, 33, 54, 80, 92, 170n14, 186n24, 188n16, 194n92, 195n2
Macoupin County Enquirer, 195n9
Magee, James Henry, 23
mail order catalogues, 186n24
manager, domestic, 48–51
Mann, Horace, 11
manufacturing, northeast, 116, 173n58
manumission, 34
March family, 38–39, 41, 57–58, 178 n37; death of Mr. March, 33, 38–39; death of Harriet, 39
marriage, xvii, 4, 7, 22, 27, 33, 34, 39–41, 59, 63, 66, 67, 71, 74, 76, 81, 82, 87, 101, 102, 114, 121, 122, 129, 138, 160, 162–64, 166, 167, 170n4, 170n14, 171n27, 178n48, 180n66, 183n45, 188n16, 195nn2–4, 195n10, 196n23; marriage, age at, 9, 195n3. *See also* wedding ceremony
Mason, James, 116, 140
Matthaei, Julia A., 172nn56–57, 174n79, 184n75

Matthews, Mitford M., 188n2, 188n4, 191n52
Mayberry, Margaret, 68, 101
Mayberry, Walter, 44, 47, 84, 85, 101
McClellan, Major Gen. George, 118
McClure brothers, 30, 84, 176n34
McCoy, Asa S., 61, 69, 74, 182n41
McElfresh family, 57, 65, 74, 88, 102, 135, 170n2, 171n23, 183n48
McKendree College, 187n44
McPherson, James M., 118, 188n12
Melton, J. Gordon, 171n26
Memphis, Tennessee, 194n93
Merrimack (ship), 148, 193n78
Messick, Daniel, 145; death of, 192n72
Methodist Church, 165, 187n39; and abolition, 18, 34, 180n6; attitude towards arts and entertainment, 23; clergy, xi, 1, 4, 7, 51, 93, 116, 120, 171n33, 177n18, 178n44, 180n66, 180–81n6, 184n67, 191n59, 191nn63–64, 193n85; clergy education, 35; conference, 1, 9, 11, 80, 92–93, 112–13, 134, 145, 175n23, 183n48, 187n45, 191n50, 191nn63–64; discipline, 9, 171n28; and education, 11, 35; emotional expression, 11, 51–52, 177n16; expulsion from, 18, 34; and literacy, 171n40; literature, 12, 171n40; liturgy, 24, 35; membership procedures, 26; missionary work of, 8–10, 75, 83, 95, 100, 164, 176n33, 177n27, 185n9, 186n29, 190n43; network of friends, 8, 22, 122, 187n38, 187n46, 188n18; North/South split, 18, 34, 53; property of, 10, 139; publications, 8, 14, 36, 54, 111; urbanization, 10–11, 35; women's role in, 1, 9, 36, 100. *See also Advocate*; Carlinville, Methodist church in; circuit rider; conversion; "good death"; Jacksonville, division of Methodist church in; Liberia; Kansas, missionary work in; Texas, missionary work in
middle class, 11, 13, 14, 20, 35, 55, 165–67, 173n59. *See also* social class
Milburn, William, Rev. 51, 52, 66, 83, 111, 120, 126, 166, 183n49, 183nn52–4, 188n14; death of, 180n69
Milligan, Ex Parte, 194n91
Milton, John, 12
missionaries. *See* Liberia; Methodist, missionary work of; Kansas, missionary work in; Texas, missionary work in
Mississippi River, 54, 73, 115, 116, 193n77, 194n93
Missouri Compromise, 18

Mitchell, Samuel, 72, 184n63
Miyakawa, T. Scott, 172n42, 175n12, 177n8, 177n10, 177n13, 177nn17–22
Monaghan, Charles, 172n43
money, 4, 10, 30, 41, 48, 49, 63, 66, 70, 77, 83, 87, 93, 100, 104, 105, 110, 112, 114, 116, 121, 125, 132, 135, 139, 147, 152, 160, 164, 166, 176n34, 181n10 196n22
Monitor (ship), 148, 193n78
Montague's Illinois and Missouri State Directory, 186n24
Morgan County, 3, 33, 103; business in, 178n37, 186n24; church property in, 10; education in, 23; immigration to, 54; politics of, 80
Morgan Journal, fire at, 99
Mormons, 18, 54. See also Dumville, Hephzibah (Bechly), views of Mormons; Utah, polygamy in
Morrill Tariff Act, 116
Motz, Marilyn, 36, 55, 174n84, 174n86, 177n26, 181n15
Murphysboro, Illinois, 188n7
musket ball, 19, 83

Nashville, battle of, 117
National Democrats, 174n5
nativist sentiment, 18
needlework, 15, 175n9
New Madrid, Missouri, 193n77
newspapers, 12–14, 17, 54, 163, 172n44, 172n47, 183n49, 186n27. See also Dumville, Hephzibah (Bechly), newspapers as source of information; *and specific newspapers*
New York City subscription library, 172n42
New York Times, 120, 174n5, 176n28, 187n41, 189n28, 189n37, 193–94n87, 194n96
New York Tribune, 172n42
Nilwood, Illinois, 3, 33, 191n57; soldiers from, 187n38, 191n57, 192n71
Norfolk, Virginia, 193n78
Normal School, 11
novels, 12, 171n40, 172n42

obituaries, 186n27, 195n9
occupation, as recorded by Census, 20, 174n80, 176n6
Odd Fellows, Independent Order of, 27, 42, 91, 92, 175n25, 185n17, 196n23
Olin, Clarinda, 189n22
Ordinance of 1015, 192n68
Oskaloosa, Iowa, 136, 191n54
oysters, 45

Palmer, G. T., 174n5
Palmer, John McAuley, 22–23, 57, 117, 129, 135, 146, 174n5, 183n50, 193n77
Palmer, Julia, 65, 77, 183n50
Palmer, Phoebe, 171n37
paper reading. *See* social activities
parades. *See* Fourth of July celebration
Paradise Lost, 12, 77, 189n27
Patten, Simon, 172–3n57
Peace Democrats, 18
Peninsular Campaign, 118
pew system, 171n34
Phi Nu literary society, 12, 14, 70, 182n31; exhibitions at, 140; fire damage, 140; readings at, 68, 82, 164
photography, 34, 42, 73, 95, 97, 102, 126, 155, 176n6, 176–7n7; Ann's photograph, xiv, 6
physicians: Dr. Hankins, 51; Dr. Long, 39; Dr. Prince, 39; Dr. Reace, 105; Dr. Shirley, 39
picnic. *See* social activities
Pilgrim's Progress, 163, 195n11
Pitner, Rev. Levi, 52, 161, 166, 178n44, 180n68
Pitner, Rev. Wilson, 43, 178n44, 182n39; cholera of, 41; death of family members, 40; slavery case, 40, 41, 53, 178n45
Pittsburg Landing (battle of Shiloh), xii, 117, 118, 147, 148, 193n79. *See also* Shiloh, battle of
Plain, Jacob, 41, 49, 74, 100, 154, 178n47
"Plea for Captain John Brown," 184–85n1
Pleasant Plains, Illinois, 171n33
poetry, 12, 175n17
political mobilization, 17, 54, 60, 62, 79, 181n9, 181n14
polygamy. *See* Utah, polygamy in
poor farm, 184n68
Pope, Alexander, 65, 183n47
Pope, Clayne L., 56, 182n20, 182n22
Port Royal, battle of, 115
Posey family, 40, 44, 64, 74, 82, 85, 102, 128, 178n43, 189nn32–33; death of Mrs. Posey, 105–6, 187nn35–36; Frances, 44, fainting of, 127–28
postage, xiii, 40, 42
postmarks, xiv, 191–92n65
Poweshiek County, Iowa, 55, 164, 179n61, 184n66, 186n23, 191n54, 196n17, 196n23
Pratt, Henry E., 185n12
preachers, charismatic appeal, 11, 35, 177n27, 178n43. *See also* church; Methodist church

Presbyterian church, 5, 106, 177n27, 178n43, 190n40
presidential elections, 1856, 18, 53, 183n44; 1860, 53, 79–80
Protestant identity, 55
Pruitt, Linda Carlisle, 175n9, 182n23
Psalm 54:5, 93, 185n20
pseudonyms, 182n24; Brother Curiosity, 57, 65, 69, 71, 76, 81, 89, 90; Mr. Consequentiality, 61; Mr. Easy, 57; Mr. Modern Refinement, 57; Mr. Punctuality, 65, 82; Mr. Watchkeeper, 57
public health measures. *See* health, public
published letters, elite perspective, 21
Punctuality, Mr. *See* pseudonyms
punctuation, 169n1; lack of, xi, 192n70

Quakers, 62, 73, 84, 94, 112, 151
Quincy College, 186n31

railroads, 12–13, 30, 33, 34, 167, 172n44, 172n47; 176n4; accidents on, 33, 63, 88, 146; completion of, 94, 127, 148; etiquette on, 88, 113; travel on, 45, 80, 152–53
Ray, Joseph, 72, 184n62
reading, 22, 163, 171n40, 175n9, 180n66, 183n59. *see also* Dumville, Hephzibah, reading of
recession of 1861–62, 115, 125, 132, 135, 152
recitation, 22, 65
Refinement, Mr. Modern. *See* pseudonyms
Reid, J. M., 171n30
religion, presence in letters, 171n25
Republican Party, 18, 19, 53, 92, 158, 173n71, 173n77, 174n5, 181n9, 189n37, 194n96
revivals. *See* church
Richardson family, 39, 85, 178n42
Richmond, battle of, 118, 135, 150, 193n78
Richmond, Virginia. *See* Balls Bluff, battle of; Peninsular Campaign
robbery, 102
Robertson, Stacy M., 173n74
Rogers, Sue: death of, 145
romances, 7, 81, 88, 90, 91, 100–101, 122, 133, 134, 160, 166, 185n15. *See also* pseudonyms, Brother Curiosity
Rose, Anne, 14, 20, 172n55, 172n57, 174n82
Rusk, Ralph Leslie, 172n42, 177n16
Rutledge, George and William: dispute between, 113, 187n47
Rutledge, Rev. William, 61

Salem, 29, 43, 44, 59, 68, 74, 84, 85, 87, 95, 123, 126, 179n57
Salmon, Lucy Maynard, 184n75
Sanders, Charles W., 72, 184n61
Saunderson family, 5, 29, 43; death of Mr., 106; death of Mrs., 102
Savannah, Georgia, 115, 164
Scanlon, Jennifer, 172n53, 172–73n57
school: attendance at, 46, 48, 51, 62, 72, 76, 94, 101, 104, 111, 112, 126, 127, 140, 151, 152, 157, 164; commendation, 24, 63; common, 11, 66, 174–5n8; establishment of, 22–23, 84, 94, 96, 97, 185n10; expense of, 1, 4; law, 86; Miss Dumville's, 63, 183n43; payment for, 30, 133, 176n38, 185n10; prayer, 24, 29; prevented from attending, 4, 13, 31, 63, 70, 158, 165, 167, 184n77; public, 174–75n8; recruitment for, 28; tuition bill, 45. *See also* Dumville, Hephzibah Bechly, desire for education; Dumville, Jemima, employment as teacher; education; teaching
School for the Deaf and Dumb, 5, 27, 175n24
Scott, Winfield, 135, 191n51
Scott County, Illinois, 170n13, 175n18, 184n64
secession of Southern states, 12, 19, 127, 129, 144, 149, 151, 152, 193n85
seeds, 126, 131, 186n24; exchanging, 94, 95, 98, 126, 131, 146, 147, 148, 158
Senate election, 1858, 79
Seneca Falls, 181n12; *Declaration of Sentiments*, 183n42
serving women, 7, 13, 21; compensation of, 7, 13, 56, 121, 130–33, 159–61, 190n46, 190n47; as consumers, 196n22; 164; vulnerabilities, 121; wages, 13, 121, 190n47. *See also* work, domestic service; work, domestic tasks
Seward, William H., 129, 189–90n37
Sewell, William G., 111, 187n41
sewers, 176n3
sewing, 14, 15, 22, 31, 63, 64, 68, 98, 100, 138, 141, 154, 173n58. *See also* fabric; fashion
Seys family: Annie, 124; death of children, 186n29, 190n39; John, 10, 129–30, 171n31; Mrs., 96, 98
Sheppard, Robert D., 180n68
Sheumaker, Helen, 173n62
Shiloh, battle of, xii, 117, 118, 147, 164, 188n9, 196n15. *See also* Pittsburg Landing
Shils, Edward, 196n20

Index

sickness. *See* disease
Sinnock, Rev., 74, 184n67
Sklar, Kathryn Kish, 171n37
slaveholding by clergy, 18, 34, 41
slavery, 62, 111, 142, 164, 176n29; as cause of war, 118, 155, 189–90n37; church, 17, 34–35, 124–25, 181n7, 181n14; as economic issue, 53, 179n49; evils of, 60, 116, 142–43; expansion of, 18, 62; and feminism, 181n14; and national elections, 53; and political conflict, 17–19, 21, 54, 80, 83, 111, 145, 167, 190n43
slaves, inheritance of, 178n45
Slidell, John, 116, 140
smallpox, 67, 68, 183n55
Smith, Carl, 176n3
Smith, G. Barnett, 192n68
Smith, Joseph, 54
Smith, Mr. (merchant), 102
Smith, Miss (dressmaker), 59
Smithsonian Institution, Library of, 186n24
smoking, 49, 100
Snow, John, 176n2
social activities: ball (dance), 40; paper readings, 14, 59, 68, 70, 82, 124, 164; parties, 44, 64, 82; picnic, 69–70, 110, 183n56; sewing, 15, 63–64; sledding, 127; sleigh ride, 68, 101; teas, 40, 74, 111; theater, 49, 193n85
social class, 13–14, 20, 35, 36, 55, 80, 81, 121, 165–67, 174n8, 189n23, 193–94n87. *See also* middle class
social cues, 186n33
social rejection, 44, 50, 61, 102, 104
soldiers, Carlinville and Jacksonville, xi, 19, 116, 153, 173n78
South Carolina, 129; secession of, 189n34
Southern sympathizers, 115, 136, 150, 152, 180n6, 191n53
Spaulding, Martha, 87, 185n14
spelling, in letters, xi, xii, 177n28
spiritual support, 29, 30, 117, 191n48; need for, 62, 107
Spooner, Matthew P., 171n31
Stamper, Anita, 179nn50–51
Stamper, Rev. Mr., 48
Stampp, Kenneth M., 173n76, 184n72
Stanton, Edwin, 117
Stanton, Elizabeth Cady, 181n14
stationery, xii, 186n25; decoration of, 118, 191n56, 192n70
Stead, Benjamin, xii, 6, 137, 143, 187n38, 192n67; letters from, 143, 149

Steckel, Richard H., 54, 180nn4–5
St. Joseph, Missouri, 162, 164
St. Louis, 3, 18, 38, 54, 147, 170n5
St. Louis Republican, 187n37
St. Louis University, 187n44
stores: drug, 46; grocery, 46, 186n24. *See also* grog shop
Stowe, Harriet Beecher, 12, 181n10
Stowe, Steven, 178n38, 187n36, 188–89n19
Stratton, Joanna, 174n4
Stribling family: character of, 120–21; health of, 31, 37, 73, 86, 97, 99, 102, 105, 120; Hephzibah's departure, 130, 133, 150, 152, 153, 159; library, 12, 152; move from Kentucky, 175n22, 182n29; Mrs. (Grandma) as employer, 31, 99, 101, 130–32; opposition to suitors, 90, 160; problems with, 28–29, 47, 58, 130; wealth of, 120, 159. *See also* Dumville, Hephzibah, departure from Striblings and relationship with Striblings; Dumville, Jemima, relationship with Striblings; visiting
Stubbs, William, 192n68
stumptailed currency, 135, 188n4, 191n52
sugar chest, 59, 182n29
suitors. *See* pseudonyms, Brother Curiosity; romances; Stribling, opposition to suitors
Sulphur Springs, 3, 164, 176n35, 187n38, 191n57, 194n92
Sunny Dell, 4, 166; in dateline, 89–91, 97, 98, 101, 104, 105, 110, 112, 122, 127, 132, 134, 137, 139, 145, 147, 149, 151, 152
Sutton, Robert P., 173n77, 180n2
Sweet, William. W., 24, 175n15
Swift, Jonathan, 182n24

Tally's War, 194n96
Taylor, Zachary, 180n1
teaching, 19–20; boarding for, 38; compensation for, 38, 45, 63, 100; 179n60; position, 38, 47, 123; training, 92. *See also* education; religion
technological advances, 6, 12, 34, 163, 172n47. *See also* gaslights; newspapers; photography; railroads; telegraph
telegraph, 12, 13, 34, 147, 172n47, 186n27
temperance, 59, 173n59
Tennessee, 17, 79, 116, 117, 182n29, 191–2n65, 194n93; Pitner estate in, 40, 41, 178nn44–45
Texas, missionaries to, 10, 30, 37, 164, 176n33, 177n31

textile mills, British, 116
Thanksgiving. *See* holidays
Thompson, George, 111, 187n42
Thomson, James, 192n75
Thoreau, Henry David, 184n1
Tiller family, 4, 37, 65, 131, 170n13, 183n51
tornado, 107, 108, 187n37, 187n40, 191n58
transcription, process of, xi–xii
travel, difficulty of, 33
Trent, British ship, 116
"true womanhood," 55, 164, 165, 172n57, 181n13
trunk, shipment of, 32–33, 37, 38, 88
Turnbull, Everett, 169–70n1, 171n17
typhoid fever, 21, 37–38, 51, 95, 105–6, 123, 163

Uncle Tom's Cabin, 12, 58, 59, 60, 176n29, 182n26, 182n36
Union Army, 19, 115–19, 122, 191n49, 191n51, 193n77, 193n86; casualties of, 19, 119, 188n1
U.S. Army, female chaplain. *See* chaplains; Hobart, Ella Gibson
U.S. Census. *See* Census, U.S.
U.S. Supreme Court, 194n91
Utah: polygamy in, 54, 60, 62; war in, 75, 184n70. *See also* Mormon; Dumville, Hephzibah (Bechly), views of Mormons

Valentines, 126
Van Winkle family, 96, 113, 138, 187n46
venetian blinds, 59, 182n28
Vicars, Captain, 12, 70, 183n59,
Vicksburg, Mississippi: battle of, 119, 120, 156, 164
view of war: by soldiers, 118; by women, 118
Virginia, Illinois, 81, 88, 90, 134, 166, 185n15
visiting, 120; Ann: 7–8, 49, 80, 95, 108, 110, 127, 141, 143; Fred, 151–52, 196n15; Hephzibah, 38, 44, 65, 68, 71, 94, 99, 102, 121, 123, 137, 148, 149, 154, 156, 160; Jemima: 80, 99, 175n2; John, 112, 157; Striblings: 26, 74, 134, 135; other, 102, 108, 111, 113, 134
voting, 55, 62, 65, 139, 181n14; regional patterns in, 18, 53–54, 79–80, 173n77

Walker, Charles, 174–75n8, 184n74
Wall, Miss J., 40, 97
Walsh, Margaret, 173n58
Walter family, 39, 44, 47, 57, 63, 64, 66, 68, 71, 74, 77, 81, 82, 85, 101; Julia, death of, 122–23; as missionaries in Texas, 37, 177n31, 178n41
War of 1812, 17, 91, 188n9
Ward, Maria, 182n37
washing. *See* laundry
Wass, Ann Buermann, 173n58, 179n51, 184n75
Watchkeeper, Mr. *See* pseudonyms
watercolors, 15
Watters, Mary, 169n5, 169n1, 170n16, 171n17, 171n20, 171n23, 172n41, 173n70, 175n9, 175n23, 182nn30–31, 182n41, 183n50, 184n60, 185n3, 185n12, 185n14, 189nn21–22, 191n61, 193n86
weather, snow, 46, 73, 101, 127, 143, 144. *See also* earthquake; tornado
wedding ceremony, 63–64, 101–2, 166; dresses, 64, 183n45; Mr. Dean and Mrs. Epler, 101–2; Hephzibah and Fred Bechly, 121; Mr. L. Huckstep, 41; Jemima and James Holme, 182; Nettie Kerr and Mr. Woods, 63–64; Mr. W. Mathers and Miss Yates, 41; Mr. McDonald and Julia March, 41; Sarah and Mr. Barrows, 114; Martha Spaulding, 87; Mr. Saunderson and Miss Hanna, 29; unnamed, 68, 81
Welter, Barbara, 172n42, 172n57, 181n13, 196n19
Wesley, John, 51, 175n14, 180n66; death of, 8. *See also* good death
West Charge Methodist Church, 1, 5, 82, 85, 185n12
Whig Party, 53, 79, 171n33
whiskey, 49, 115
Whitaker genealogy, 179n57
Whittaker, Mr., 51
Williams, children: death of, 38–39, 98–99, 196n23; health of, 83; play, 84, 94; school for, 94, 96, 104, 127, 151; sickness of, 94, 96, 112
Williams, Mrs. Eli: death of, 67
Williams, Elias, 73, 184n66
Williams, Elizabeth Dumville: age of, 1, 112, 159; death of, 164; dissatisfaction with Iowa, 46; farm tasks, 25, 94; grave of, 196n17; immigration of, 4; literacy of, 4, 172n45; marriage of, 4; place of burial, 196n23; property of, 164; work of, 94, 140
Williams, John: crops of, 83–84, 94, 104, 112, 114, 136; death of, 164; debt, 104, 136, 151; first trip to Iowa, 42; letters of 1855,

45–46; letters of 1857, 72–73; 1858, 83–84; letters of 1859, 94–96; letters of 1860, 104, 112, 114; letters of 1861; 126–27, 135–36; letters of 1862, 150–51; loan to, 135, 151–52; military service of, 164; move to Iowa, 45–46; place of burial, 196n17, 196n23; views of Civil War, 127; views of Lincoln, 114; views of the South, 127, 149, 151; work, farm, 25, 45, 46, 87, 94, 112, 135, 136, 140, 153. *See also* visiting

Williams, Josiah, 72, 104, 184n64; letter of, 107

Williams, Margaret Emily: letters of, 151, 157–59

women: education of, 81, 165; and markets, 172n57; political roles of, 55, 62, 80–81, 184n76; social roles of, 66–67, 81, 165; suffrage, 55, 81, 181n12, 181n14, 183n42. *See also* domesticity; "true womanhood"

work: domestic service, 19, 20, 183n51, 190n44; domestic tasks, 14, 19, 25, 58, 59, 66, 140, 141; farm tasks, 49, 66, 87, 94, 124, 136, 140, 153; teaching tasks, 77, 89, 98, 100, 105, 107, 141, 147, 164, 177n28. *See also* apple drying; childcare; domestic management; farm management; flowers; gardening; knitting; laundry; sewing; teaching

Wright, Charlotte M, 174n4

Yale College, missionaries from, 177n27
Yates, Congressman Richard, 33, 39, 178n40

Zboray, Ronald J., 169n4, 171n40, 172n42, 172nn44–45, 172n48

ANNE M. HEINZ is the former Assistant Dean of the Division of the Social Sciences at the University of Chicago and the coauthor of *Crime and City Politics*.

JOHN P. HEINZ is the former Director of the American Bar Foundation and Owen L. Coon Professor Emeritus at the Northwestern University School of Law. He is the coauthor of *Urban Lawyers: The New Social Structure of the Bar*.

The University of Illinois Press
is a founding member of the
Association of American University Presses.

Composed in 10.5/13 Adobe Minion Pro
by Kirsten Dennison
at the University of Illinois Press
Manufactured by Sheridan Books, Inc.

University of Illinois Press
1325 South Oak Street
Champaign, IL 61820-6903
www.press.uillinois.edu